Modelling the Logistics of Mantzikert

Modelling the Logistics of Mantzikert

Philip Murgatroyd, Vincent Gaffney, John Haldon
and Georgios Theodoropoulos

ARCHAEOPRESS ARCHAEOLOGY

ARCHAEOPRESS PUBLISHING LTD
Summertown Pavilion
18-24 Middle Way
Summertown
Oxford OX2 7LG

www.archaeopress.com

ISBN 978-1-80327-799-8
ISBN 978-1-80327-800-1 (e-Pdf)

Cover: A 3D representation of MWGrid agents in the landscape.

This book is available direct from Archaeopress or from our website www.archaeopress.com

Contents

List of Figures

List of Tables

Acknowledgements

This publication is a result of an AHRC-EPSRC-Jisc e-Science grant, awarded to Vincent Gaffney, John Haldon and Georgios Theodoropoulos in 2007. We are extremely grateful for the foresight shown by these funding bodies in setting up the e-Science projects. The ability to produce a project which combines computer simulation and historical research was an opportunity that, at the time, was not widely available elsewhere.

Several specialists contributed vital assistance and advice throughout the project and beyond. Mike Ford greatly assisted in our understanding of the literature around human energy requirements and exercise. Warren Eastwood helped us get to grips with the environmental data. Rob Minson and Bart Craenen not only developed a distributed simulation infrastructure, but also helped Phil Murgatroyd acquire the necessary technical skills to produce the simulation software. John and Patricia Carman were a great help in introducing us to the wider military history community. Gary Sheffield had a vital, albeit brief, role in pointing us to George Armand Furse's 'The Art of Marching'. Without this piece of advice, this book would have been completed a lot closer to the project's end date of 2011, but neither it, nor the process of researching it, would have been half as interesting.

Archie Dunn was always available to provide Byzantine historical context. The staff and students of the University of Birmingham's VISTA centre were instrumental in providing a framework within which this kind of digital archaeology project could thrive, including Simon Fitch, Ellie Ramsey, Henry Chapman, Eamonn Baldwin, Nigel Dodds, Helen Moulden, Anneley Hadland, Emma Kitchen, Andrew Lewis, Emma Login, Simon Hartley and others. Preparatory work for this project was carried out by Helen Gaffney, Helen Goodchild, Gino Bellavia and others, and this work can be found in the Brill publication of 2006. Eugene Ch'ng has always been a valuable source of technical help and his comments, along with those of the other examiner, Julian Richards, greatly improved Phil Murgatroyd's PhD thesis. Stuart Dunn, of the Arts and Humanities e-Science Support Centre, gave valuable assistance during the 'Medieval Warfare on the Grid' project. He also served on the project management committee, along with Steve Wilkes, Paul Hatton, Steve Turner, Georgios Theodoropoulos and Vince Gaffney. Jason Roche was always happy to discuss the overlaps between the Mantzikert campaign and the Crusades, and his local knowledge of the routes between Nikaia and Dorylaion has been most useful. We are extremely grateful to all these who contributed to the research in this book. Any mistakes are, of course, our own.

Phil would like to thank his Mum and Dad and his wife, Jenn, for their endless support. John Dore and Mike Burns were supportive from the start but sadly never got to see the end results. They are both greatly missed. To the rest of my family and friends, thanks, and sorry it's taken so long.

Chapter 1 – Introduction

An organised military has always been a key feature of an organised state, and whether the military succeeds or fails can have a massive impact on societies in general. For this reason, a key part of state bureaucracy, particularly in pre-modern states, is the organisation of the military for offensive and defensive action. Yet despite its importance as a key method by which states can be maintained, the study of the mechanisms by which armies are raised, moved, fed and equipped has attracted less attention than the study of strategy and tactics and the personalities of generals and political leaders. Military logistics is a term that covers the organisations and methods that ensure sufficient people are in the right place at the right time and in the right condition to threaten or achieve military supremacy. Strategy and tactics are important in achieving military supremacy but if armies cannot be moved or fed then strategic and tactical ability become moot points. Armies can be destroyed without fighting and armies that are moved and fed effectively can have a critically important advantage in battle.

The historical focus on battles and leaders is partly because far more of the primary sources focus on these topics,[1] but also because the relationships between the systems included within military logistics are complex and the evidence for these systems is often inaccurate and/or incomplete. Raising an army requires resources and organisation, and moving it is dependent on transport infrastructure and, especially in the pre-modern world before effective food preservation and railways, the amount and location of food surpluses. Surplus food is dependent on agricultural productivity and demography, both of which also affect tax income. Military campaigns can have extensive effects on the availability of food surpluses, even if those campaigns are fought away from home soil. If enemy action impacts on home territories then this can have drastic effects on demography, agricultural productivity and therefore also on tax income. With such an interrelated web of complex systems, it's unsurprising that historians, both ancient and modern, have focused on the character of famous generals and the turning points of decisive battles. These stories have clearer narratives and more exciting plot twists than can usually be found in a description of the organisation of a baggage train or a list of required foodstuffs.

However, gaining a more complete understanding of military logistics, including the mechanisms that support it and the effects of moving large groups of people across a pre-industrial landscape is not only important in researching the significant military campaigns of history but also a way of gaining new insights into other aspects of society. If we can quantify the amount of food required to sustain an army in a campaign we are able to say something about the agricultural productivity, demography and transport networks of the lands they travel through. Each of these aspects of society are complex systems, with complex relationships between them. The complexity inherent in the systems that underpin military logistics has its pros and cons. It makes understanding these systems a more difficult task, but it also means that work on one piece of the puzzle can maybe help us with the other pieces too.[2] As Gotthold Ephraim Lessing, along with many students of esoteric, environmental and sociological topics may contend, 'everything is connected'.[3] This statement does not just hold for nature, as Lessing originally intended, but also applies to this book, in which Byzantine history, computer science, graph search algorithms, the spread of the railroads, Microsoft, the 19th-century British Army and the Roman roads of Anatolia all play a role.

In 2007, the *Medieval Warfare on the Grid* project commenced at the University of Birmingham, with funding from a joint AHRC-EPSRC-Jisc e-Science research grant. Its aim was to find some way of reaching beyond the limits of the historical sources by using new technology to try and access this interrelated network of complex systems underpinning pre-modern military logistics. Research into complexity in the second half of the 20th century had resulted in computer simulation techniques that had been profitably used to research the behaviour of complex systems. If these could be used on the systems that constitute the elements of military logistics in a pre-modern state, then we could not only approach military campaigns from a bold new direction but also use this to understand more about the societies that supported the armies that protected them. The work undertaken during the *Medieval Warfare on the Grid* project forms the basis of this book, though much has been added since then to incorporate new sources of information on military logistics.

[1] Luttwak 1993, 5–6

[2] Haldon 2006a
[3] Lessing 1889, 399

What is military logistics?

According to the United Kingdom Ministry of Defence,

> Logistics is the science of planning and carrying out the movement and maintenance of forces. Logistics comprises the development, acquisition, storage, movement, distribution, maintenance, recovery and disposal of materiel; transport of personnel, acquisition and construction; maintenance, operation and disposal of facilities; acquisition or furnishing of services; and medical and health services.[4]

The above quote is the definition of logistics from the 2017 UK tactical doctrine for land operating environments, but it is sufficiently generic to apply to military logistics of any era. It is designed, along with administrative support, to be the means by which armies can be sustained for as long as operationally necessary. The word itself is derived from the Greek, *logistikos*, meaning 'skilled in calculation', and has been used in its current form since at least 1838 when Jomini used it to refer rather vaguely to essential tasks for warfare that are not strategy or tactics.[5]

The importance of logistics

The areas covered by our definition of logistics are key factors in the ability to keep an army in the field. George Armand Furse, writing in the 19th century and drawing from examples in which the British Army had campaigned against nations with less developed logistical infrastructures in Africa and Asia, stated that local forces which can travel light and are highly mobile pay 'an enormous price, which is the impossibility of carrying on protracted operations'.[6] The implication here is that the British Army's logistics infrastructure made their forces less mobile. Nevertheless, the British army's support structures, expensive and complicated as they were, allowed forces to be kept in the field longer than their opponents, thus securing a critical advantage.

This trade-off between mobility and endurance is just one of a series of complex relationships and factors involved with moving and feeding an army. Although there are methods of organising an army that are more, or less, effective than others, the individual circumstances of each campaign are important and undermine any attempt to define a 'one size fits all' idealised approach to military logistics.

> Marching is indeed an art in itself, and a complicated one too, as so many circumstances, amongst others the season of the year, the nature of the climate, the state of the roads, the actual physical and moral condition of the troops, the attitude of the population, and the urgency of the situation, have all to be taken into account. The more numerous an army is, the more difficult it becomes to move it, the more imperative becomes the necessity for methodical arrangements in everything which concerns its transition, down to the most minute details.[7]

Mantzikert - our case study

In 1071, the Byzantine Emperor, Romanos IV Diogenes, marched an army of native soldiers and foreign mercenaries from west to east across Anatolia in order to decisively engage the Seljuk Turk Sultan, Alp Arslan, in battle. We have writings regarding the character of the leaders and the events of the battle but, in common with most pre-modern campaigns, we cannot say precisely how large the armies were nor do we possess all the information we would like in order to say exactly how they were organized, fed or moved, what effect they had on the communities that will have supplied them or what life on the road was like for the vast majority of the combatants in a battle that would have significant effects for the Byzantine Empire and the whole of the Middle East.

The march of the Byzantine army across medieval Anatolia to the Battle of Mantzikert in 1071 was chosen as a case study for the *Medieval Warfare on the Grid* project as it is recorded in a number of contemporary and near-contemporary historical accounts and takes place across a reasonably well-researched landscape and yet there are crucial details missing from our knowledge of the campaign and the areas through which it passed. The sources of our knowledge of this campaign have been thoroughly discussed by many researchers and, absent new data, all we can do is revisit the same accounts and reargue the same points, *ad infinitum*. Carole Hillenbrand in her study of the Muslim historical writing about the battle suggests 'the only way to shed any really new light on the 'event' lies within the discipline of military archaeology'[8], but we hope to demonstrate that archaeology, history and computer science can combine to provide an approach to the Mantzikert campaign that gives a radical new perspective. We also hope to demonstrate that this approach is applicable to a wide variety of pre-modern military campaigns, and even to some from more recent history.

The historical context

In 1068 the Byzantine Empire was in a more precarious military position than it had been for almost a century.

4 Land Warfare Development Centre 2017
5 Leighton and Coakley 1955, 11
6 Furse 1882, 34

7 Furse 1901, 4
8 Hillenbrand 2007, 4

Figure 1: Byzantine Anatolia at the time of the Turkish raids.

Basil II (976-1025) left Byzantium with an expanded empire, a strong successful army and a healthy treasury when he died, childless, leaving his brother Constantine VIII as head of the Empire. From the 1040s in particular, Byzantine military strength had been jeopardised by civil wars, rebellions and a preponderance of bureaucratic emperors who favoured the metropolitan elites above the provincial military aristocracy.[9] Basil II's successes ensured that the Bulgars in the west no longer presented a threat, and in the east the aggression from Muslim lands was limited. Due to a series of military revolts in the 11th century, driven by the anti-military policies of the emperors, the thematic levies, citizen soldiers recruited from the Empire's own provinces, had been unused and in some cases disbanded in favour of regionally recruited field armies, known as tagmata, whereas the existing field armies had been partially replaced by foreign mercenaries.[10] Nevertheless, there is evidence to suggest that properly led Byzantine armies had some measure of success up to the 1060s.[11]

By 1068 the reduction in defences protecting the east had led to a series of raids by Turkish nomads[12] (Figure 1). The nomads were encouraged by the Seljuk Turk rulers to prey on Byzantine Anatolia instead of Seljuk-controlled areas further east.[13] Seljuk successes against Armenia, including the sack of Ani in 1064, had met with no strong resistance from the distracted or inept Byzantine rulers, so when the Empress Eudokia's

husband Constantine X Doukas died in 1067 it became clear to even the pro-bureaucrat empress that a strong military leader would benefit the empire. It was in this spirit that the general Romanos Diogenes, brought to Constantinople in order to be punished for leading a revolt, was instead chosen by the empress to be her husband and the next emperor.[14]

Romanos IV Diogenes, as he then became, established as his first priority the need to stop the Turkish nomads from raiding Anatolia. Hampered by the lack of experience of the thematic troops and the hostile, bureaucratic Doukas family in Constantinople, he hastily assembled an army to try to engage the nomads in battle. The nomads themselves consisted of a series of mobile bands which were elusive and difficult to commit to an engagement. Romanos reasoned that if he were to engage them in pitched battle then superior Byzantine organisation, numbers and heavy troops would triumph over Turkish mobility. During 1068, Romanos chased the nomads across Anatolia without ever being able to decisively engage them. A similar campaign took place in 1069.[15] In 1070, Romanos left the general Manuel Komnenos to fight the Turks while the emperor stayed in Constantinople attempting to secure his position on the throne. Manuel Komnenos had no more success than Romanos had done, although none of these campaigns could be said to be a complete failure either.[16] At least there was now a more hostile environment in Anatolia for the nomadic raiders.

---

[9] Angold 2004; Cheynet 1990; Holmes 2008; Lauxtermann and Whittow 2017
[10] Haldon 2008, 165
[11] Haldon 2003
[12] Attaleiates 2012
[13] Haldon 2008, 168

[14] Holmes 2008
[15] Vratimos-Chatzopoulos 2005
[16] Attaleiates 2012, 253

In 1071 the emperor set out with an army that the Armenian monk Matthew of Edessa called 'more numerous than the sands of the sea'[17], although he was hardly a neutral observer and his description of the size of the army probably reflects his sympathies, which were most likely with the Turks, or at least against the Byzantines. Although Byzantine sources give no numbers and those quoted by Arabic sources are likely to be inflated to emphasise the scale of the Byzantine defeat, it seems that this army was much larger than those used in the previous three years. As the Arabic historian, al-Husayni, recorded in the early 13th century, 'Byzantium threw its own lifeblood at the Sultan and the Earth brought forth its burdens of men and equipment'[18], although, like Matthew of Edessa, al-Husayni had no reason to downplay the size of the Byzantine force. The emperor's aim was to engage the Seljuk Turk Sultan in battle and destroy Seljuk military strength on the eastern borders. Alp Arslan had in 1070 taken the border fortress of Mantzikert and also besieged Edessa in 1071 although he was subsequently more involved with action against the Fatimids than he was with battling the Byzantine Empire.

In March or April 1071, Romanos sent ambassadors to Alp Arslan demanding that he abandon his siege of Edessa and withdraw from the eastern border of the empire, although by this point Romanos had already left Constantinople with his army so the extent to which the emperor expected the Turkish Sultan to comply is debated.[19] Alp Arslan reacted by hastily assembling a force to resist the Byzantine army, although Romanos thought he had headed back to Persia to do this. In actual fact Alp Arslan had gathered a reasonably sized army on the eastern borders of the Byzantine Empire long before Romanos had expected him to be able to do so. There are suggestions from some later Byzantine historians that this was the result of a secret arrangement with Romanos' political enemies as part of a plan to use the Seljuks to remove the emperor.[20] By the time Romanos reached Mantzikert and recaptured the fortress without a fight, Alp Arslan was in the area with a sizeable force.[21]

Romanos headed out of the fortress on August 26th and arrayed his forces for battle. Advancing towards the Seljuk Sultan's camp the army were peppered with arrows from the bands of nomads, who used their mobility to avoid close combat. By the time the day was coming to a close the Byzantine army had still not been able to force the Turks into close quarters and were prepared to retreat back to the fortress and try again the following day. It was at this point that a

fatal political flaw of the emperor's was made manifest. Romanos had brought a member of the Doukas clan, Andronikos Doukas, along with him despite knowing that his loyalty was questionable to say the least.[22] This was probably done so that he would act as a hostage to guard against any traitorous moves back at the capital while the emperor was away. Andronikos had however been given command of the rear guard. When Romanos reversed his banner to signal the retreat, the rear guard should have covered the army as it left the field. As it was, Andronikos spread the rumour that the emperor had been killed then ordered his units to retreat back to the fortress. Bereft of cover the other parts of the army were left to fend for themselves against the opportunistically attacking Turks.

The centre of the army was savaged, and the emperor captured. Possibly preferring an emperor that could be beaten as opposed to an unknown successor, Alp Arslan treated Romanos relatively well. He extracted agreements from the emperor, kept the emperor's lavish baggage train that had been captured in the aftermath of the battle, and released him after a week. By this time, however, word had got back to Constantinople that Romanos had been slain and the Doukai took advantage of the situation and siezed control of the empire.[23] Romanos attempted to regain his throne by force, but his revolt was defeated and he was captured. He was blinded by the new emperor, Michael VII Doukas, with the intention of being confined to the monastery at Proti but died from the effects of the blinding soon afterwards.

The importance of Mantzikert

Mantzikert is a pivotal moment in medieval history and affected areas far removed from Eastern Anatolia. Runciman called it 'the most decisive disaster in Byzantine history'.[24] The Byzantine Empire was afflicted by a period of civil wars from the defeat at Mantzikert until Alexios I Komnenos took the throne in 1081.[25] It was this unrest more than the military defeat at Mantzikert that weakened the empire[26] but the usurping of the throne by the Doukas family marked the beginning of this unrest. The Byzantines never again controlled all of Anatolia and the Turkic peoples were never fully driven out, culminating in the fall of Constantinople in 1453 and the triumph of the Ottomans. The defeat at Mantzikert also stoked European fears of the Muslim world and was in small part a catalyst of the First Crusade.[27] The Ottomans in their turn gave way to the modern Republic of Turkey, with Mantzikert being the

---

[17] Dostourian 1972, 231
[18] Hillenbrand 2007, 53
[19] Haldon 2008, 169
[20] Vratimos 2018
[21] Friendly 1981, 173

[22] Haldon 2008, 170
[23] Angold 2004; Holmes 2008
[24] Runciman 1951, 61
[25] Cheynet 1980
[26] Haldon 2008, 165
[27] Hillenbrand 2007, 1

first major military victory of Turkic peoples within the borders of what is today the modern state of Turkey. As such it is a well-established event in the modern Turkish historical tradition and in Turkish popular ideology. Within the town of Malazgirt, the modern name for Mantzikert, there is a statue to the Seljuk Sultan Alp Arslan. Mantzikert occupies a similar status as a pivotal event for the modern state of Turkey as the Battle of Hastings does for England.[28] As the Byzantine Empire was a direct continuation of the Eastern part of the Roman Empire the Battle of Mantzikert resonates through the ancient, medieval and modern worlds.

The campaign

Of the actual campaign, we know relatively little. Contemporary Byzantine sources include Michael Psellus, an anti-military bureaucrat and scholar, who disliked Romanos and stayed behind in Constantinople,[29] and Michael Attaleiates, a military nobleman who accompanied the emperor on the campaign.[30] A few decades after the battle, Nikephoros Bryennios, the grandson of a general of the same name who was on the Mantzikert campaign, wrote an account.[31] From contemporary sources, we know that the emperor left Constantinople for Mantzikert in either late February or early March, crossed the River Halys (the modern Kızılırmak River) near a place called Krya Pege where he expelled some German mercenaries from the army,[32] travelled via Sebastea (modern Sivas) and Theodosiopolis (modern Erzurum) and split his army into two parts not far from Lake Van and ordered half his forces to take the fortress at Khliat (modern Ahlat).[33] There is no mention of any specific logistical problems *en route* so we can provisionally assume no exceptional disasters regarding provisioning or movement occurred. Attaleiates[34] does mention that at some point the emperor split his own entourage away from the rest of the army and travelled independently but we do not know where this happened or for how long this arrangement lasted.

What is missing?

The historical records have very different priorities than providing a practical account of the Byzantine army's logistical requirements. Michael Psellus was a committed supporter of the bureaucratic faction at court and his account is mainly concerned with emphasising Romanos' failings as a leader. In any case, he stayed behind in Constantinople while the army

went on campaign, although he would undoubtedly have had contact with survivors of the campaign on their return. Michael Attaleiates was on the campaign and was a supporter of Romanos, but focussed more on the events surrounding the battle than on the march. As eyewitness accounts provide inadequate information specific to the Mantzikert campaign, we must look to other works in an attempt to provide specific details as to how the army might have organised itself. Military treatises and accounts of campaigns are sparse from the middle of the 11th century as this was a comparatively peaceful period of Byzantine history. In comparison, the 10th century saw the publication of the three military treatises associated with Constantine Porphyrogennetos[35] along with the *Taktika* of Leo the VI,[36] originally written in the late 9th or early 10th century but subsequently expanded in around 1000 by Nikephoros Ouranos. The three military treatises translated by Dennis[37] also belong to the 10th century, as does the *Sylloge Tacticorum*,[38] but only the *Strategikon* of Kekaumenos remains as a major military work from the pre-Mantzikert 11th century. That is not to say that these works are of no use at all. Even the *Strategikon* of Maurice,[39] written in the late sixth century, carries useful organisational detail that may well have remained current until the 11th century. The 10th century treatise translated by Dennis as *Campaign Organisation and Tactics* for instance[40] provides details on how the Byzantine army should set out its camp. It also provides some practical details useful in moving the army, such as the need to send surveyors a day in advance to set out the following evening's camp site. More detailed discussion of the 10th century Byzantine military context is available in the works of McGeer[41] and Chatzelis and Harris.[42]

However certain key facts are missing from the historical record. The size of the Byzantine army on the Mantzikert campaign is a matter of conjecture, discussed by Haldon[43] and Cheynet[44] among others, although it is possible to make estimates based on the recorded detail of specific units. Modern estimates ranging from 40-60,000 are considered reasonable but lack conclusive evidence.[45] No numbers are given by Byzantine sources at all, although not because Byzantine historians were reticent to exaggerate numbers on principle. Leo the Deacon claimed a total of 400,000 for the army of Nikephoros II Phokas which was almost certainly much

[28] Hillenbrand 2007, 205
[29] Psellus 1966
[30] Attaleiates 2012
[31] Bryennios and Gautier 1975
[32] Friendly 1981, 168
[33] Cheynet 1980, 424
[34] Attaleiates 2012, 267
[35] Constantine Porphyrogenitus 1990
[36] Dennis 2010
[37] Dennis 1985
[38] Chatzelis and Harris 2017
[39] Dennis 2001
[40] Dennis 1985
[41] McGeer 1995
[42] Chatzelis and Harris 2017
[43] Haldon 2008, 172
[44] Cheynet 1980
[45] Haldon 2006b, 13

too large for a field army of the time, to such an extent that there is uncertainty regarding whether he ever meant it to be taken literally.[46]

Some Arabic sources give numbers of soldiers for the Byzantine army at Mantzikert, but these seem more motivated by the desire to exaggerate the scale of the defeat than to provide accurate information. The numbers quoted in Arabic sources, often written hundreds of years after the battle, range from 50,000 through 100,000 and 300,000 to 600,000 soldiers (Table 1). When plotted on a graph against the date of death of the historian, used in the absence of reliable data regarding when each source was written, it reveals an unexpected pattern. Interestingly, it seems the size of the Byzantine army in the Arabic literature tends to get smaller over time (Figure 2), the tale shrinks in the telling.

Table 1: Size of the Byzantine army from Arabic sources

Historian (approximate date of death)	Size of Byzantine army	Page number in Hillenbrand, 2007
Aqsara'I (1333)	50,000	96
Rashid al-Din (1318)	100,000	260
Ibn al-Athir (1233)	200,000	64
Ibn al-Azraq al-Fariqi (1177)	300,000	34
Ibn al-Jawzi (1200)	300,000	38
Nishapuri (1187)	300,000	36
Sibt ibn al-Jawzi (1256)	about 300,000	69
al-Husayni (1225)	over 300,000	53
al-Bundari (1226)	300,000	59
Rawandi (early 13th c.)	600,000	259
al-Turtushi (1126)	600,000	27
Ibn al-Qalanisi (1160)	600,000	30

Numbers in excess of 100,000 are considered highly unlikely by modern historians, but the fact that the practical implications of moving large numbers of troops around Anatolia cannot be demonstrated is significant. Historians have, as yet, no framework within which to evaluate these numbers except via other, often contradictory, historical sources. Existing theories based on historical research suffer from a lack of testability.[47] Other gaps are apparent from the historical record. Although certain points along the route are known, the exact route is not detailed. No

mention is made of the effect that the passage of the army had on the communities that it passed through. Direct archaeological evidence of the march of the army is non-existent due to the ephemeral nature of an army on the march.

This lack of quantified data also applies to the military treatises, indeed there is a lack of quantifiable evidence throughout all areas of the historical debate.[48] No systematic survey has been recorded in which armies of various sizes marching various distances over various terrains are detailed along with departure times, arrival times and lengths of column. This information is important in enabling us to recreate the Byzantine methods of moving their armies. The military treatises themselves survive as a selection of hints and tips rather than a comprehensive 'how to' guide to moving and supplying an army.

The need to model

Much of archaeology consists of the discovery of patterns, whether they are the patterns of finds on an excavation site or the distribution of sites in a landscape. Interpreting these patterns involves creating hypothetical processes to explain how these patterns came to be created and discovered. Why are the sites we research or the objects we find located where they are? Is it an artefact of our recording methods or does it reflect past behaviours? If we are seeing evidence of human activity, what form did it take? What processes can explain the patterns? Archaeologists can create mental models of these processes, but these mental models remain theoretical and untestable. One area of archaeology, experimental archaeology, seeks to work the other way around. These explanatory processes are reattempted in order to determine whether they actually do create the patterns seen in the archaeological record. Hence, people have worked iron to try to associate patterns of hammerscale with different metalworking tasks and conditions.[49] They have knapped flint to compare the results to excavated assemblages.[50] They have dragged a replica *ahu* across Easter Island and erected it with primitive tools and equipment.[51] However, some processes are more amenable to this kind of physical, real world simulation than others.

As the Byzantine army no longer exists it cannot be studied directly, and even if it did it would be a costly and complex endeavour to observe it in all circumstances. The impracticality of marching tens of thousands of people across hundreds of miles in varying conditions

---

[46] Talbot and Sullivan 2005, 104
[47] Haldon 2006b, 4

[48] Haldon 2006b, 2
[49] Dungworth and Wilkes 2007
[50] Aubry *et al.* 2008
[51] Van Tilburg and Ralston 2005

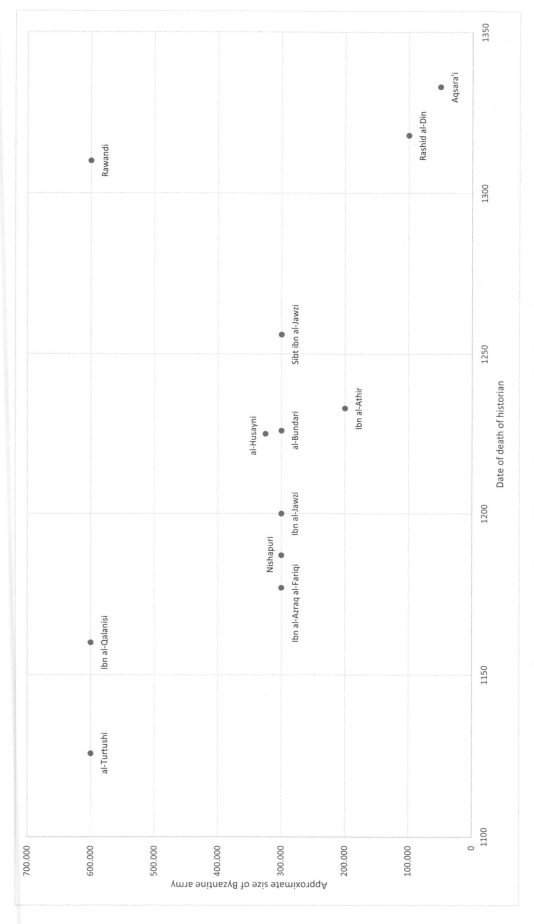

Figure 2: Estimates of the size of the Byzantine army at Mantzikert from Muslim sources.

7

and with varying types of organization should be obvious. Much more practical is the option of creating a model of the Byzantine army within a computer. Rules can be created in order to simulate an army on the march which can then be modified and altered, and the results compared with each other and with the historical facts as we know them.

A model is an abstraction of the system to be studied, containing only the aspects relevant to our research. The values we put in are often hypothetical values, but these can be rooted in real world metrics in order to provide an element of testability. The models can be used to express hypotheses and run simulations over time, producing results which we can compare with both the historical record and the results of other, slightly different, models. Simulation is not re-creation, and the objective is not to build an exact model of the Byzantine army on the march, with the exact number of participants moving in the exact way that they did in 1071. Instead, we are seeking to examine the processes involved with moving the army and how they interact to create the large-scale behaviours of the army as a whole. For this reason, several models must be created and run multiple times with differing parameters in order to provide comparative data. The hypotheses can then be tested against each other and against historical data in order to draw conclusions. The difference between the models' outputs and both the historical record and the outputs of other models will provide new evidence within which to frame the debate over the events of the Mantzikert campaign.

If the results of the models agree with the historical data, it does not necessarily follow that the model is an exact representation of our research target, different processes may produce the same end state. Similarly, if the results of the simulation do not fit observed data it does not mean that the model is of no use, the differences may be caused by known phenomena that are not included in the model. In the end, the models will not produce an image of what *did* happen, but they will be able to indicate what *could* have happened and may allow us to eliminate certain hypotheses that *could not* have happened.

Why can this not be filled with conventional research?

Although much work has been done on Byzantine military organisation and logistics,[52] the information given in military treatises and historical accounts can only take us so far. There is rarely enough information given for us to recreate the mechanisms of transport that were used, even if they were homogeneous across all circumstances. Despite the recommendations

detailed in military treatises, there may have been situations in which the established order was altered to fit the circumstances. The issue of competence is also relevant; even if the treatises describe best practice it does not necessarily follow that this was adhered to.

In the case of Mantzikert, the historical sources have been exhausted in the search for this information. All that is left from a historical point of view are arguments of claim and counterclaim. No new evidence is likely to appear unless a previously undocumented account is discovered. However, it is possible to construct a model of the army, containing within it the characteristics we need to create new evidence within which we can frame the historical debate. Human and animal dietary requirements are well studied by medical professionals, veterinary biologists and sports scientists.[53] There is no reason to think that the space a human being or animal takes up in a marching column and speed at which it travels have changed significantly since Mantzikert, or even within the last 10,000 years. It is possible to use these values to construct hypothetical models of an army on the march in order to test certain practical circumstances. This approach has been used outside of a computer environment by, among others, Jonathan Roth[54] in his work on the Roman army, Donald Engels[55] on the Macedonian army of Alexander the Great, John Lazenby[56] and Stephen O'Connor[57] on the soldiers and sailors of Ancient Greece, John Pryor[58] and Bernard Bachrach[59] on the times of the Crusades and John Haldon on the Byzantine Empire.[60]

The model-based approach

Just such a system utilising fairly simple maths and no computing power beyond that of a calculator was used by Donald Engels in his book about the logistics of the army of Alexander the Great. Although top-down, statistical modelling of an army's logistical arrangements had been attempted for modern defence situations,[61] Engels' book was the first comprehensive attempt to do so with the aim of researching a pre-modern campaign. Working from the historical record and filling in the gaps with more modern terrain and physiological data, Engels constructed a compelling model of the Macedonian army that was able to demonstrate that certain types of logistical arrangements were necessary in order to keep Alexander's force supplied. Working on the basis that each human required 3 lbs of grain and 2 quarts of water per day he was able to calculate

---

[52] McGeer 1995

[53] Carpenter 1921
[54] Roth 1999
[55] Engels 1978
[56] Lazenby 1994
[57] O'Connor 2013; 2015
[58] Pryor 2006
[59] Bachrach 2006
[60] e.g. Haldon 2006a
[61] e.g. Holliday and Gurfield 1968

a total weight of the food and drink requirements of the army. Adding to this the weight of food and water for the animals, he could calculate the number of pack animals required for various sizes of armies marching for various numbers of days between resupply. He was able to take into account areas where water would be abundant, and therefore unnecessary to be carried in bulk, and areas such as the Gedrosian Desert where water would not have occurred at all. This practical approach allowed him to calculate the diminishing amount of space on each pack animal available for the food of others as increased capacity was taken by its own food. With this he could demonstrate quite clearly the ever-increasing number of pack animals required as the length between resupply locations increased. In one example, an army that required 1,121 pack animals to carry one day's worth of supplies would require 2,340 for two days, rising to 40,350 for 15 days and 107,600 for 20 days.[62]

By consulting the historical accounts, he was able to produce a hypothetical size of the army at each point of its route and calculate how many pack animals it would need to get from supply point to supply point. In the process, he demonstrated that without sophisticated logistical arrangements the Macedonian army could never have successfully travelled the distances that it did. By eliminating unlikely or impossible hypotheses he was able to demonstrate not only that Alexander's logistical arrangements frequently involved arranging in advance with the states on his route to provide resources but that logistical considerations at many times dictated how and where he would move.

Pryor uses the same approach slightly differently, to examine the journey of Bohemond and his troops on their march to Thessaloniki in 1096.[63] He used an in-depth examination of the historical records and contemporary evidence for supply requirements to attempt to frame Bohemond's journey in a practical context. He used a hypothetical size and organisational framework of the marching column to estimate the column length and calls on Engels' work and others to examine the food requirements of both human and animal participants. Although basic and highly conjectural, as admitted in the concluding remarks, Pryor's work adds new evidence to a historical problem.

Yuval Harari constructed a hypothetical medieval army of 10,000 combatants in order to examine the practical implications of supply on strategy, and vice versa.[64] Like Engels, he worked with averages for food consumption and the calorie content of foodstuffs in a top-down model with fairly simple maths that can be done with

pencil and paper. Like Engels, his model is a useful step beyond the majority of work that has gone before, but is too simple to explore some of the implications of the results that it delivers.

The problem of complexity

The approaches detailed above are relatively simple to calculate, consisting of a series of values multiplied by the number of individuals. They take top down, systemic approaches to determining the behaviour of the army as a whole. However, the army is not one organism for the purposes of movement, but its overall progress is affected by the interactions between the individuals that comprise it. If one part of the army moves slowly, succeeding units must either bypass the hold-up or be reduced to the same speed. Various tactics can be used to mitigate against this kind of situation, from moving in a broad column where possible to splitting the army over several parallel columns or even marching parts of the army along the same route on subsequent days. Different types of organisation can be used within the column and different combinations of cavalry and infantry are likely to change the overall dynamic. Larger armies should, all other things being equal, move slower than smaller forces, though not necessarily by a predictable amount. This all indicates that the system at work when an army moves is more complex than can be adequately modelled by the approach taken by Engels, Pryor, Harari and others.

But if we are to model the movement and provisioning of an army to a greater level of detail that that used by Engels and others, we would require more detail on these aspects of logistics than is contained in the Byzantine military treatises. Comparative data for our models is supplied by 19th-century military writing, particularly the work of George Armand Furse, which is a largely untapped source of information regarding the movement of armies in conditions comparable to those of the Mantzikert campaign. These more modern sources can be used to fill in detail entirely absent from medieval sources, with caution, enabling plausible models to be created which have details of small interactions between agents and large-scale validation of data.

A system in which the overall behaviour depends on a series of much smaller interactions between its constituent parts and in which this overall behaviour cannot be predicted by examining the constituent parts individually is known as a complex system. Complex systems consist of many small, simple interactions and are evidenced in the forming of snowflakes, the flocking of birds and the behaviour of an ant colony.[65] Complex systems with emergent behaviour, behaviour

---

[62] Engels 1978, 19
[63] Pryor 2006
[64] Harari 2000

[65] Gilbert and Troitzsch 2005, 11

that emerges from a mass of simple interactions, cannot be easily predicted just by knowing the parameters that control the behaviour of one of the individuals involved. If you know the speed of a car on an empty motorway you can calculate how long it will take to reach its destination. If, however, 100 other cars are using the same part of the motorway then knowing the maximum possible speed of one car will not be enough information to help determine its arrival time at its destination. This is because its progress is also affected by its interactions with other road users. It will be able to speed up when the road is clear but will have to slow down when other vehicles impede its progress. You would have to model the whole system in order to accurately estimate its arrival time. The whole system however has no overall controller determining how each car behaves. Each vehicle has its own rules determining its behaviour and it is the interactions of these individuals that gives us the state of the motorway as a whole. So it is with moving large bodies of people.

Agent-based modelling (ABM) is a computer modelling technique whose structure replicates complex systems such as these.[66] ABM contains two main elements: the agents and their environment. The agents are autonomous software units that contain within themselves the rules for their behaviour and the characteristics that describe their relevant attributes. The environment is the area within which these agents act, and can be as sparse or as rich as required. The overall behaviour of the system comes from the interactions between the agents, and between the agents and the environment. This system of autonomous agents operating within an environment is ideal for examining military logistics as it replicates the structure created by large numbers of individuals travelling across, and interacting with, a landscape.

A brief history of ABM

The concept of agent-based modelling has been around since the middle of the 20th century, but it was not until the 1990s that computing power had advanced to the point where it became widely adopted. Prior to that, Conway's 'Game of Life'[67] and the cellular automata of von Neumann and Ulam[68] had laid the theoretical underpinnings while remaining low technology, with Ulam's cellular automata being worked out on sheets of paper. Craig Reynolds' models of the flocking behaviours of birds were among the first that would be recognisable as modern computerised agent-based models and were an early example of how a group of individuals with simple internal rules could replicate

real world phenomena.[69] Agent-based modelling became much more technically feasible once Object Oriented Programming (OOP) languages such as C++ and Java could be combined with sufficient computing power to take advantage of them. OOP emphasises interactions between encapsulated data fields and methods in a way that makes ABM easier to implement. Since then, the technique has been applied in a wide variety of disciplines, from architectural planning and emergency management[70] to more abstract applications in social science.[71]

ABM in archaeology

Although ABM, the modelling of the actions and interactions of autonomous agents within an environment, can be traced back through Conway's 'Game of Life' to the beginnings of cellular automata in the 1940s, its use in archaeology has a much shorter history. As early as the 1960s and 70s, interest was growing in computing's ability to explore general systems theory,[72] however computational power had not advanced to the levels required to model complex systems dynamics.

From the mid-90s onwards archaeologists started to appreciate the use of ABM for exploring the interactions involved in socionatural systems, systems that incorporate both human society and culture as well as natural, environmental factors. ABM's constituent elements of an environment containing autonomous agents acting within it have naturally attracted archaeologists interested in the development of societies. Taking archaeological evidence and using ABM to construct 'what if?' scenarios in an attempt to fill in the inevitable gaps in our knowledge has enabled archaeologists to examine such problems as the rise of settlement complexity in the Bronze Age Fertile Crescent,[73] the emergence of states in Central Asia[74] and the link between ecology and observed settlement patterns in the American south west.[75] State-level ABMs dealing with societal complexity typically require data from many different fields as these systems are affected by many variables. This typically results in large, multidisciplinary projects which are comprised of a wide range of specialists.

The Village Ecodynamics Project (VEP) ran from 2001-2014 and involved archaeologists, geologists, geographers, computer scientists and economists among others in seeking to explain key aspects of

---

[66] Gilbert and Troitzsch 2005, 172
[67] Gardner 1970
[68] Von Neumann 1951

[69] Reynolds 1987
[70] Thompson and Marchant 1995
[71] Epstein and Axtell 1996
[72] Doran 1970
[73] Wilkinson *et al.* 2007
[74] Cioffi-Revilla *et al.* 2007
[75] Kohler 2010

the societies inhabiting the area around south west Colorado between 600-1300.[76] It coupled detailed modelling of terrain and weather with human societies, plant and animal resources and water availability. By treating these elements as one socionatural system they have provided a complex model with which to test established theories and propose new ones. Building on established work such as Van West's published estimates of landscape carrying capacity when used for maize agriculture,[77] the VEP were able to add detail to this work by incorporating it into an environment that simulated temperature and rainfall. The series of models developed as part of the project allowed archaeologists to investigate aspects of the landscape and its use by its inhabitants, including use of resources, location of settlements, societal complexity and possible reasons for the study area's apparent depopulation in the 13th century AD.[78]

Archaeological ABMs do not just consist of large interdisciplinary projects such as the VEP, that amass large quantities of data in order to research a specific subject. More abstract models exist that focus on either one small aspect of a historical situation or a general process appropriate to various places and times. These projects require smaller teams, often being the product of just one or two researchers, Smith and Jung-Kyoo Choi's work on inequality[79] and Shawn Graham's NetLogo models of Roman civic violence[80] being examples. These are unable to draw upon the breadth of knowledge that a large multidisciplinary project can muster but are typically smaller and more accessible, commonly enabling independent researchers to download and alter them at will on easily available platforms such as a standard home PC.

Archaeology as a discipline is making increasing use of ABMs in order to fill gaps where archaeological and historical methods of enquiry cannot provide a full picture due to the very nature of the evidence they draw upon. The new types of evidence being created by ABMs are enabling archaeologists to ask questions previously considered unanswerable, whether they concern specific instances or more general themes. Due to modelling's modular nature, facilitated by its basis in OOP, individual elements can be reshaped and reused by further projects. The ability to take individual elements from previous projects and retest and tune them in a different setting means that future models will be easier to create and more thoroughly validated. Each project leaves a legacy, not only in conclusions on a specific topic, but also in a further set of tools to be utilised by future modellers.

Military historical simulation

ABM's architecture of agents within an environment has lent itself to examining interactions between individuals and their surroundings. Socionatural systems,[81] systems in which both social and natural factors have an effect, are common research topics for ABM within archaeology. Military applications have been less common, despite the long history of simulation use within modern military environments. The solution of military problems was a significant driver in the development of electronic digital computing[82] and the use of simulation for strategic planning, logistical organisation and tactical training has a much older pedigree than computing itself. Kriegsspiel, a proto-wargame developed for the Prussian army in 1812, though leaning on even earlier work, was a battle simulation system that was used to train Prussian army officers in generalship and battlefield tactics.[83] It used a table with modular terrain tiles and wooden blocks to represent forces but allowed replaying of historical battles and the development of 'what if?' scenarios to enable officers to run through possible future engagements without the organisation and expense involved with full-scale military manoeuvres. Its rules were initially very complex, being designed to be as accurate as possible, resulting in simulated battles that often took longer than the real thing. As this was inconvenient and somewhat removed the need to quickly react to the kind of surprising circumstances that crop up on the battlefield, a sleeker version, 'free Kriegsspiel', was developed. Although free Kriegsspiel was more immediate and took less time, it sacrificed some of the earlier version's complex rule system in favour of snap judgments by experienced referees. It took until the development of digital computing for military simulation to develop the ability to maintain complexity whilst allowing fast-paced simulations.

By the 1960s, computing power had advanced to the level where state-supported organisations could use simulation to provide effective training simulators and also to be able to examine the systems used in military organisations and suggest improvements. Computers could now calculate events based on real world data and feed the results back in real time. Mainframe-based software was being used to solve problems of logistics,[84] command and communications,[85] deployment by air,[86] and equipment maintenance,[87] with 200-300 simulation projects being carried out over 3 years in the United

[76] Kohler and Varien 2012
[77] Van West 1994
[78] Kohler et al. 2012
[79] Smith and Choi 2007
[80] Graham 2009

[81] Kohler and van der Leeuw 2007
[82] Copeland 2004
[83] Wintjes 2015
[84] Davis 1967
[85] Tiede and Leake 1971
[86] Sharpe 1965
[87] Conway 1964

States alone by the mid-1960s.[88] More recently, there are enough modern military simulation papers for academic journals to be dedicated to the subject (e.g. The Journal of Defense Modeling and Simulation: Applications, Methodology, Technology), with subjects ranging from the strategy of guerrilla warfare[89] to the damage caused to equipment by IEDs.[90] The focus has moved from the systems-based equations of the 1960s to ABMs such as the U.S Marine Corps' ISAAC [91] and Project Albert.[92]

Although ABMs are used extensively within modern military environments, their use for studying military activity in the past is much rarer. With the exceptions of a game-theory examination of the World War II U-boat campaign in the Bay of Biscay,[93] a brief simulation of Roman military communications along Hadrian's Wall[94] and several models regarding military tactics published with the involvement of Xavier Rubio Campillo,[95] there is very little impact of ABM in military history or archaeology. The majority of recent work on pre-modern military logistics[96] uses technology available in the 19th century and therefore cannot examine the complex systems and emergent behaviours accessible to agent-based approaches.

Is the Byzantine army a complex system?

If agent-based models are ideal for studying complex systems that result from emergent behaviour, can we say that the Byzantine army on the march is such a system? Our answer is yes! Complexity theory shows that where emergent behaviours occur, our knowledge of an individual's state and behaviours will not allow us to predict the behaviour of the system as a whole.[97] This is a situation that applies to an army on the march, as the interactions between the agents and the constraints of the environment prevent accurate predictions of overall speed of the army based on the speed of its constituent elements. There is a concertina effect of stops and starts that prevents soldiers simply moving from one location to another at whatever speed they like. This is eloquently described by George Armand Furse in his book, *The Art of Marching*.

This lengthening is brought about by the oscillations which the column undergoes, owing to the want of uniformity in the individual movements, which have

their origin within the column itself like the wave of the oscillatory motion in a hanging rope. Every single oscillation produces a contracted wave, in which all the individuals are compelled to stop, to this follows a rarefied wave, in which the individuals accelerate their pace. But the checks being instantaneous, as it is natural and laid down, the individual quickening being gradual, the rarefied wave is always greater than the contracted, from which ensues gradually an abnormal lengthening out of the formation.[98]

The limitations of ABM

All models are wrong but some are useful[99]

ABM is only a modelling technique; it may be the most applicable to certain real-world phenomena, but it works within the limits of all models. In creating a model of an army on the march it is not saying that the model is a reproduction of the events of the Mantzikert campaign. A model is a hypothesis to be tested, ready to be refuted or upheld until a better model comes along that more plausibly describes reality. In modelling the march of the Byzantine army, it is accepted that it is not possible to model all aspects of every individual in the marching column, or even just all aspects thought to be relevant. It is, however, possible to model enough of the important aspects to have a model whose results can be compared to the historical record to useful effect. The model will not show what did happen, it will show what would have happened should certain conditions be met. This can then serve as a benchmark against which existing theories about the Mantzikert campaign can be compared.

ABMs, particularly within archaeology where the actual processes involved can no longer be observed, can suffer from the problems associated with equifinality. Equifinality describes the condition whereby a particular end state may have come about by several different processes.[100] Just because there is a model that produces a similar end state to that seen in the archaeological and historical record it does not necessarily follow that the model accurately reflects the system at work. It may be that an entirely different system is responsible, and it will fall to other, possibly more traditional, sources of data to be able to determine when this is happening. Simulation is an addition to other methods of research, rather than a replacement for them.

Archaeology presents many specific problems to ABM. Unlike other topics such as medicine or physics, archaeological modelling generally starts with only a

[88] Dalkey 1967
[89] Doran 2005
[90] Gabrovsek *et al.* 2016
[91] Ilachinski 2000
[92] Horne and Leonardi 2001
[93] Hill *et al.* 2004
[94] Gotts 2017
[95] e.g. Rubio-Campillo *et al.* 2013; 2015; Wittek and Rubio-Campillo 2012
[96] e.g. Bachrach 2006; France 2006
[97] Gilbert and Troitzsch 2005, 10

[98] Furse 1901, 206
[99] Box 1979, 2
[100] Premo 2010

very small percentage of the originally available data. Similarly, the end state of the process to be modelled will be poorly evidenced and may be largely unknown.

The potential of ABM

Making models is a key part of scientific research. Mental models representing hypotheses to be tested are formed when trying to fit data into a coherent system. There are many advantages, however, to formalising these models in a computer system:

- Computer models allow quantification.
- Computer models are replicable.
- Computer models can be easier to show to others.
- Computer models can be expanded and altered by others.
- The process of modelling is useful to hypothesis formation.

Computer models allow real world quantities and metrics to be reliably used. The classical Greek word *'logistike'*, when used in a military context, specifically refers to any strategic or tactical operations based on quantitative calculation.[101] Mathematical equations can be easily represented and resolved allowing data to be calculated reliably and quickly. The ability of modern computers to handle large amounts of data means that computer models can reach sizes impossible with mental models. Computer models can be replicated, either by the original creator or other interested parties. They can be run with exactly the same parameters to verify that the model produces consistent output or with different parameters to compare the results. These parameters must be explicit as computer models deal with absolutes. It should be possible to examine all the data involved with a model and the processes that are enacted upon it. The processing and output of computer models can be used to explain hypotheses to others, whether it is another specialist seeking to examine the methodology behind the model or a generally interested observer. Even just the process of modelling often forces a researcher to think of circumstances and aspects of a problem that are often ignored, even if a computer model itself is never created.[102]

Among the many different types of computer model, agent-based models have specific advantages that make them useful to military logistics researchers:

- They are modular.
- Their structure mirrors that of an army.
- They can make use of similar work in other disciplines.

The modular nature of agent-based models allows elements of the model to be changed easily. Agent types, behaviours and environment variables can be easily varied in order to compare with results from other models. It is this characteristic that makes them so suitable to OOP languages, whose own approach is that of a series of modular entities with their own rules and characteristics. Their modular nature allows elements from other disciplines to be fitted into the system as a whole. Specialists from other subjects can work on individual modules that can be plugged into the system when finished, with only the inputs and outputs needing to be specified beforehand. The hierarchical and modular nature of OOP mirrors that of the army itself, with divisions consisting of several brigades which are made up of several smaller units, right down to the individual level. The hierarchy of classes in the software is similar to the hierarchy within the army itself.

Summary

Despite good work by Engels and others, there are still a lot of unanswered questions regarding how pre-modern armies move and how their practical requirements impact the states which raise and direct them and the lands through which they move. We now have access to tools such as ABM which are suitable for examining the complex interactions between individuals that exist in an army on the march, yet little work has so far been attempted using such methods to research military logistics. By using the case study of Mantzikert, a significant turning point in history with supporting historic accounts which largely ignore logistical concerns, we can demonstrate how ABM can complement traditional historical methods of research. This approach can then be used to provide a new angle with which to approach age old questions regarding other military campaigns.

A note on names and dates

All dates are AD, unless specified. Names have been rendered as closely as possible to their Greek usage at the time of the Mantzikert campaign, except where individuals or places are more well known by their anglicised equivalent.

---

[101] Roth 1999, 1
[102] Aldenderfer 1981

Chapter 2 – The Historical Context

Introduction

When building a model, it often helps to have some data on which to base the characteristics and behaviours of that model. We also need some data against which to validate our model. If we do not know what happened at all on the march to Mantzikert or were entirely ignorant of how the Byzantine army may have moved or fed itself, how do would we know whether the behaviours in our model have any relation to what happened on the campaign? In the case of Mantzikert, the majority of this data comes from the historical literature, not just of late 11th-century Byzantium but further afield in both time and space.

There are three main categories of written records that can help us create a model of the Byzantine army on the march to the Battle of Mantzikert:

- historical accounts of the campaign itself.
- historical accounts of the Byzantine army at other times and in other situations that may give clues to how the army may have been organised.
- military treatises that were intended to help generals organise and use armies, and which may have been studied by the commanders of the Byzantine army in 1071.

These each tend to have their strengths and weaknesses. Obviously, accounts of the army's march to Mantzikert are of paramount importance as they deal with the specific situation that we wish to model. Any details particular to the march have to be taken into account. However, it is the deficiencies in this record that create the need for an alternative way of examining the Mantzikert campaign. The sources omit much of interest and allow little scope for analysis of the processes involved with moving an army. Military treatises were generally written with a view to providing practical details to help the commanders of armies raise, equip, organise and manoeuvre their troops but the extent to which their advice was followed in general, let alone on the Mantzikert campaign specifically, is debatable. Accounts of other campaigns may give us some information regarding how things actually worked in practice, providing examples of behaviours not recorded for the march to Mantzikert. Given enough comparable accounts we may start to understand what classed as usual behaviour for the army under different conditions, enabling the specifics of the Mantzikert campaign to be put into context. However, like military treatises, the details of campaigns which are removed in space and time from Anatolia in 1071 will have to be used with care if applied to the Mantzikert campaign.

In this chapter we will summarise the historical accounts relevant to the march of the army across Anatolia in 1071 from both Byzantine and foreign sources and then assess the military treatises in order to gain as complete a picture as possible of how the Byzantine army behaved in general and how the specific circumstances of the Mantzikert campaign could have changed this.

Byzantine and contemporary sources for the Mantzikert campaign

There are many historical accounts that deal with the events around Mantzikert, both from a Byzantine perspective as well as those from other cultures. Most were written long after the event, in some cases hundreds of years later. Contemporary accounts consist of that of Michael Attaleiates,[103] a military judge who was on the Mantzikert campaign and was an eyewitness to events, Michael Psellus,[104] a noted historian who stayed behind in Constantinople during the campaign, and Skylitzes Continuatus,[105] who extended the writings of John Skylitzes and was likely to have been Skylitzes himself.[106] Of these three, the most comprehensive coverage comes from Michael Attaleiates. Attaleiates' account is largely, though not entirely, favourable to the emperor, while Psellus is very much anti-Romanos. Skylitzes Continuatus' account is primarily based on Michael Attaleiates, although this may not necessarily have been due to a bias towards Romanos IV Diogenes. The Mantzikert campaign is also covered from a semi-neutral position by the Armenians Matthew of Edessa and Aristakes Lastivertc'i as well as by a large number of Arabic historians, some contemporary, most not.

The historical accounts share similar characteristics. They focus on the battle itself rather than the march across Anatolia, they tend to draw moral conclusions from the result, and they are inconsistent in their accounts of the size of the armies. Byzantine sources omit any specific quantification of the size of the army at all, while Arabic sources tend to exaggerate the numbers in the Byzantine army to enhance the Turkish

---

[103] Attaleiates 2012
[104] Psellus 1966
[105] McGeer and Nesbitt 2020
[106] McGeer and Nesbitt 2020, 5

victory and therefore the moral lessons that can be drawn from it.

Michael Attaleiates

Michael Attaleiates was born sometime around 1025 and died before 1085. He studied law in Constantinople and slowly but surely worked his way up in society until he had reached sufficient prestige that he sat on the court that tried Romanos IV Diogenes for rebellion prior to his ascent to the throne. It is testament to his political skills that he could then become a trusted advisor to the new emperor as well as keeping high office after Romanos was deposed, serving the subsequent emperors Michael VII Doukas and Nikephoros III Botaneiates.[107] He dedicated his *History* to Botaneiates which, due to his short reign, dates the work to the years 1078-1081. Attaleiates was a military judge, accompanying Romanos on his three campaigns to rid Anatolia of the Turks and, while he is somewhat of an apologist for his friend, provides an essential eyewitness account of the Mantzikert campaign and those which preceded it.

Attaleiates is doubly useful to our efforts to simulate the Mantzikert campaign as not only is he an eyewitness and historian, but he also shows some concern for the issues regarding the funding and feeding of the empire's soldiers. He records an incident in which a leader of a unit of soldiers had defected to the enemy due in part to not receiving the money with which to pay for rations for his men.[108] He paints a bleak picture of the martial competence of the Imperial decision makers and contrasts this with the brave, sensible, pious Romanos. Attaleiates states that the three months taken by Romanos to prepare the supplies and equipment for a military operation in 1068 were not usually considered enough.[109] Attaleiates joined the 1068 campaign as the man in charge of the military tribunal and so was able to watch the emperor in charge of the army at first hand. Romanos strengthened an army that was supposedly in poor shape and intercepted a band of raiding Turks, albeit by over-extending the horses of his cavalry force.[110] In fact Attaleiates states that Romanos' cavalry force travelled for eight days without their own supplies, presumably picking up whatever they could from the settlements they passed through. This may explain the poor state of the horses if either inappropriate or inadequate supplies were available or if the horses were marched continuously, generally requiring a rest day per week to maintain condition. Attaleiates records 'only' three days' rest at Sebasteia,[111] implying more was normal under the circumstances. He also records an attempt by the Turks to ambush a party of Imperial troops sent out to purchase grain.[112] Logistical considerations again affect the emperor's decision making when an attack on the fortress of Azas is decided upon due to the large amounts of water in the fortress, but subsequently abandoned due to the lack of water outside for the besieging army.[113] He also avoids Antioch in 1068 as it had poor stocks of grain that would be further depleted if the town had to support his army[114] and counsels against heading into a previously ravaged area due to the likely lack of food to sustain a force that, by this time, was much reduced anyway.[115]

Attaleiates and the Mantzikert campaign

Attaleiates records that the emperor set out from Constantinople on March 13th, 1071.[116] He spent a few days on the Asian side of the Bosphorus and then sailed to Helenopolis. He then proceeded east to the Anatolikon province.[117] The Emperor at this point crossed the River Sangarios over a bridge called Zompos[118] where he began to assemble his remaining forces. Attaleiates records that the emperor did not always travel with the army at this point, instead breaking off to supervise his own lands every now and then. When the army crossed the River Halys, the emperor was not with them, but once they were into the Charsianon province he no longer spent time away from the army, staying with it from then until Mantzikert. Attaleiates says 'he did not allow the bulk of the army to enter the city of Kaisereia',[119] which may imply that the army travelled close to it. They camped at a place called Krya Pege (meaning 'Cold Spring'), which 'was lacking in no necessity', an interesting phrase as the necessities listed were firewood and drinkable, cold water. The army spent several days at Krya Pege but moved on when it became obvious that the needs of the army were laying waste to the formerly pleasant location. Interestingly, the punishment for a band of Nemitzoi who had staged a display of disobedience was to move them from the bodyguard to 'last place'.[120] Was this just a social slight or did travelling at the rear of the column also bring with it unwanted practical consequences?

From Krya Pege the army marched to Sebasteia and on to the 'country of the Iberians'. Outside Sebasteia on the road to Koloneia they hit a fork in the road. Romanos chose the route to the left, inadvertently leading the army past the corpses of Manuel Komnenos' campaign of the year before. From here the army continued 'day

---

[107] Attaleiates 2012, ix
[108] Attaleiates 2012, 173
[109] Attaleiates 2012, 189
[110] Attaleiates 2012, 195
[111] Attaleiates 2012, 197
[112] Attaleiates 2012, 197
[113] Attaleiates 2012, 213
[114] Attaleiates 2012, 219
[115] Attaleiates 2012, 249
[116] Attaleiates 2012, 261
[117] Attaleiates 2012, 265
[118] Attaleiates 2012, 267
[119] Attaleiates 2012, 267
[120] Attaleiates 2012, 269

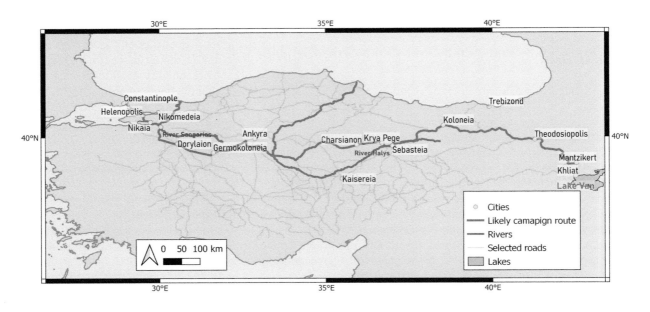

Figure 3: Locations mentioned in the Byzantine historical accounts of the campaign.

after day' to the deserted town of Theodosiopolis, although the former inhabitants had not moved far so there would have been supplies in the area. It was here that the emperor 'remained for not a few days and issued a proclamation that everyone should supply himself with provisions for two months'.[121] This is explained as being necessary due to the wasted nature of the land from hereon in. From here, Romanos sent out foraging parties of Scythians 'as he had done on previous occasions' towards Khliat with the intention of leading the rest of the army in taking back the fortress of Mantzikert and swinging back round to rejoin the Scythians and attack Khliat. With the Scythians were also some Germans and 'another large part of the army' as Romanos considered the garrison of Mantzikert to be weak and he had heard there may have been a large force moving on Khliat. The Scythians, Germans and others sent to Khliat had instructions to prevent the inhabitants gathering the crops in from the fields and denying them to what the emperor hoped would soon be his besieging army.

Once at Mantzikert, the emperor made a fortified camp and prepared for an assault, aided by siege towers 'carefully prepared of huge logs of various kinds of wood and transported on almost a thousand wagons'.[122] Attaleiates also records that 'innumerable' flocks of animals had been brought along. Considering the fact that Romanos considered the area beyond Theodosiopolis waste and that it was here he ordered to collection of two months' worth of supplies, it seems

reasonable that some of these flocks and wagons came from Theodosiopolis at least. The fortress at Mantzikert was taken relatively easily but a force that had been sent outside the fortress was ambushed and, despite a show of force from the emperor, the Turks attacked some people not able to camp within the fortress, including 'those selling army supplies'.[123]

The amount of relevant detail in Attaleiates' account of the Mantzikert campaign and the preceding marches around Anatolia make it an invaluable resource. Attaleiates has an eye for military detail, is not solely concerned with the battle itself or the moralizing aspects of the tale and provides a much more extensive account than that of his contemporary, Michael Psellus. Nevertheless, despite being the most useful of the accounts of the Mantzikert campaign, the logistical detail consists of useful fragments of data, rather than the extensive, detailed account of processes and their results that would be required to build a simulation of the army on the march.

Michael Psellus

The *Chronographia* of Michael Psellus is by far his best-known work. Finished sometime late in the reign of Michael VII Doukas (1071-1078) and therefore predating Attaleiates' *History*, it consists of two parts. The first is the history of the emperors from the ascension of Basil II in 976 to the abdication of Isaac I Komnenos in 1058. The second continues from then until the mid-late 1070s but is heavily slanted in favour

---

[121] Attaleiates 2012, 271
[122] Attaleiates 2012, 277

[123] Attaleiates 2012, 285

of the Doukas family whom Michael knew very well. It is this bias that makes some of the events detailed in the *Chronographia* problematic to analyse, but the bias is at least fairly transparent. Michael Psellus himself spent much of his adult life in and around the Constantinopolitan elite, being an advisor to many emperors, including Constantine IX Monomachus and Constantine X Doukas. He was a highly educated man and an entertaining writer.

His account of the Mantzikert campaign is that of an eyewitness to certain events. He remained in Constantinople during the actual campaign but was in court during the reign of Romanos IV Diogenes and will have spoken to some of those who took part on their return. His chief contribution to the actual events was to support the Doukas family's usurpation of Romanos' throne after the defeat and his supposed bitter regret at the blinding of the emperor comes across as largely hollow considering his partisan views.

Psellus emphasises his military knowledge, remarking that he 'had made a complete study of everything pertaining to military formations, the building of war-machines, the capture of cities, and all the other things that a general has to consider'. However, his writing does not tend to include the kind of useful detail that imply that Psellus has any real interest in military matters, unlike Attaleiates. He says he was reluctantly brought on Romanos' expedition in 1069 but provides only so much information to tell us that Romanos was foolish and that his advisors (himself excepted, obviously) were evil.

Of the Mantzikert campaign, Psellus notes that Romanos took his army to Caesarea and considered a retreat to Byzantium but decided against it. The rest of his account concerns the battle, where Andronikos Doukas' treachery is predictably ignored, and Romanos is given the blame for failing to secure his rear.

Skylitzes Continuatus

The *Continuation of the Chronicle of John Skylitzes*, commonly referred to as *Skylitzes Continuatus*, is so called because it forms a subsequent addition to the history compiled by John Skylitzes. Although uncertain, it is thought that the author was likely to have been John Skylitzes himself, though the two parts of the whole text are still sometimes treated separately. Whereas the main text of John Skylitzes' history ends at 1057, *Skylitzes Continuatus* covers the years between 1057-1079, and therefore is of relevance to our study of the Mantzikert campaign. Skylitzes relied on the works of others to compile his accounts and, as a result, less is known of his life and opinions than of some other historians such as Attaleiates and Psellus. His account

of the Mantzikert campaign is based heavily on the work of Attaleiates, but *Continuatus* as a whole also incorporates some of the work of Psellus, plus some unknown sources. As Skylitzes himself was thought to have lived between 1040-1110,[124] it is not impossible that some of these unknown sources may have been eyewitnesses to events.

There are some differences between *Skylitzes Continuatus* and the *History* of Attaleiates, and it is uncertain whether they arise from some unknown historical source or from conversation Skylitzes may have had with eyewitnesses. Skylitzes states that the Uzes and Franks which split from the army after Theodosiopolis did so because they were heading to Khliat to obtain provisions. He also names Joseph Tarchaneiotes as the man who persuaded the forces sent to Khliat to ignore the emperor's request for reinforcements.[125]

Matthew of Edessa

The *Chronicle* of Matthew of Edessa was completed sometime between 1130 and 1137.[126] Matthew's *Chronicle* covers the years between 952 and 1128 and provides an account of the Mantzikert campaign. Although it is not clear when the *Chronicle* was started, it is unlikely to have been earlier than 1101, 30 years after Mantzikert. Matthew's date of birth is also unknown, but it can be reasonably accurately, but not precisely, dated to the last quarter of the eleventh century. This means that although Matthew had probably not been born at the time the Mantzikert campaign happened, he will almost certainly have spoken to people who may have had personal recollections to share. Being an Armenian monk, Matthew has a different perspective on the battle between the Byzantines and the Turks.

> *Thus, a very great and formidable number of troops was gathered together from the entire country of the Goths, from all the Bulgars, from all the distant islands, from Cappadocia and all of Bithynia, from Cilicia and Antioch, from Trebizond, and [last but not least] from Armenia – whose remnants of very courageous soldiers still existed; moreover, Diogenes had mercenaries from the infidels of Khuzistan brought, and thus the emperor gathered together a formidable army as numerous as the sands of the sea.*[127]

Matthew records Romanos pillaging Sebasteia as a result of some friction between the Byzantines and the Armenians and claiming to intend to do away with the Armenian faith on his return from the campaign, although this may be an attempt to portray Romanos as

[124] McGeer and Nesbitt 2020, 6
[125] McGeer and Nesbitt 2020, 121
[126] Andrews 2016, 1
[127] Dostourian 1972, 231

falling foul of God and therefore setting himself up for the coming military failure.

Matthew records some details regarding the movement of Alp Arslan through the area in the prelude to the battle at Mantzikert. He says that he received horses, mules and food from the dux of Edessa and lost 'countless' horses and camels on a forced march.[128]

Aristakes Lastivertc'i

Little is known of the life of Aristakes but he is believed to be an Armenian cleric and historian who wrote his *History* sometime between 1072-1079. The village of Lastivert is thought to be in the region of Theodosiopolis and so it's possible that Aristakes may have seen Romanos' army travel through on their way to Mantzikert. Aristakes gives a brief description of the battle which shares some characteristics with the Byzantine sources but seems to be a poor reflection of the actual events of the campaign. He emphasizes Romanos' pride in a similar way to Michael Psellus, but this may have been for the purposes of drawing a religious lesson from the story. Aristakes does, however, mention some brief details about the Byzantine journey to Mantzikert. He states that 'halting in Biwt'ania, he assembled a countless host'. He also records that 'with an unbecoming plan, [the emperor] sent numerous troops under commanders along a different road, while he himself with a great host travelled East until he reached the great city of T'eodupolis [Karin/Erzurum], where he arranged the cavalry'. It is tempting to interpret this as a misunderstanding of the division of the force that occurred after Theodosiopolis but that event seems to be referred to a little later in the narrative, so it may be a reference to an actual event on the march to Mantzikert that is omitted from all other accounts. The fact that Aristakes was writing shortly after the battle leaves open the possibility that this was a real event ignored by his contemporaries and deemed too uninteresting to be repeated by the historians who followed.

Muslim historians

The earliest Islamic source for the Battle of Mantzikert is that of al-Turtushi.[129] Although his account is written long after Mantzikert, al-Turtushi may have met eyewitnesses to the battle during his travels round the Middle East in the 1080s. He puts the size of the Byzantine forces at 600,000, surely too large for an army of the time, and the Seljuk force at 12,000. He also includes some highly unlikely details not found in any other account. Several of the Arabic and Persian sources mention Byzantine siege engines, their presence

supported by Attaleiates, as well as the large baggage train that was pillaged by the Turks after the battle. The message of Mantzikert, that of the triumph of Islam over Christianity despite overwhelming odds, is repeated by various writers through the Middle Ages, long after the Seljuks had ceased to be a recognisable group. The Muslim sources gives figures for the sizes of the Seljuk and Byzantine forces, but these vary wildly and are highly unreliable. In the end, Carole Hillenbrand is forced to conclude 'it is fruitless to hope to reconstruct a battle from medieval Muslim sources'[130].

Relevant sources for the Byzantine army in other situations

Historical accounts of the Byzantine army in action at other times may give us information that can be assumed correct for the Mantzikert campaign. It can also provide comparative information that help us to understand the sources that directly deal with the campaign. Thanks to the relative paucity of information on the Mantzikert campaign itself, any account that provides information regarding the size, organisation or behaviour of armies is potentially useful. Some writers are largely uninterested in military matters, but others actually went on campaigns and provide plausible details not found in military treatises. The obvious caveat is that the army changes over time and the size and composition of the army, and therefore presumably some of the mechanisms used to support it, differs from campaign to campaign. Nevertheless, there are commonalities associated with the practical aspects of moving people, animals and goods over a landscape that would apply to armies both before and after Mantzikert.

Leo the Deacon

Leo the Deacon was born sometime around 950 and published his *History* before the end of the millennium.[131] In it he covers the reigns of four emperors: Romanos II, Nikephoros II Phokas, John I Tzimiskes, and Basil II, the latter only briefly. Leo participated in the Bulgarian campaign of 986 and was present at the Battle of Trajan's Gate. Somewhat unusually for a man of the cloth, his work mainly focusses on military matters and can therefore be a useful source of information regarding the Byzantine army. He recounts the military campaigns of emperors and generals and his work mainly serves to confirm that the advice given in the military treatises is followed in real life. He notes that Nikephoros II Phokas sets out from Constantinople for a campaign against the Arabs around the Spring equinox, which was around the same time of year as Romanos

---

[128] Dostourian 1972, 234
[129] Hillenbrand 2007, 26

[130] Hillenbrand 2007, 137
[131] Talbot and Sullivan 2005

IV Diogenes set out for Mantzikert.[132] He records that Nikephoros stopped to muster his army in Cappadocia before heading to Mopsuestia, which he besieges and takes by late Autumn, which leaves the possibility that the march to Mopsuestia took a similar amount of time to Romanos' march to Mantzikert. There are other suggestions of a set campaigning season, raising questions of exactly how this would have been supported and what constrains it placed on army size and movement. Shorter campaigns still started in the springtime, John Tzimiskes' attack on the Rus in Bulgaria in 971 for instance was already besieging Preslav by Easter,[133] implying that either Spring was the ideal time to start a campaign, or it was the earliest possible time and Emperors tended to err on the side of caution when deciding how long a campaign would last. The *Taktika* of Nikephoros Ouranos claims that campaigns should begin in winter, autumn or spring to warm, fertile regions, and in spring, summer or autumn for cool and temperate regions, indicating that spring works well for either.[134]

Army sizes in the *History* tend to number in the tens of thousands, with one noted exception of a Byzantine army of 400,000. This number is so out of place that the translators make efforts to explain its outlying nature.[135] Examples in the tens of thousands need no such explanation, being considered plausible when compared with other accounts, but the practical foundations for these assumptions are largely unexplored.

One aspect of Leo's *History* that would add a note of caution to any attempt to use it as a direct source of information for modelling the Mantzikert campaign is that the vast majority of manoeuvres described within it take place under threat of enemy action, giving them a different character to the march towards Mantzikert. Nevertheless, as a historical source which confirms the validity of the military treatises, Leo's *History* is a useful document.

John Skylitzes

John Skylitzes produced his *Synopsis historion*, translated into English under the title 'A Synopsis of Byzantine History 811-1057'[136], as a compilation of other, earlier works. Little is known of John Skylitzes himself although it seems likely he was born before 1050 and may have lived well into the 12th century.[137] His work survives in two forms: a shorter version dealing with the years 811-1057 and a longer version containing

the previously mentioned Skylitzes Continuatus, that covers the period of the Battle of Mantzikert and continues up until 1079 and the reign of Nikephoros III Botaneiates.[138] Although the main part of the *Synopsis historion* deals with events before Mantzikert, it is still useful in places.

Although not as focussed on military matters as Leo the Deacon, Skylitzes includes some details regarding the size of armies and their movement during campaigns. Skylitzes' *Synopsis* was clearly well known and widely used within the Empire as it survives via a comparatively large number of extant manuscripts. One of these manuscripts, known as the Madrid Skylitzes, is fabulously illustrated and serves as an unparalleled source of imagery from the Byzantine late 12th century.[139] The Madrid Skylitzes also provides some rare examples of almost contemporary illustrations of soldiers with their equipment, providing some supporting data to the equipment descriptions in the military treatises. Skylitzes sought to produce a chronography, a retelling of history largely stripped of the eulogies and censure that skewed the work of other historians, although he displays some clear bias for or against some of his subjects. It reads largely as a chronological description of the reigns of emperors and focusses almost exclusively on events within the empire itself. Sometimes Skylitzes seems to reproduce his sources with little alteration, but his work remains extremely valuable as many of his sources are lost to us, surviving primarily through Skylitzes' *Synopsis*.

Military treatises

Military treatises are known from various points of the lifetime of the Byzantine Empire, particularly the tenth century. They were compiled by, or at the behest of, emperors and high-ranking officers. Their general purpose was to pass on useful information regarding raising, equipping, feeding and moving an army as well as tactics for winning battles against the likely enemies of the day. Of the Byzantine writings dealing with military logistics, the most prominent include Maurice's *Strategikon*,[140] the treatise on *Campaign Organization and Tactics*,[141] the military treatises of Constantine VII Porphyrogenitus[142] and the *Taktika* of Leo VI.[143]

Strategikon of Maurice

The *Strategikon* of Maurice was written in either the late 6th or early 7th century, probably sometime between

---

[132] Talbot and Sullivan 2005, 101
[133] Talbot and Sullivan 2005, 181
[134] McGeer 1995, 143
[135] Talbot and Sullivan 2005, 104
[136] Skylitzes and Wortley 2010
[137] Skylitzes and Wortley 2010, x
[138] Skylitzes and Wortley 2010, xxxi
[139] Skylitzes and Wortley 2010, xxx
[140] Dennis 2001
[141] Dennis 1985
[142] Constantine Porphyrogenitus 1990
[143] Dennis 2010

592-610.[144] There is an element of debate regarding whether it was actually written by the emperor Maurice (582-602), his brother-in-law, Philippicus, or by an unknown author. Whoever the author is, they clearly had experience leading men into battle on both the eastern and western parts of the empire and yet also knew aspects of military law and had studied the writings of earlier military works. While apparently dating from well before the period of study relevant to the Mantzikert campaign, the *Strategikon* was a tremendously significant book, influencing works all the way through the Byzantine period. Sections were reused in the military writing of Leo VI and, while the battle tactics of more contemporary works are quite different, enough organisational and logistical details are sufficiently similar to conclude that moving and feeding the army of Mantzikert would have involved problems and solutions familiar to the emperor Maurice.

The *Strategikon* places most emphasis on the equipment, organisation and use of cavalry, reflecting the composition of armies of the time. There is, however, some discussion of mixed forces and the formations they might take up. It distinguishes between marches performed away from the threat of enemy action and marches performed with the enemy nearby, a distinction also made in other works such as *Campaign Organisation and Tactics*. It contains sections on battlefield tactics, the characteristics of the likely opponents of the empire at that time and, of more relevance to the Mantzikert campaign, how to organise the army's movement and camping. It goes into useful detail regarding the day-to-day mechanisms of moving the force in different circumstances and provides some detail of the routines used when in camp. Although some mention is made of how foraging for animal fodder works, it largely omits discussion of mechanisms of supply, quantities of food, the means by which foodstuffs were procured and the effects that this may have had on the communities which provided for the army.

Maurice devotes an entire section of the *Strategikon* to the practice of marching through one's own country with no threat of enemy activity, which is particularly appropriate to the Mantzikert campaign.[145] Among his recommendations are:

- the army should not be mustered in one place as this will generate discord amongst the earliest arrivals who would be waiting too long.
- the commanding general should be at the head with his specially selected troops.

- the general should stay around at river crossings to ensure everything is done in an orderly fashion.
- cultivated fields should be avoided where possible.
- if the army is small then it should avoid inhabited areas in case spies observe it and relay the information back to the enemy.

Taktika of Leo VI

The *Taktika* of Leo VI[146] differs from some other military treatises such as the *Strategikon* of Maurice or the works of the Nikephoros', Phokas and Ouranos, in that Leo VI never led an army into battle and had very little personal experience to contribute. Instead, Leo compiled a text consisting of works by earlier writers and his own observations, fitted into a format that largely follows the order of the campaigning year. It starts with the qualities required of a general before moving on to planning, organisation, equipment, logistics, camps, preparations for battle and the battle itself before also covering sieges, surprise attacks, the characteristics of some of Byzantium's enemies and naval warfare. Leo mainly relies on Maurice's *Strategikon* but also uses the work of more ancient authors such as Onasander, Aelian and Polyaenus.[147]

Leo's motivation for compiling the text was to provide an updated version of the advice given by proven earlier authorities to his generals to serve as a practical handbook to guide them in their duties.[148] Leo was a prolific writer and was known as Leo The Wise. He produced works on a variety of topics related to government and religion. His *Taktika* was written in the very early 900s and, although it is largely a reworking of earlier texts, its format and content proved influential among writers of military works throughout the tenth century,[149] although the extent to which it was actually used by generals in the field is uncertain. Although it relies on the *Strategikon* for much of its content, some of the advice is changed in a way that indicates an attempt to move away from the source material if required. Maurice's *Strategikon* prioritises cavalry forces whereas the *Taktika* contains much more information regarding infantry equipment and tactics and places more emphasis on combined forces of cavalry and infantry.[150]

Sylloge Tacticorum

The *Sylloge Tacticorum* dates from the first half of the tenth century and its name translates as *A Compilation*

---

[144] Dennis 2001, xvi
[145] Dennis 2001, 20–22

[146] Dennis 2010
[147] Haldon 2014, 25
[148] Dennis 2010, 7
[149] Haldon 2014, 17
[150] Haldon 2014, 79

of Tactics.[151] Like many Byzantine military treatises, it is a compilation of advice from earlier works, both fairly recent sources like the *Taktika* of Leo VI and sources from classical antiquity such as Onasander. It dates itself to 903-4, but this date has been largely rejected by modern scholars who disagree as to the actual date of composition.[152] It is possible that the work dates from the second quarter of the tenth century and the earlier attribution was an attempt by Constantine VII Porphyrogenitus to avoid giving credit to his hated father-in-law Romanos I Lekapenos, during whose reign it may have been created. The fact that it seems to have been revised at some point after its creation muddies the waters even further, as does the fact that the earliest known manuscript is from over four hundred years after its creation. The fact that the *Sylloge Tacticorum* contains mainly recycled information is not of significant detriment to its usefulness, as it is in the choices made regarding what has been used, or not, and what has been discarded from earlier works that we can learn about what the compiler considered worth preserving.

The *Sylloge Tacticorum* is an eclectic mix of organisational details, advice for armies on the march, descriptions of the correct equipment for soldiers and a compilation of ruses to be aware of when campaigning against the empire's enemies. It contains a section that compiles and summarises events from classical antiquity so that contemporary generals can learn from the distant past. There is little regarding the march of an army that is not echoed in other works, particularly the *Taktika* of Leo VI. It contains a useful description of a mixed infantry and cavalry force of 26,184 men, of which 19,414 (74%) are infantry and 6,770 cavalry. This provides a useful model on which to base the size and composition of any hypothetical Mantzikert army. Whether a Byzantine army of exactly this size ever set out or not, it is presumably representative of the kind of force the compiler expected his audience to have to lead.

Constantine VII Porphyrogenitus

The Byzantine Emperor Constantine VII Porphyrogenitus had some involvement with three military treatises.

- A very short treatise involving a list of mustering points (*aplekta*), and which forces are to muster at each on an expedition to the east.
- A fairly short overview of some of the preparations required before setting out on an expedition and some organisational detail of how the army moves. This is presented as a description of how Constantine the Great and

Julius Caesar organised expeditions, but it seems clear that this is just a literary device to present the advice as reputable.
- A much longer compilation of advice from Constantine VII to his son, Romanos II.

Although the modern published translation is entitled *'Constantine Porphyrogenitus: Three Treatises on Imperial Military Expeditions'*,[153] it is likely that the second of the three was a military treatise by Leo Katakylas, compiled during the reign of Leo VI, possibly around 903-912.[154] The third seems to be mainly written by Constantine VII Porphyrogenitus at some point before the late 950s, though possibly revised later, and was addressed to his son, Romanos II. Constantine was a keen scholar but never led an army and so the information contained in the third treatise is drawn from a variety of sources, including the second treatise by Leo Katakylas. It is plausible that this third treatise was compiled in order to provide Constantine's son with a useful handbook to help him succeed in the kinds of military endeavours that Constantine himself had not been able to take part in. The first treatise is a list of gathering points for the army that seems to have been put together by a later redactor from notes left by Constantine.[155]

This highlights a significant factor in trying to piece together Byzantine military practice from the treatises available. Large-scale military expeditions were not particularly common, and decades could pass between them. If it had been 30-40 years since the last significant campaign, then anyone seeking advice on how to proceed would have had to rely on the texts written as a result of previous experiences. Therefore, the absence of up-to-date military treatises from the years before Mantzikert may have been a situation presented to Romanos IV Diogenes himself, in addition to being a problem for the 21st-century military simulation builder. Of course, smaller scale military activity will have been taking place on an almost constant basis, however, coping with a large body of troops provides unique challenges not faced in the task of moving forces an order of magnitude smaller.

Constantine is one of the few treatise writers to acknowledge that, as military practices can change over time, an explicit statement was required about when the procedures contained in the text were considered current. He attests that the practices he describes had remained current since his grandfather Basil's days, making them potentially almost 100 years old.[156]

---

[151] Chatzelis and Harris 2017
[152] Chatzelis and Harris 2017, 5–7

[153] Constantine Porphyrogenitus 1990
[154] Constantine Porphyrogenitus 1990, 66
[155] Constantine Porphyrogenitus 1990, 63
[156] Constantine Porphyrogenitus 1990, 97

Constantine's treatise differs from most of the others in that it mainly deals with military campaigns from the point of view of an emperor who does not share in his soldier's misery. It contains no recommendations for suitable sites to set up camp or which battlefield formations suit which enemies. Instead, it concerns itself with the duties of an emperor from a ceremonial point of view and as the head of the Imperial household. It has much more information on the baggage requirements of the Imperial retinue and what the pack animals are actually carrying than the other treatises described here. It is, in short, a treatise written by a scholar who lived a luxurious lifestyle of ceremony and who had never, and would never, need to command an army in battle.

Nikephoros Phokas

The *Praecepta militaria* of Nikephoros Phokas was written around 965,[157] and it is at least plausible, if not likely, that it was written by the emperor himself rather than merely being attributed to him.[158] Nikephoros Phokas had extensive military experience before becoming emperor and his reign was one of the most militarily successful in the empire's history so the *Praecepta militaria* comes to us with the highest credentials. It is mainly concerned with infantry and cavalry battlefield organisation but also includes some useful information on encampments and the organisation of baggage. It was a synthesis of previous work combined with the experiences of the author and although Nikephoros was clearly familiar with ancient military works, the *Praecepta militaria* is intended as a manual to help generals cope with the battlefield as it was at the time.

Campaign Organisation and Tactics

Campaign Organisation and Tactics is a treatise that was translated and published in English by George T Dennis as part of his *Three Byzantine Treatises* book.[159] It's authorship and date are uncertain, but Dennis is inclined to ascribe it to Nikephoros Ouranos as advice given by him to a young Basil II during the early 990s when the Byzantine Empire was on the offensive against the Bulgarians.[160] The treatise consists mainly of practical advice for an army on the march, including distances, procedures and recommendations. The treatise starts with some regulations regarding the arranging and setting up of camps to protect the army overnight. It then sets out the process for breaking camp on the day of a march using a series of trumpet blasts to indicate at what point certain procedures should take place. There are a series of practical bits of advice regarding the

actual movement of the army, both when the enemy is near and also when the army is in safe, friendly territory. The author is clearly both educated and sober and his recommendation to avoid showy equipment in favour of good quality items made of plain iron is typical of the tone of this treatise.[161] The effectiveness of the army is paramount throughout. Interestingly, the author states that it is not possible to transport more than 24 days' supply of barley for an army's horses.[162] This is very close to the theoretical maximum derived by Donald Engels' work on the army of Alexander the Great in which his hypothetical pack animals could carry 250lbs in weight and required 10lbs of food per day.[163] The treatise goes on to deal with certain aspects of siege warfare and recommends ensuring the army is kept active, well recorded and is able to practice setting up camp a few times in friendly territory before moving into more threatening areas.

With its emphasis on practical advice about the essentials of moving and feeding an army, it's not hard to imagine a hypothetical, friendly and very interesting conversation between its author and the great Victorian student of logistics, George Armand Furse, whose work will be introduced later on.

Taktika of Nikephoros Ouranos

The *Taktika* of Nikephoros Ouranos was written around the end of the tenth century.[164] Nikephoros Ouranos was a civil official and soldier of the late tenth century and the complete *Taktika* comprises 178 chapters, although not all have been translated and published.[165] It is largely based on earlier works, among them the *Taktika* of Leo VI and the *Praecepta militaria* of Nikephoros Phokas.[166] The section published by Eric McGeer in *Sowing the Dragon's Teeth* is a revised and expanded version of the *Praecepta militaria* with original additions by Nikephoros Ouranos. The fact that Ouranos, an experienced soldier, largely reproduces the work of Phokas implies that it is a text which had proved useful in his own career. He provides supplementary advice gained from his military experience and his role as governor of Antioch. Nikephoros mentions in an original addition of his own that 'The men of old, in their conduct of siege warfare, constructed many devices such as rams, wooden towers, scaling ladders, with various features, as well as tortoises and all kinds of other things which our generation has never ever seen'.[167] This apparent lack of such siege machinery contrasts with Attaleiates' claims of such machinery's presence at Mantzikert, implying

---

[157] McGeer 1995, vii
[158] McGeer 1995, 173
[159] Dennis 1985
[160] Dennis 1985, 243

[161] Dennis 1985, 289
[162] Dennis 1985, 303
[163] Engels 1978, 19
[164] McGeer 1995, vii
[165] McGeer 1995, 79
[166] McGeer 1995, 80
[167] McGeer 1995, 161

that either they had come back into fashion by 1071 or Ouranos is referring only to certain specific types of siege machinery.

Conclusion

The accounts of people who were on the Mantzikert campaign, or who may have met people who were, provide some information that we can use to simulate the Byzantine army's march. Michael Attaleiates especially, provides useful information regarding the route taken and some extra logistical detail that cannot be ignored due to its comprehensive and authoritative nature. It goes a long way from providing the kind of detail required to build a model of the army on the march, let alone tell us about the effects it may have had on the settlements along the route, though. Anecdotal evidence is available from other historians, particularly those from the 10th and 11th centuries. This can plausibly fill in some of the gaps, though the concerns of these writers were far removed from documenting the practical aspects of moving and feeding an army. Military treatises are more specifically relevant in this regard, although these are all written at some remove from the events of Mantzikert as well as being debatable in how well the advice they contain maps onto the actual behaviours of an army on the march. Overall, though, the Byzantine historical record gives us a solid starting point in our attempts to model the army's march through Anatolia.

However, there are critical gaps in our knowledge that can only be filled by other types of evidence. These gaps include how the army was supported by the settlements through which it passed and what effect this may have had on those people. As the army is intimately linked to many different areas of the Byzantine state and society there are many aspects of this complex system of interactions that the historical accounts do not help us with. We will continue by looking at the wider context of Byzantine society as revealed by history and archaeology and then go on to describe a possibly surprising source of useful data.

Chapter 3 - The Byzantine World

The march to Mantzikert did not take place in a vacuum and there are many aspects of Byzantine society that affected, and were in turn affected by, the planning and execution of the emperor's campaign to confront the Seljuks. This poses problems as, in order to properly research the army's march, we would ideally first have to know about everything else of relevance to the army, which turns out to be almost everything about Byzantine society in one way or another. On the plus side, the process of researching the logistics of the army can help us expand our knowledge of these many areas of Byzantine life.

The context for the army's march includes aspects of Byzantine demography, economy, geography and the relationship between the state and society. The army must be raised, moved, fed, watered, organised, equipped, paid, disciplined when necessary, convinced that God is behind them and at the end of the march, set loose on the enemy in a sufficiently capable condition to win a battle. In order to do this, the Byzantine state would need administrators, quartermasters, surveyors, judges, foragers, guides, muleteers, arms manufactories, horse ranches, a compliant population with some surplus food, knowledge of the road network, and an understanding of how the changing of the seasons affects water courses and harvests.

The fact that a military campaign involves many areas of society and relies on many aspects of government, the environment and even, in the case of the road network, the history of Anatolia, presents both problems and opportunities. If our goal was re-creation of the Mantzikert campaign, the sheer amount of data that we would need renders the task impossible. Yet this is not our goal, as we are using simulation to work our way out from certain known points in an attempt to gain new perspectives on both the movement of the army and the elements of society and the environment on which it depends.

For this reason, this chapter provides a summary of the wider historical context surrounding the march, including some detail on the organisations and factors that will have affected the campaign, from finance and food to transport infrastructure and settlement patterns. This provides an overview of the world within which the march to Mantzikert took place, a world within which the simulation's results must function and about which the results may provide views unavailable via more traditional methods.

Byzantine taxation

The finances of the empire, and especially the way it funded military campaigns, are areas in which the kind of data that we would need in order to build complex models are largely absent. We can plausibly state, however, that the military was the recipient of a significant, probably the largest, percentage of tax revenue.[168] In the ninth century, an anonymous treatise was able to say that most tax revenues were spent on the army,[169] and the situation was unlikely to have been much different in the late 11th century. Other matters of public importance were funded from taxes such as the building of ships or walls, however paying the military represented the largest outgoings on the state's balance sheet.[170]

Tax was mainly derived from two sources: commerce and agriculture.[171] The nature and rates of these sources of taxation varied over time and the amount of both commerce and agriculture that could be taxed also varied, with the size and affluence of the empire and its neighbours being key variables. The Byzantine economy was overwhelmingly agrarian, like most economies up to the modern era. Large amounts of tax were collected from agricultural productivity, whether in kind or commuted to cash via economic exchange. Commerce played a much smaller role in taxation, but a large role in mobilising agrarian wealth.[172]

Taxation was collected either in cash or in kind and this included the provision of food or equipment for military campaigns. It should be mentioned, however, that payment of foodstuffs in kind for military campaigning could have been levied as an extraordinary tax. This might also have been separate from regular taxation schemes, and offset against future tax payments although, in reality, this was liable to be forgotten. These supplemental taxes could be levied at any time, and functioned as a way of filling the gap created by uncertain expenditure and uncertain tax income. The downside to supporting an army via special taxation was that it risked alienating the taxed population and reducing their support for both the campaign and the emperor who instigated it.

---

[168] Hendy 2008, 157
[169] Haldon 2015, 345
[170] Dennis 1985, 13
[171] Haldon 2015, 347
[172] Angold 2007

As a factor in campaign planning, finances would have formed a separate but related consideration to the provisioning of the army. Determining the affordability of an expedition was a necessary preliminary step according to Leo Katakylas,[173] implying that intended expeditions could be changed or cancelled if the financial resources were not sufficient. This includes both the financial resources to raise an army and also those required to support it on campaign. Tactics and generalship are favoured by Maurice over large numbers of men as 'the former provide security and advantage to men who know how to use them well, whereas the other brings trouble and financial ruin'.[174] This was probably more true of the 11th century than preceding periods, as an army that had previously been partly composed of subjects providing military service in exchange for land had largely given way to one that was paid for with cash.

An earlier system that required military service from people across the Empire had, by the 11th century, been transformed into one in which such service was rendered via a payment that could be used to equip native soldiers and hire mercenaries.[175] This increased the flexibility of the army but resulted in a heterogeneous mix of nationalities and types of troops. Troops were supported at locations across the empire and field armies of both native and foreign troops were also stationed around Constantinople, but individual mercenary units could also be hired on an *ad hoc* basis for individual campaigns. Foreign troops could be hired for cash but could also be acquired as part of treaty arrangements.[176]

How much money was needed to pay for an expedition of the size of Mantzikert is debatable. Although there are some records regarding specific amounts that soldiers were paid, uncertainty over how often they were paid and how much food and equipment they were provided with render it impossible to state with any certainty how much the Mantzikert campaign cost. The records allow us to examine differences in pay between different types and ranks of troops but not to determine how much money the army would have had to take with it. We do know that Manuel I spent 2,160,000 gold coins, approximately 8 tons of gold, on a military expedition to Italy in 1155.[177] The expenses for this expedition would have included significant 'gifts' to local rulers and the expedition did not end until 1158 so the circumstances were very different to those of Mantzikert. Lavish spending such as this, however, is recorded throughout the pre-Mantzikert eleventh century and there is no indication that the treasury

was unduly stretched by the cost of the Mantzikert campaign.[178] The financial cost of the Mantzikert campaign must also be measured against the cost of not going on campaign, as the Turks who raided eastern Anatolia would have been taking their toll on agricultural productivity, livestock and lives.

The affordability of a campaign was not just dependent on tax income but also the cash reserves built up by the current and preceding emperors. The history of the Byzantine empire is replete with rulers either building up surpluses in the treasury or squandering those built up by their predecessors, whether by military expenditure, displays of largesse or extravagant public works. Further back in Byzantine history the unsuccessful expedition of Leo I against the Vandals in 468 reportedly costed over 60,000 lbs of gold and virtually bankrupted the empire.[179] Closer in time to the events of Mantzikert, Basil II's success in building up the Imperial treasury were squandered by Constantine IX Monomachos and the Empress Zoe in the mid eleventh century.[180]

In the absence of specific details in historical accounts, it is a difficult task to quantify how much money Romanos had at his disposal when he assumed the role of emperor in 1068. There is a complicated relationship between the empire's economy, its Imperial reserves and its coinage. There was a steady debasement in the gold content of the coinage from the reign of Constantine IX which extended beyond Romanos IV Diogenes to the reign of Nikephoros III Botaneiates, which ended in 1081.[181] It is tempting to draw a straight line between this debasement and a lack of Imperial reserves and therefore a weakening of economic activity, yet there are other indicators of a strong economy within the empire in the decades before Mantzikert. We should therefore be circumspect about oversimplifying the complex Byzantine economic situation. Nevertheless, it is hard to ignore that some areas of the economy may have been in trouble before Mantzikert and the chaos of the decade which followed Mantzikert is unlikely to have improved things.

Cecile Morrisson's analysis of the monetary 'devaluations' of the eleventh century allows us to distinguish between an expansionary phase (lasting until approximately 1067) and a subsequent recessionary phase (beginning with the reign of Romanos IV Diogenes), during which a veritable monetary crisis raged, linked to military defeats and to the need to replenish a treasury that had been left high and dry.[182]

---

[173] Constantine Porphyrogenitus 1990, 85
[174] Dennis 2001, 64
[175] Haldon 1999, 125
[176] Haldon 1999, 126
[177] Laiou 2002, 3

[178] Laiou 2002, 738
[179] Hendy 2008, 221
[180] Hendy 2008
[181] Hendy 2008, 509
[182] Laiou 2002, 402

Taking this as a starting point, there is circumstantial evidence that the Byzantine economy was not in particularly rude health at the time of the Mantzikert campaign but no direct evidence that the cost of the campaign unduly stretched the resources of the empire. The increased pace of coinage debasement after Mantzikert may well have been more reflective of the cost of the effects of Seljuk raids on the Anatolian economy and the subsequent loss of control over large areas of central Anatolia.

Due to the links between tax, commerce and agriculture, the fact that the Mantzikert campaign may have been a drain on resources could give us a method of using the cost of the campaign to draw tentative conclusions regarding other aspects of society. Attempts have been made to assess the rate of land tax in the Byzantine Empire[183] and this could give us a start at examining the relationship between agricultural productivity and supplying an army on the march. The nature of this relationship is, like most other things related to the Mantzikert campaign, complex.

Byzantine agriculture

Knowing that the state consists of three elements—the army, the clergy, and agriculture— you have devoted no less care to the latter, which is best able to preserve human life.[184]

The above quote comes from a dedication to Constantine VII Porphyrogenitus and is an acknowledgement of the essential role of agriculture in 10th-century Byzantine society, though it is applicable to all periods of the empire. Food is a critical part of military logistics and the amount and location of the food required can dictate when and where armies march.[185] The amount and location of food supplies will largely depend on where food is produced and at what point of the growing cycle the demand occurs, although storage of previous surplus is also relevant. In order to create an agricultural context within which the march can take place we need to create a model, albeit not necessarily a computerised model, of Byzantine agriculture, including which foods are produced where and at which part of the year they become available. This is initially a challenging task due to the lack of quantitative data in the primary sources, however this subject has attracted historians whose research can be productively reused. One of the limited number of relevant data points from the Byzantine Empire's military history states that 'Eustathios Maleinos in Asia Minor had been able to receive and feed Emperor Basil II and his army of at least 20,000 men on their way to fight the Arabs around

the year 1000'.[186] While this event lacks information on how long the army was fed for and what the effect was on the food supplies in the area which supported them, it does suggest that armies similar in size to the lower estimates of that used on the Mantzikert campaign seem to have been supplied without significant problems, although this is hardly a ground breaking finding.

Nevertheless, the fact remains that the agrarian history of the empire contains significant data voids. Quantified data, as usual, are particularly absent, with manpower, yields, crop values, herd sizes and areas under cultivation all insufficiently recorded for the late 11th century. Comparative data from other areas and periods is not hard to find, however, and plausible models can be made, with the proviso that this data often masks a tremendous amount of variability between different years. The complex interrelations of climate, demography, national political situation and local social organisation conspire against authoritative recreation of the Byzantine managed landscape. No wonder then, that previous research has mainly dealt with coarse averages,[187] or avoided quantitative details entirely.[188] Nevertheless, it is the interactions and variations of the elements of the agricultural system that contain interesting patterns that could be teased apart within a computer simulation, regardless of the completeness of primary sources. However, without the time to devote significant attention to modelling Byzantine food production, this project can only take a broad view of how the army may have been fed and how this might have impacted the settlements on which the burden of supplying the army fell.

The army marching to Mantzikert will have spent most of its time marching through central Anatolia, excepting the initial stages in the west and the more complex logistical situation beyond Theodosiopolis. The cooler, drier climate on the Central Anatolian Plateau favoured stock rearing while the lower, wetter river valleys around the coast were more conducive to the growing of grain, fruit, vines and olives. The difficulties of long-distance land transport of goods would have ensured that the demand for a variety of foodstuffs in Central Anatolia would usually be satisfied by local suppliers, clustered around those smaller areas which suited agriculture in the case of agrarian staples such as wheat.

The agricultural technology available to Byzantine farmers was similar to that of Western Europe, with iron tools, water mills and irrigation systems all in use. One difference was the sole ard, which was in much more widespread use than the plough, which

---

[183] as summarised in Haldon 2015, 361
[184] Laiou 2002, 231
[185] Engels 1978

[186] Lefort 2002, 293
[187] Lefort 2002
[188] Hendy 2008

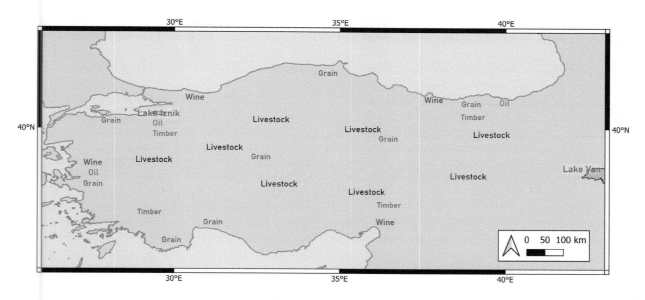

Figure 4: Resource availability in Byzantine Anatolia (after Hendy 2008, 70).

was favoured further west, although there is a debate regarding whether the ard would be more suitable for the thinner soils typical in Anatolia.[189] Draft animals such as donkeys, mules and oxen would have been in common usage by even the poorest farmers, who could have shared such resources with neighbours.

Large estates owned either by members of the aristocracy or by the state were a common feature of the landscape but were not ubiquitous, with villages of smallholders also common. As the eleventh century progressed, the state became more active in taking control of whatever land it could plausibly claim, at the expense of the villages.[190] The social order comprised slaves and wage labourers at the lowest level of wealth, through tenant farmers and smallholders to minor members of the aristocracy and above. Merchants and artisans also occupied this spectrum, with support from activities such as smithing present in many villages.[191]

When the farmers near the bottom of the social order were not being overly taxed or having their land confiscated by local landowners or the state, life for them was probably not terrible. We have little reliable data for 11th-century Anatolia but the average peasant in 14th-century Thessalonike would have had an ox, a cow, a pig, four goats or sheep and an unrecorded number of chickens.[192] Those whose livelihood relied on raising stock rather than growing crops would have had many more. They also had an average of two beehives each, being a source of both honey and wax. There are

no reports of significant extreme weather events or crop failures in immediately pre-Mantzikert Anatolia, and the assumption is that food provision in general was at least adequate, possibly even comfortably sufficient.[193]

The availability of the different foodstuffs which formed a significant part of the Byzantine diet would not have been uniform across the empire, with different areas suiting different crops and transport costs being reasonably high for transport away from the coasts. Central Anatolia was not a conducive climate for olive cultivation, and olives or oil would have to have been brought from coastal areas. Butter is likely to have been the predominant source of fat due to the primacy of stock rearing in these areas. Likewise, the plateau is not a good environment to grow vines and therefore much of their wine would have been transported in, raising its price. Cereals were so essential that they would have been cultivated in the most favourable spots available, even on the plateau, and the dry climate of Anatolia may not necessarily have been a significant barrier to effective cereal cultivation.

Production and harvest, particularly in the case of annual plants, depend more on the pattern of rainfall than on its annual volume, which, in theory at least, is always sufficient. Thus the Anatolian plateau, in spite of its long dry season (more than five to six months) and relatively scanty precipitation (which can shrink to less than 200 mm per year), is relatively favorable to the cultivation of cereals thanks to a pattern of rainfall that is characterized by a spring maximum.[194]

---

[189]   Lefort 2002
[190]   Lefort 2002, 288
[191]   Lefort 2002, 235
[192]   Lefort 2002, 246
[193]   Laiou 2002, 738
[194]   Geyer 2002, 35

Our view of the likely agricultural capacity of central Anatolia is also warped by the landscape's high potential for 'negative evolution'.[195] The thin soils are swiftly eroded, and their re-establishment is difficult. This means that the march to Mantzikert may well have taken place through a more fertile landscape than that seen today, with erosive processes degrading the soils in the intervening centuries. Nevertheless, tax rates from the tenth or eleventh century indicate that central Anatolia was considered generally less fertile than the Balkans, which in turn was less fertile than southwest Anatolia.[196]

Much of the Central Anatolian Plateau is likely to have relied heavily on stock rearing and cereal production for its food supply, with wheat, barley, flax and millet all represented in archaeobotanical remains found during excavation. These would have been supplemented by beans and peas, which are also recorded.[197] Animal bone assemblages are dominated by cattle, sheep, goat and pig.[198] Any army travelling through central Anatolia would have found grain, meat and cheese as the most readily available means of sustenance. This may have been reflected in the foodstuffs transported by the army from areas further west, with olives, oil and wine possibly forming the bulk of the food supplies carried by the army out of the lower, more densely populated areas around Nikaia, with the promise of plentiful grain and meat supplies available on the plateau.

Supply to the army, however, does not just rely on production and transportation, with more complex political factors also playing a role. Although the empire was not a democracy, there were many reasons to respect the population of the lands that were being travelled through. Although the immediate concern would be access to foodstuffs on the march, a rebellious population may provide materiel support to any future challengers to the throne. A supportive population who could expect fair treatment would be more likely to provide food and equipment than one who expected to have to hide resources to avoid it being impressed or stolen by the army. This was known to Byzantine generals, as recorded in military treatises (see p83) and seems to be a universal consideration for armies moving through their own territories. In the American War of Independence, administrative problems and a reluctance to undermine political support among the populace by resorting to impressment of goods and services meant that sometimes food was plentiful for the residents of an area, but not for the army which marched through it.[199]

There are no Byzantine records of home territories being reduced to desolation by the demands of a friendly but hungry army. However, the fact that Romanos' expeditions in 1068, 1069 and 1071 all seemed to travel different routes is indicative that there may have been an impact on the settlements through which the army travelled, making it problematic and unfair to place the burden on the same settlements each year. Though we have no direct evidence regarding the Mantzikert campaign, it is possible for the impact of human events on the agriculture of Anatolia to be visible in the environmental evidence retrieved from lake sediment cores and pollen data.[200] Although climate clearly has a role to play, the Arab invasions and subsequent return to relative security left traces in the landscape that can be seen in the environmental data. No such signal is readily apparent from any specific military campaign, indicating that if any problems were the result of military manoeuvres, they were at least of short-term impact.

The broader agricultural context of the march to Mantzikert provides an image of a landscape of differential availability of common foodstuffs but with enough quantity to comfortably sustain the population. How that may translate into the ease of supply of an army consisting of tens of thousands of individuals would depend on how many people the landscape usually supported, and how long the army stayed around for.

Byzantine demography

The demography of Anatolia has an important role to play in the logistics of the march to Mantzikert. There is, broadly speaking, a relationship between the size of a population and the size of the armies they can provide for.[201] The size of the population as a whole is also related to the size and pattern of settlements. These will have a complex relationship with the road network through which the army would have travelled. The amount of surplus foodstuffs that a settlement can provide would depend on the size of the settlement as well as the surrounding environment and the weather. So, if we could find out how large the population of Anatolia was and how it was distributed it would help in the attempt to understand how the army marched across Anatolia. Likewise, our attempt to understand the march of the army could help provide an insight into Byzantine demography.

Agricultural technology is one factor driving availability of supplies for the army but 'given the slow advances of technology, demography is of primary importance in the development of the countryside, production being

---

[195] Geyer 2002, 38
[196] Lefort 2002, 300
[197] Haldon *et al.* 2018, 151
[198] Haldon *et al.* 2018, 154
[199] Huston 1966, 27

[200] Haldon *et al.* 2014
[201] Haldon *et al.* 2011

a function of the increase or decrease in population'.[202] Angeliki Laiou arrives at an estimated rural population of the empire of 18 million in 1025.[203] This incorporates a rural population density of 17 people per square kilometre for Anatolia, but these would have been unevenly distributed. It's possible that there would also be a lower population necessary for stock-raising compared to that required for agrarian agriculture, so the population density around the route of march may, on average, have been less than 17 people per square kilometre, with a higher density in the more fertile coastal areas.

If we take Laiou's 18 million rural population as a plausible base, we can somewhat arbitrarily add maybe another million to cover the urban population and to cope with the hypothesis that 'a slow and steady demographic rise during the eleventh and twelfth centuries affected both towns and the countryside.'[204]

Byzantine towns are perhaps to lesser extent the successors of ancient cities than they are of fifth- and sixth-century large rural agglomerations, which had been fortified relatively early in their history in order to resist invaders, and in which basic cottage industries developed.[205]

Small towns would have housed populations of around 1000-2000 inhabitants, with medium sized towns somewhat bigger at around 5-15,000.[206] Thus the army marching to Mantzikert would have represented the equivalent of a large Anatolian town, constantly on the move. However, it is important to recognise the distinction between urban and rural societies. Towns would have represented focal points for the surrounding rural areas rather than being the source of population and commercial activity they have subsequently become. Thus, just because a medium-sized town might have had a population of around 10,000 people, its ability to gather supplies would be much greater than is implied by solely focussing on this number. The estates, villages, ranches and smallholdings that formed the hinterland of a settlement would all have been able to contribute towards supplying the army, as might areas further afield if enough notice was given.

The route of the march passed through some larger settlements such as Nikaia, Dorylaion and Ankyra although Byzantine cities were typically fairly small in plan, Constantinople aside, and the area encompassed by their walls would not have had enough space for anything other than a small force to camp within. There will no doubt have been fields of produce in the immediate periphery so the army may well have had to camp a short distance from any city that its route went 'through'. The army's main concern would have been to camp close enough to easily tap into a city's surplus food.

It is not just the size and distribution of people throughout Anatolia that is of interest to us. Although the Battle of Mantzikert has been framed as a clash of two Empires, the Byzantines and the Seljuk Turks, this applies a veneer of simplicity to the human geography of the conflict that is not supported by the evidence. Although the Byzantine Empire could be described as Orthodox Hellenic, the army, and the people who inhabited Anatolia in 1071, were by no means homogenous. Regional groupings existed throughout Anatolia and local loyalties could be particularly strong. Armenians and Syriac Christians were widespread and powerful in the East. The Seljuks themselves combined features from their nomadic past on the steppe along with Persian and Muslim traditions and culture. They were disparate bands of Islamicized Oghuz Turks who had served with Karakhanid and Ghaznawid armies and whose commitment to the Seljuk cause had a strong streak of self-interest. [207]

The Byzantine road network

As previously mentioned, the road network of Anatolia has a complex relationship with the patterns of settlement, whereby settlements tend to grow up in areas accessible to the road network and roads tend to be built between settlements. The Byzantine road system, and indeed its settlements, did not form in a vacuum. The system was, to a large extent, based on the one developed by the Romans. This in turn was not developed independently of those that came before, in the same way that the road network of Britain contains within it traces of Medieval, Roman, Bronze Age and perhaps even earlier routes. This supports the view of the Byzantine road system as a palimpsest, built up over millennia and as a result of changing priorities and conditions. One main change that is seen in the archaeological record that would have had an effect on the Mantzikert campaign was a tendency around the fourth to the sixth centuries to introduce steps on steeper parts of some roads, reducing their utility to wheeled vehicles but increasing their practicality for pack animals.[208] This can be contrasted with the more cart friendly road network from the height of the unified Roman Empire. Even ancient Greece had wagon-navigable roads to some quite remote, obscure parts,[209] so the Byzantine system clearly differed in ways which made the mitigations required for easy cart travel largely unviable.

[202] Laiou 2002, 47
[203] Laiou 2002, 51
[204] Laiou 2002, 401
[205] Laiou 2002, 394
[206] Laiou 2002, 394

[207] Beihammer 2017
[208] Belke 2017, 29
[209] Lazenby 1994, 8

Although some research has been done on the road network of Byzantine Anatolia,[210] ancient roads are notoriously hard to date without extensive archaeological excavation, and even then they are likely to be the result of patterns of construction, reconstruction, use, upkeep and abandonment that are not easily identified or dated from the evidence left behind. The most comprehensive overview of the Byzantine roads system is contained within the publications of the *Tabula Imperii Byzantini*, an ongoing project run by the Austrian Academy of Sciences. The maps contained within the *Tabula Imperii Byzantini* volumes contain the routes of roads, but these have no dating information and can be only regarded as a first draft of any comprehensive knowledge of the system, valuable though they are. Paved roads may just be upgrades of dirt tracks which follow the same route, and these routes may continue during and after the decay of the paved surface. The surface itself may be kept to a good standard in stretches where the need is great, or resources are plentiful, but could be left to go to ruin elsewhere along what was originally the same road. Nevertheless, there is ample historical evidence of road travel throughout Anatolia by carts, pack animals, goods and armies. Available information attests to a road network which was at least functional, even though a precise snapshot of how it would have looked in 1071 eludes us. The importance of such a network is magnified by the fact that, although there were some navigable rivers in Anatolia, there were none that would have allowed transport of troops or goods at any significant scale.

It is likely that the road network of Anatolia in 1071 was highly heterogeneous, with some well maintained, important highways but also a lot of poorly maintained roads and a considerable number of dirt tracks whose utility varied with the weather. This view is borne out by the historical record in which carts, which require flatter, smoother surfaces, were mainly used for short distance transport of goods whereas longer distance trade tended to be via pack animals, which can cope better with more difficult terrain.[211] Just because a road was present, it does not necessarily follow that easy movement was assured. Passes through the mountains could necessitate single file for both pack animals and travellers. The effects that these restricted routes had on the movement of an army was a strategic

consideration for the route planning of Romanos' 1069 campaign.[212]

The roads, along with the postal service, intelligence gathering and foreign affairs, were the responsibility of an official with the title, the Logothete of the Dromos,[213] and although the state had the main responsibility for the construction of infrastructure, local settlements could take matters into their own hands at times. In one instance, 'the inhabitants of the village of Bouzaia in Gordiane built a bridge over the Tembros for their own convenience and that of travelers'.[214]

The extent to which roads were adhered to by armies marching across Anatolia would depend on a number of factors. Certainly, restricting the army to the road network would have helped with route finding and prevented units from wandering off and getting lost. It would also have made absconding harder. In many areas, sticking to the road would have been a necessity due to the terrain on either side. Roads would also have often been constructed on the quickest route between two settlements, and the supply situation would have heavily favoured a route that travelled from town to town. There may have been areas of more open countryside in which the army could spread out a bit, but they would still have had to avoid agricultural areas due to the possibility of damaging crops, causing ill will between the army and the local community. Nevertheless, there were doubtless areas in which the army could spread out a little, especially in flatter areas with pastoral usage.

Summary

Although the context of the Byzantine world is critical when examining the Mantzikert campaign, there are significant gaps in our knowledge about important subjects such as agriculture, demography, economy and transport systems. Any progress in any of these areas can possibly help us in the others if we have a unified model, however sparse, within which these elements fit. A closer look at the circumstances and mechanisms of moving an army during the Mantzikert campaign will allow us to focus on areas where these elements intersect, showing areas with the potential to help us understand the interlinked aspects of Byzantine society.

[210] notably French 1981 and the works of Klaus Belke
[211] Belke 2008, 301
[212] Attaleiates 2012, 249
[213] Miller 1966
[214] Laiou 2002, 62

Chapter 4 - Logistical Considerations

From within the preceding historical context, we need to attempt to find some specifics upon which to build our models. A general knowledge of the Byzantine world based on modern scholarship, including archaeology and history, is a sound base, but computer programmes require specific instructions regarding the behaviour of each element within them. Certain aspects such as the amount of space a person, animal or wagon takes up and the speed that they can travel are likely to be easy to encapsulate with plausible values. Other variables such as the amount and weight of food and equipment carried are liable to be more speculative. This chapter contains a summary of the different aspects of supplying and moving the Byzantine army and a review of the available evidence, but the following chapter will deal with the largely untapped source of quantitative details which will be essential in our attempts to build a useful model of an army on the march.

Quantitative details are highly beneficial for use in computational models as computers require precise, though not necessarily accurate, numbers to work with. Byzantine sources often lack quantitative detail and when they do, this detail sometimes requires careful analysis. After the defeat of the Rus at the Battle of Dorostolon in 971, Leo the Deacon recalls the Byzantines giving the 22,000 remaining Rus two *medimnoi* of grain each to stave off their hunger.[215] This amounts to a total of over 150,000kg of grain, although it is not known for how long the Rus would have had to survive on this. Knowing this could drastically change our attitudes to the charitable nature of the Byzantine gift. As this campaign was supported by a Byzantine fleet it also does not necessarily tell us much about land transportation either.

In addition to a lack of quantitative detail, the use of Byzantine sources is complicated by the difference between ancient and modern units of measurement and the fact that ancient units of measurement are not always apparent, fixed, or known, when they are mentioned at all. For example, the standard unit of measurement in the Byzantine world for foodstuffs such as grain was the *modios*, but there is no easy way to convert this to modern weights as the *modios* is a measure of volume rather than weight and there were different varieties of *modios* in existence. Therefore, although the *annonikos modios* has been suggested as the most appropriate type of *modios*, and has been

translated to the modern value of 8.7kg, this value has potentially more precision than accuracy.[216] Within this work, all ancient weights and volumes have been translated into standard modern weights and measures but it's always best to bear in mind the uncertainty that surrounds these.

It's also important to remember that the purpose of the models is to examine different scenarios regarding the march of the army, not to build one model that closely replicates the march. We may not know how much siege equipment was carried from Constantinople, but we are able to examine the implications of the many possible permutations. We cannot know how optimal the amount of food carried by the army was, but we can model different scenarios and suggest consequences resulting from being too cautious, or not cautious enough, regarding food and resupply. Within this framework, exact modern equivalents of ancient weights and measures are desirable, but not essential. When moving a real army, however, accuracy becomes more critical.

Military rations

Therefore, before war is commenced, careful consideration should be given to supplies and their issue in order that fodder, grain and other army provisions customarily requisitioned from provincials may be exacted in good time, and quantities always more than sufficient be assembled at points well-placed for waging war and very well-fortified. But if the taxes in kind be insufficient, everything (needed) should be compulsorily purchased from advance payments in gold.[217]

Food is a critical part of military logistics, and its procurement, transport, storage and delivery are essential duties of the quartermaster. To ease calculations, armies often have a set ration per person per day. This will depend on circumstance, location and cultural values but across many areas and points in time, it has often been centred around bread of some kind. For the purposes of our models, the important aspects are the weight of the food and the calories that it provides, although to create a plausible model of this we need some idea of what the food consists of. We have no primary data regarding the standard daily food ration for a member of the Byzantine army during

---

[215] Talbot and Sullivan 2005, 199

[216] Haldon 2005, 88
[217] Vegetius 2011, III, 3

the Mantzikert campaign so we will have to construct our models using other data. Thankfully there is quite a lot of data to draw on from other times and places and there is a general agreement to much of it. The standard soldier's ration varies over time and space, but not radically so.

Byzantine military rations

As we have no record of the typical daily ration from the Mantzikert campaign, the data will have to come from elsewhere. It seems likely that, while there will have been a target ration, adjustments may have been made to accommodate the different availability of certain types of foodstuffs along the route. It would have undoubtedly revolved around bread of some kind, whether soft bread that would be familiar to us today or the more robust, but less palatable, twice-baked bread variously referred to as biscuit, hard tack, *bucellatum* by the Romans or *paximadion/paximation* by the Byzantines.[218] However, bread alone was insufficient to provide all the elements to keep an army healthy. Supplementary protein, along with certain vitamins and minerals would have been essential, or at least very important. Marching across Anatolia, performing arduous tasks such as constructing camp and being exposed to diseases from around the empire would have meant that a balanced diet would have been rewarded. Meat, cheese, wine, vinegar, oil, salt, pulses and vegetables would all have been available to a greater or lesser extent. To a certain extent, the nature of the task of simulating the rations of the army on the march to Mantzikert is complicated by the sophistication of our models, compared to previous works. Donald Engels' model of the army of Alexander required a single weight to be assigned to a daily ration, which was deemed to apply to all humans in the army. Now that we can simulate an Anatolia of various resources, and various availabilities throughout the year, we can move beyond Engels' simplification and start to model an army where not everyone eats the same food and not all foods are available all the time.

Specific references to Byzantine military rations indicate a diet mainly based around bread, with the main additions being meat and/or cheese. We have evidence for a diet that rotated every three days, with bread on one day and *paximadion* on two, along with additional salt pork on one day and mutton on two. We have a record of one Roman pound (327g) of meat and/or 2-3 Roman pounds (654g – 981g) of bread per day for stationary troops, although these figures would have had to increase to take into account the added calorie consumption of marching.[219] Wheat was the primary grain used for bread, although barley and millet could have been used for *paximadion*.

Jonathan Roth states that the ancient Roman infantryman would have received a grain ration of two *sextarii* (1.08 litres) per day and that this would have represented up to 75% of both the weight of the total daily ration and the calorific content.[220] Cavalry and officers would have received more which would have allowed them to feed any servants that they may have had. Ancient amounts of grain, like those used by the Byzantines, were based on volume rather than weight, which would have sped up the measuring out process. Estimates of the weight of grain per litre vary from 0.75-0.825kg.[221] Grain, primarily wheat, though sometimes barley, was a staple foodstuff in the pre-modern world and its ubiquity on military campaigns was driven by its portability and durability. It could be carried in grain form in which it is fairly robust and keeps well, then milled into flour when required to make either soft bread or harder biscuit. Hand-mills are a fairly essential item which are mentioned often in military writings of both classical antique and Byzantine periods. Hand mills were heavy but were required if grain, rather than flour, was transported with the army. They were also fairly effective, allowing 4-6 men to mill up to 220lbs of grain in one hour.[222]

Soft bread, baked once, was preferred, but was larger, harder to store and more vulnerable to moisture than its twice-baked alternative. *Paximadion* was baked twice to drive out more moisture and was therefore more robust, resistant to mould and, unfortunately, could be quite a challenge to eat. It could be gnawed on the march, performing the role of chewing gum today, but was only really edible when soaked in liquid such as a stew or broth. In the American Civil War, soldiers would drop it into their coffee which had the dual purpose of softening the hardtack and killing any weevils, which could be skimmed off the top once their dead bodies had floated to the surface.[223]

Although grain often formed the backbone of military rations due to its easy availability and portable nature, rations could be quite varied. In 1775, the United States Congress set the standard daily ration as: 1lb of beef or salt fish or 3/4lb of pork, 1lb bread or flour, 1pt milk or 1/72 of a dollar, 1qt cider or spruce beer. In addition to this, the ration included: 3pt peas or beans per week, 1pt corn meal or 1/2pt rice per week, 9gal molasses per 100 men per week, 3lbs candles per 100 men per week and 24lbs salt or 8lbs hard soap per 100 men per week.[224] The carriers of the Chinese Expeditionary Corps in 1860

---

[218] Haldon 2005, 87
[219] Haldon 2005, 86

[220] Roth 1999, 19
[221] Roth 1999, 24
[222] Haldon 2005, 87
[223] Billings 1887, 116
[224] Huston 1966, 26

had a somewhat plainer diet, receiving 906g of rice and 225g salt meat or fish per day.[225] Emperors, of course, fared much better. Constantine VII Porphyrogenitus notes that 'from the departure of the baggage train, the head of the table should load the 80 pack animals with all the imperial requirement, and should obtain from the *protonotarios* 100 suckling lambs, 500 rams, 50 cattle, 200 chickens and 100 geese, for consumption at the imperial table and for feasts.'[226]

In addition to grain and meat, cheese was also an important foodstuff, both on campaign and in society generally. It was widely produced within the empire, with Cretan cheese being especially important. 'In 1022 or somewhat earlier the Venetian Leone da Molin arrived in Constantinople with some 2,860 kg. cheese, the provenance of which is not stated. However, it is likely that this was high-grade Cretan cheese and that its import was not an isolated case'.[227] The provision of Cretan cheese was also attested to in 1402, when 2.5 tons were provided for a Venetian naval expedition to Constantinople.[228]

The Byzantine army during the time of the Mantzikert campaign contained a number of troops from different cultures, including Germans, Armenians and steppe nomads. The extent to which these troops were supplied with different rations is unknown, although they were treated differently at times. When feasts were appropriate, likely to be during religious festivals, the Byzantine soldiers of the tenth century received one animal for 10 persons whereas foreign troops received 1 cow per 30.[229] It would, however, certainly be more straightforward to issue all troops with a standard ration and let them sort any differences out themselves by means such as purchase from sutlers or local settlements on the march route and by trading foodstuffs with other units within the army. The extent to which these options were practiced, or even possible, is open to conjecture.

Counting calories

There are two approaches to the subject of calories with regards food provision in the Byzantine army: produce a daily ration and calculate how many calories it would provide or decide on a calorific requirement and work out how this need can be met. Donald Engels calculated the food requirement of the Macedonian army based on a requirement of 3600 kilocalories per day, a figure supplied by the US army in the 1970s.[230] This he converted to a typical ration based on likely available foodstuffs. Jonathan Roth uses a model height, weight and age of a typical Roman soldier to arrive at a daily calorie requirement of 3000 per day.[231] The diet of a Viet Cong combat soldier was reckoned to be around 4000 kilocalories per day, although less was expected to be consumed if in garrison or on light duty.[232] Previous works have made calorie estimates from daily rations within the range of 2750-5000+ kilocalories per day.[233]

Once again, the need to assign a daily calorific requirement is a function of the simplicity of the models within which this data is used. With more complex computational models we can measure calorie expenditure at an individual level, using modern medical science data to estimate the energy expended by marching. This will allow us to research the complex relationship between the amount of supplies being transported, the speed of the army, the route taken and the amount of food required. The harder the route and the harder the march, the more calories would be required to keep the army in good condition, which in turn leads to a greater requirement for food transport, but also those supplies being more quickly depleted. This is most definitely too complex for models such as Engels' but is practical with computational help.

Sources of rations

Food was likely to have come from three main sources:

- supplied by settlements *en route* as the result of a prior arrangement with government officials.
- supplied by settlements *en route* by means of ad hoc commercial transactions.
- supplied commercially by travelling merchants.

A system that provided advance notice of the amount and types of foodstuffs, arms, armour and supplies required by an army as it passed through a region had been in operation since at least the time of Justinian and, broadly speaking, was still in effect in 1071.[234] Imperial stud farms and arms manufactories had given way to more local manufacture of arms and provision of animals but the shift from levied troops to standing units of mercenaries may have resulted in a smaller requirement for the equipment of war to be collected *en route*. Foodstuffs and consumables such as firewood or charcoal were still likely to have been required from settlements along the way and advance notice would have been given so that areas had enough time to produce or collect the surplus required by the army.

---

[225] Furse 1882, 72
[226] Constantine Porphyrogenitus 1990, 129
[227] Jacoby 2010, 128
[228] Jacoby 2010, 130
[229] Constantine Porphyrogenitus 1990, 133
[230] Engels 1978, 123

[231] Roth 1999, 12
[232] Holliday and Gurfield 1968, 32
[233] Harari 2000, 303
[234] Haldon 1999, 139–148

It is also likely that other less essential items or foodstuffs will have been made available by the settlements through which the army passed. This would have benefitted the inhabitants of those settlements who will have temporarily gained a large new market for whatever produce they had which was not covered by any pre-existing contract, and seasonal, local produce would have spiced up an otherwise, fairly monotonous diet for the troops.

The provision of goods via merchants is attested by the *Taktika* of Leo VI, which advises 'See that they [merchants] are not unfairly treated and so come to bear a grievance that may lead them to discontinue furnishing the supplies we need.'[235] This implies that they not only provided extras for the soldiers but also could contribute to the demand for essentials if required, for a price. The price of wheat appears to vary significantly across time and place in the Byzantine empire[236] but this is partly due to the limited number of data points we have in the historical record. It was likely to be fairly stable across the area of Anatolia at the temporal resolution needed to study the Mantzikert campaign, although the campaign itself is likely to have skewed prices to a certain extent. Prices of other necessities such as wine or livestock are even less well attested.[237]

The question of whether settlements along the route would have been required to provide only the types of provisions that they could produce within their area or would have needed to provide items traded from further afield is an interesting one. Massive amounts of goods made their way by sea to Constantinople and could be transported to any port in Anatolia if required. Land transport was slower, costlier and less efficient, rendering the supply of goods produced in areas local to the route of march more valuable. If this stripped an area of surplus, it is possible that existing trade links could have resupplied that surplus over time after the army had moved on.

Some common items such as olive oil could not have been widely produced on the Central Anatolian Plateau due to the characteristics of the olive tree. These trees cannot withstand frost and were only widely cultivated in the coastal areas of Anatolia. There would have been extensive trade networks for oil throughout the region, though, and so it would have been possible to collect some *en route* rather than bringing the whole army's supply from the regions that cultivated the olive near the beginning of the march. Existing trade routes could have been used to accumulate surplus goods in advance of the army's arrival, in addition to being used to restock once the army had moved on.

The actual situation though, is likely to have been a mixed bag of mainly local products supplemented by items acquired via long distance trade. Olive oil is likely to have been a more prominent part of the army's diet in the earlier stages of the route where it was more abundant and, thanks to the economies related to transportation, cheaper. The journey up to the more pastoral areas of the plateau is likely to have seen a gradual switch from oil and grain to butter and meat, but with neither oil nor grain disappearing from the menu.

Water

It is a terrible thing to have to engage in two battles. I mean the one against the enemy and the one against the heat when water is lacking.[238]

Water is an even more important resource than food for both the humans and animals of the army. The recommendations to set up camp near a water source, if kept, would have ensured that no more water than required for the time marching between camps would need to have been carried. Nevertheless, Donald Engels' work on the transit of Alexander's army across the Gedrosian Desert shows that if water was unavailable then it quickly became a very significant aspect of the logistical situation.[239] Skylitzes records an event from the reign of Romanos III Argyros in which the emperor disregards the warnings of his generals not to campaign in Syria in the summer due to the lack of water. The Byzantine army was subsequently trapped in a place with insufficient water and, as a consequence of their weakened state, were routed in battle.[240]

Water transport problems were sometimes solved in unorthodox ways. The Arab historian al-Ṭabarī relates a story that occurred on a march from Iraq to Syria around 632 in which the commander of a force of 500-800 soldiers obtained both food and water in a 5-day trek across a desert by allowing 30 camels to drink their fill and then slaughtering them for food and to access the water stored in their stomachs during the march.[241]

Water, of course, is used for more than just drinking, just as not all things that are drunk are water. The total requirement of water for both humans and animals is unrecorded for Byzantine contexts, but data from elsewhere is available. Furse records that 'men need about five gallons (22.7 litres) of water per diem for

---

[235] Dennis 2010, 197
[236] Laiou 2002, 822–829
[237] Laiou 2002, 835

[238] Dennis 1985, 285
[239] Engels 1978, 111
[240] Skylitzes and Wortley 2010, 359
[241] Muhammad 2009, 91

all purposes, horses eight to twelve gallons (36.3 - 54.5 litres), oxen six to seven (27.3-31.8 litres).'[242]

Water sources were sought out as essential elements of camping locations and therefore preparation by the Byzantine army was unlikely to have consisted of more than the provision of personal water skins for individuals. A more frequent practical concern may have been organising access to these water sources. Thousands of horses and people are unable to access even a large source simultaneously and the action of hooves and boots can churn up the ground at the edge of a river, making the approach harder and less pleasant for anyone following. Maurice recommended that horses should be watered downstream to avoid muddying the waters, allowing humans to take drinking water from the cleaner areas upstream.[243] Solutions such as foldable leather drinking troughs or half barrels[244] can mitigate the need for all animals to make the trip to the river themselves, and the staggered arrival of units into camp will also help. The practicalities regarding the watering of humans and animals at the end of a day's march would make an interesting agent-based model but are sadly outside the scope of this work.

Climate

The climate could have affected the Mantzikert campaign directly, with temperature and/or precipitation making movement difficult, or indirectly at a larger temporal and spatial scale by affecting agricultural productivity, and therefore also food availability. Temperature and the availability of fresh water would have had an impact on the soldiers of the army as they marched, with each factor being, to a certain extent, interdependent. Marching in hot weather would have increased the amount of water required for both the humans and animals in the army and may also have reduced the availability of water sources, which would also have been affected by precipitation.

We have no information regarding the weather along the march to Mantzikert which presumably indicates no major climate-related complications. The climate data which does exist has both a large temporal and spatial scale, but this does not provide any direct evidence for climate-related problems either. The climate at Nar Golu, in central Anatolia but south of the route to Mantzikert, has been described as 'moderately wet' at this point, implying warm conditions not drastically different from the climate today.[245]

Therefore, there is no realistic prospect of reconstructing the daily temperature and rainfall data of 1071 precisely. The climate can either be plausibly modelled from longer term data or ignored if it is likely not to significantly impact on the campaign. Downscaling coarse data into finer resolution data which more closely conform to small scale patterns is a valid approach[246] but this is likely to result in minimal implications for the march. A cursory glance at modern data from the Central Anatolian Plateau indicates that the hottest times of the year were spent in some of the cooler locales, with the high elevation of the areas around Theodosiopolis resulting in temperatures which should cause few problems for marching, especially at the rates likely to apply to a large army. Overall, climate has the potential to impact the march of the army, but the complexities involved and the likelihood of significant changes to the existing models mean that this will remain outside the scope of this project.

Animals and loads

Sources

One of the most important aspects of logistics is the transportation of food and equipment. Prior to the widespread use of the internal combustion engine, and even afterwards in certain circumstances, the primary method of moving items in bulk over land involved the use of pack animals and/or carts pulled by draft animals. Pack animals and carts are frequently mentioned in Byzantine sources but, like so many other areas important to military logistics, quantitative data is largely absent. One exception is a mid-tenth century text that specifies three types of load: saddled horses carrying a person could carry four *modioi* each (34kg), unridden, saddled horses could carry eight *modioi* (68kg), and pack animals could carry ten *modioi* (85kg). Even here there are uncertainties regarding the weight of a saddle and the type of pack animal, usually assumed also to be a horse.[247]

Quantitative data can be found in more modern sources, with George Armand Furse dealing with pack and draft animals in several publications, especially his 1882 publication, *Military Transport*.[248] In fact both of Furse's first two books were on the subject of military transport and both emphasise its importance.

Military Transport contains a large amount of detail regarding animals, loads and methods of organisation that are far beyond anything recorded in Byzantine texts. This is obviously helpful when modelling Byzantine logistics as it also discusses marches in

[242] Furse 1901, 562
[243] Dennis 2001, 160
[244] Furse 1882, 252
[245] Haldon *et al.* 2014, 142

[246] Contreras *et al.* 2019
[247] Haldon 2005, 96
[248] Furse 1882

many different circumstances, some with very similar parameters to the Mantzikert campaign, and explains why different arrangements are needed for each. This allows assumptions regarding how animal transport was used on the march to Mantzikert to be based around practical experience, albeit that of the 19th century. There are a variety of more modern sources, going all the way up to a training document for US Special Forces published in 2004 that covers the use of pack animals in detail.[249] The 19th-century military writing of Furse and others will be more comprehensively covered in the next chapter.

Where did the animals come from?

We do have some specific information regarding the Byzantine army's approach to the provision of transport for a military campaign. Reckoning up the number of pack animals required and adding some additional animals to cope with losses due to lameness and injury was an important preliminary step in an expedition according to Leo Katakylas.[250] Given a gestation period of around a year, not much could be done at short notice about the available numbers of horses and donkeys in time for a campaign to begin. Consequently, early planning must have ensured that there were enough of the empire's stock of pack animals, whether in Imperial or private hands, in roughly the right place at the right time to be useful. Another factor to be taken into account when planning a campaign is that horses which are usually in pasture will take 4-6 weeks to get into condition and habituated to the kind of work that would be required of them.[251] Animals could have been bought from other areas around the Mediterranean in the same manner as the British Empire procured pack animals in the 19th century, shipping them from around the world to wherever needed. This is not mentioned in contemporary sources and there will have been few places with the infrastructure to breed large numbers of pack animals that might not also have been worried that they would be used in a campaign against them.

Although the Empire would have had its own store of pack and draft animals, suitable animals in private hands were likely to have been very common. A clue to the availability of pack animals within society at large can be found in an example from an early twelfth century Macedonian village named Radolibos, which broke 129 peasants down into the following categories:[252]

Owning no oxen – 38
Owning one ox – 39
Owning a team of oxen - 32

Owning one or more donkeys – 17

It's uncertain how representative of villages in Anatolia this data might be, but it implies that oxen and donkeys were not rare, even at the lower end of society. If these animals were required for local transport work, they could probably be easily requisitioned for the army. Larger rural estates and merchants would no doubt have access to reasonable numbers of trained pack animals that could be rented for local work or to supplement permanent army transport as required. Furse states that 'in well populated, industrious countries, where the soil is regularly tilled, and good roads are plentiful, there will be no serious difficulty in requisitioning means of transport'.[253] However, the extent to which of these characteristics applies to the march route across Anatolia is debatable. They are more likely to be appropriate in Western Anatolia where the towns were more densely packed and the land more suitable to agriculture.

How were they organised?

Pack and draft animals could be owned by the government and permanently travel with the army, be hired for the duration of the campaign or be hired for only a part of the march. There is no comprehensive data on which of these options were used during the march to Mantzikert, but the differences caused by these options can be simulated in order to determine whether the likely outcomes differ significantly. In all likelihood each of these would have been used to some extent and, for the purposes of how much the army can carry and how fast it can move, the first two are functionally identical, differing only in total cost and the eventual fate of the animals at the end of the campaign.

Furse stresses the usefulness of making temporary use of local transport to move equipment and food across a limited stretch of the journey. This enables pack animals and wagons to be used which are appropriate to the local conditions and come with knowledgeable operators invested in their animals' condition.[254] If animals are used only within easy reach of home it also frees the army from having to provide forage for the animals or food for their operators.

Picking the right animal for the job

Pack transport and draft transport have fundamental differences that make them more or less suited to specific circumstances. In areas with good roads, pack transport is less convenient than wheeled transport and occupies a larger space in the marching column.

---

[249] U.S. Army 2004
[250] Constantine Porphyrogenitus 1990, 85
[251] Furse 1882, 77
[252] Lefort 2002, 246

[253] Furse 1882, 21
[254] Furse 1882, 28

Wheeled transport can stay packed during rest stops and overnight, whereas pack animals need to be unloaded and reloaded, preferably by an experienced packer.[255] Wheeled transport is also more efficient, carrying more per animal than pack animals can, reducing the amount of animal food required, therefore reducing the amount of baggage carrying capacity required. However, wheeled transport is much harder to move through broken or steep terrain, and repairs to carts are harder to effect than repairs to a pack saddle. Losing a pack animal removes the capacity to carry a single animal's load whereas losing a draft animal can render the whole cart and its load immobile, or its mobility severely compromised.

Differences do not just occur between draft and pack animal transportation. Animals also vary considerably, even amongst the same species and from the same source. Sir Charles Napier's logistical arrangements in India in 1844-45 included tablets specific to the individual animal hung round their neck indicating the maximum load each was to be loaded with.[256]

The choice of pack and draft animals is based on a number of criteria, including availability, suitability to the forage of the campaign route, type of work to be done, availability of water during the march and climate. These do not just affect the species of animal used but also the size and breed. In the Zulu War of 1879, the British Army brought mules from around the world but the ones that performed best were those from climates and environments that more closely resembled South Africa.[257] Condition is important when determining how much an animal can carry. Poor forage ensured that loads carried by horses and mules during the Abyssinian Expedition of 1868 were reduced to 100 lbs (45 kg) from a more usual 150-160 lbs.[258]

Even if animals were physically homogenous, the fact that they are sentient beings with individual personalities can be a source of complication to the unprepared. Horses and mules have a social hierarchy that can cause trouble if new animals are quickly introduced into the pack. Working with this hierarchy would make organisation easier while fighting against it could cause conflict and injury.[259]

The primary means of transport potentially available to the Byzantine army during the Mantzikert campaign were:

- Horses
- Mules
- Donkeys
- Camels
- Oxen
- Carts
- Humans

We are certainly not in a position to determine exactly how many of each species were used and in what way during the Mantzikert campaign, but we can examine the parameters within which each mode of transport works and examine the implications of favouring one particular mode of transport over another.

Horses

Horses could be used as both pack and draft animals, but they were less commonly used to carry equipment due to the fact that other animals were more suited for that task and also because horses were more useful in other roles, particularly as cavalry mounts. Horses that were not primarily pack animals could still have been used to carry small loads temporarily as a useful reserve, when required. This would have to have been balanced by the need to keep any horses required for combat use in good condition. As horses were a vital part of the army due to their use as cavalry mounts, their needs could affect the overall strategic situation of the army. Attaleiates' recounts that the effects of rough terrain on their horses' hooves was a factor preventing the Turks following Romanos' disordered Byzantine army at Mount Tauros in 1069.[260]

The US Special Forces training pack does not distinguish between weights carried by horses, mules and donkeys, instead giving the maximum as 35% of the weight of the animal.[261] Furse quotes a Thomas Moore as using 30% as a guide to how much a mule can carry, although the lack of referencing leaves us unsure as to which of the many Thomas Moores he is quoting.[262]

Modern US information states that a horse or mule can travel 20-30 miles per day with maximum load over mountainous terrain.[263] Strong, compact, placid horses between 14.2 and 15 hands high (1.44-1.52m) are preferred as pack animals although their usefulness for riding and draft means that they are rarely used as such.[264]

Mules

A mule is the sterile offspring of a horse and a donkey. The fact that a mule cannot be used to create more mules would seem to make them less attractive than

---

[255] Furse 1882, 74
[256] Furse 1882, 40
[257] Furse 1882, 66
[258] Furse 1882, 74
[259] U.S. Army 2004, 2–13

[260] Attaleiates 2012, 245
[261] U.S. Army 2004, 1–1
[262] Furse 1882, 83
[263] U.S. Army 2004, 1–1
[264] Furse 1882, 76

either the horse or the donkey for packing or pulling carts. They do however possess certain characteristics that have made them a popular choice for military logistics across many ages. Broadly speaking, they have the food requirements of a donkey with the carrying capacity of a horse. This makes them more efficient than either, when looked at purely in terms of the ratio of carrying capacity to food requirements. Mules are also preferred to horses for pack work as they are hardier, calmer under heavy burden, have higher resistance to skin chafing, sun and rain, are more surefooted, are longer lived and of lower price.[265] The United States Quartermaster-General's report of 1865 states that mules had replaced almost all horses in the army's baggage trains.[266] Their only drawbacks compared to horses are that their illnesses, while fewer, tend to be more serious and they can be more easily startled by loud noises.[267]

Mules carry more weight on their back legs than horses do, which makes them more surefooted in rugged terrain.[268] The two can be effectively combined as mules form close bonds with horses, particularly mares, and strings of mules can be controlled by controlling the mare. The mules can even be let loose at night knowing that they will not stray far from the mare.[269] This advice is given in both the modern US Special Forces training info and the Army and Navy Journal of 1881.[270]

Mules can be worked from 4-25 years of age and are best between 14-15 hands high (1.42-1.52m) for convenience of loading and to avoid some problems, such as weak limbs, which are associated with larger animals. A loaded mule will walk a little over 3mph and will move quickly uphill but slowly downhill.[271]

Wellington specified one spare mule for every 6 and that a laden mule could travel 12 leagues (around 36 miles or 58km) in 3 days, quicker if unladen.[272] This agrees with the information provided by Furse for the Peninsular War in which mules were hired to carry loads of 200 lbs for 10-12 miles (16-19km) loaded and 15-16 (24-26km) unloaded.[273] A pack horse or mule takes up 4 yards (3.66m) in the column of march, including the interval between itself and the following animal.[274] Roth notes that Wellington's Spanish mules were given 2.3kg of barley and 4.5kg of straw each day and surmises that 2kg of hard fodder could be sufficient.[275]

The actions of a Mr. W. Anderson, described as 'one of the best mule packers in the States', might act as a hard limit for mule performance. He had mules that were specially bred for packing and of a superior quality loaded with 300 lbs (136kg) but they gave out completely after two weeks. Few of his mules could pack over 250 lbs (113kg) and that, after travelling 300 miles with 50 mules packing an average of 250 lbs the mules required four weeks' rest to recover. It is worth bearing in mind that mule packing is a situation more favourable to mule performance than operating in the baggage train of an army as the pace and routine of travel can be dictated by the mules rather than strategic or logistical necessity. Even in these conditions, Mr. Anderson found that an average of no more than 200 lbs (91kg) was sustainable.[276] The 336 lbs (152kg) claimed by Sir Charles MacGregor for the weight that a Persian mule could carry over bad roads, indefinitely, is treated with great suspicion by Furse.[277]

It is worth noting that care should be taken when using quantitative data regarding modern mules in a Byzantine context. It may be that modern mules, and indeed horses and donkeys, are both larger and stronger than their Byzantine counterparts. Firm conclusions are difficult to draw due to the relative lack of archaeological evidence regarding Byzantine mules, however. This is not only due to a lack of samples but also the ease with which mule bones can be misidentified as other equids.[278]

Donkeys

Donkeys were considered by Furse to be good pack animals if certain conditions are met. They should not be too young and should be of good size and breed. They are surefooted, have good endurance and are easily led. The maximum load is listed by Furse as 100 lbs (45.4kg).[279] Donkeys range in size from 36 inches (0.91m) to over 56 inches (1.42m) in height, although pack animals are recommended to be between 55 (1.40m) and 62 inches (1.57m) for ease of loading and overall load handling capacity, meaning large donkeys are more suitable.[280]

Donkeys have several advantages over horses, including that they manage water more efficiently than horses and therefore have lower requirements.[281] Donkeys are not easily spooked and are easy to work with.[282] Donkeys are also less selective regarding their diet, compared to horses, and are more capable of withstanding periods

[265] Furse 1882, 77
[266] Furse 1882, 78
[267] Furse 1882, 78
[268] U.S. Army 2004, 2–1
[269] U.S. Army 2004, 2–1
[270] Furse 1882, 79
[271] Furse 1882, 79
[272] Wellington 1838, 409
[273] Furse 1882, 84
[274] Furse 1882, 103
[275] Roth 1999, 66

[276] Furse 1882, 83
[277] Furse 1882, 84
[278] Kroll 2012, 99
[279] Furse 1882, 85
[280] U.S. Army 2004, 2–9
[281] U.S. Army 2004, 2–2
[282] U.S. Army 2004, 2–4

of hunger.[283] The fact that they are able to carry less weight than an average horse or mule while taking up almost the same amount of space in the column of march means that their use would extend the line to a longer length than would be the case with either of their main alternatives.

Camels

Camels have been used as pack animals extensively throughout the areas of the world to which they are suited but they have certain characteristics that make them problematic outside of these constraints. They are unsuited to hilly terrain if raised on the plains and vice versa, and take a long time to recover once sick. They do however possess some useful traits which can make them excellent members of the baggage train. As camels carry more than mules or ponies but eat around the same amount, they are economical and will occupy less space in the line of march than the number of mules that would be required to carry the same amount of equipment.[284]

US Special Forces training information states that Dromedaries can carry packs weighing 600-700 pounds (272-318 kg) for 7-8 hours over distances of 25-35 miles (40-56km). Bactrians can carry loads of 900-1000 pounds (408-454 kg) for the same time over the same distance.[285] These maximum loads are almost twice the amount that Furse gives as a realistic load for camels, which is specified as 320-450 lbs (145-204kg). Whether this is related to a comparative lack of knowledge regarding pack camels in the modern US forces or whether Furse's figures were based on practical loads for a camel on an extended campaign rather than a shorter period is unknown. It may even point to differences in camel abilities between the 19th and 21st centuries. Furse recommended Anatolian camels that are crosses between Bactrian and Dromedaries as the best breed. He cites Major Sir B. P. Bromhead as recommending rum as being highly effective in combatting camel exhaustion.[286]

Camels seem to have more individual variation in their load carrying capabilities as there is a record of a camel carrying 1,120 lbs (508 kg), although this is only recorded due to it being a very unusual amount, roughly equal to the weight of the camel itself.[287]

Camels can travel further without water than other pack animals but are slow grazers and need plenty of time to feed.[288] Camels should only be fed at the end of the working day.[289] They can travel up to 3 mph but 2-2½ mph is more realistic for a laden camel. They are cheap to maintain but if sick, require a long time to recover and are unlikely to do so in time to rejoin a campaign as short as Mantzikert. Sir Charles Napier split his camels into two groups, strong and weak, and gave each one a wooden label specifying the weight they could carry. These were 300 lbs (136kg) for the strong and 200 lbs (90.7kg) for the weak, the relatively low figures being a reflection of the nature of the country he was operating in.[290]

The length of a camel, including the space between it and the following camel, is 5-6 yards (4.57-5.49m), which is greater than the 4 yards (3.66m) recorded for mules.[291] Sebeos records the Arabs tying the legs of their camels with cords to stop them wandering at night or at rests on the march.[292]

Oxen

Due to the inefficiency of Byzantine equid harnessing techniques, cattle were a popular choice for plough teams and, when used as draft animals, for heavy loads, although their high water requirements made them less frequently used in arid areas.[293] Oxen have been used as both draught and pack animals but are very slow, especially up or down hill. Draught bullocks do not usually exceed 1½ mph and pack bullocks are only slightly faster at 2 mph.[294] Pack bullocks can carry around 160 lbs (72.6kg) but require a lot of food and water and are not particularly disease resistant. Oxen should graze for at least six hours a day, or more if grazing is scarce or low quality. They also benefit from a mid-day break in which they feed.[295]

Carts

> As two horses can draw at least as much as eight pack animals can carry, this alone will show what a saving of animals, drivers, food, and forage can be obtained by the use of wheel transport in all countries which are intersected by good roads.[296]

The use of animal-drawn carts for carrying military supplies is attested all the way back to ancient Greece, with Xenophon's *Cyropaedia* giving a maximum load per yoke of around 25 talents (646.5kg). [297] Maurice's *Strategikon* recommends one light wagon per infantry dekarchy or squad, containing 'a hand mill, an axe,

[283] Roth 1999, 65
[284] Furse 1882, 87–88
[285] U.S. Army 2004, 10–6
[286] Furse 1882, 90
[287] Furse 1882, 101
[288] Furse 1882, 85
[289] Furse 1882, 251
[290] Furse 1882, 101
[291] Furse 1882, 95
[292] Muhammad 2009, 93
[293] Kroll 2012, 98
[294] Furse 1882, 90
[295] Furse 1882, 251
[296] Furse 1882, 95
[297] Miller 1914 6.1.54

hatchets, an adz, a saw, two picks, a hammer, two shovels, a basket, some coarse cloth, a scythe, lead-pointed darts, caltrops tied together with light cords attached to an iron peg'.[298] The main problem which carts present to the student of military logistics is their heterogeneity. They can be drawn by a single animal, or anywhere up to 14. They subsequently display a large variation in maximum weights, speeds and distances taken up in the column of march. Their usefulness made them almost ubiquitous despite their drawbacks, with all but the most swiftly moving armies making at least some use of them.

Wagon transport can be pulled by horses, mules or oxen and its practicality is determined by several factors, including the state of the roads,[299] and the availability of trained drivers, spare parts and experienced repairers. Wagons range from small and light to large, heavy wagons requiring many draft animals. Each has advantages and disadvantages that would have been well known to the transport organisers of the Byzantine army. One significant factor for suitability is the state of the roads; it is likely that wagons hired from their own home would have been suitable for the roads found in that area. In areas where the roads render wagon transport unsuitable, there are likely to be no wagons to hire due to their impracticality. The extent to which bad roads slow the progress of wheeled vehicles, increase fatigue in draft animals and extend the length of the column are unquantified, but it seems uncontroversial to suggest that they will. George Head records a journey of 400-500 yards across muddy ground taking five hours due to artillery carriages continually becoming stuck in the mud.[300]

Yet where roads are conducive, wagon transport was clearly preferred to pack animals. It is more efficient and easier on the animals as there is no load on them during periods where they are not moving. Pack animals can struggle during the wait between being loaded and setting off whereas draft animals have no such problem. Furse recommends wagons that are strong, light and cheap, that will work well during the war and realise a good value afterwards.[301] Slow work requires wagons not weighing more than 17 cwt (864 kg) that are able to carry a load of 3,000 lbs (1,361 kg), and quick work requires wagons weight around 10 cwt (508 kg), able to carry around 15 cwt (762 kg). A pair of bullocks on good roads will draw a load of 800 lbs (362.9kg).[302] Major-General Sir E. Wood recommended large wagons pulled by 18 oxen or 10 mules in South Africa, carrying loads of 4,500 lbs (2,041 kg) or 2,200 lbs

(998 kg), respectively.[303] The ox wagons could travel 10-16 miles (16-26km) per day whereas the mule wagons could travel around 15 miles (24km) or up to 10 miles more if the mules are corn fed. Furse suggests that it will take about 30 minutes to get 50 carts moving.[304]

Two-wheeled carts can be pulled by one animal and are easier to drive, can travel on roads that larger carts cannot and can be turned around in smaller spaces. They are also easier to upset, have no method of braking when travelling downhill and are more destructive to road surfaces on account of their weight being split across two points rather than four.[305] Byzantine sources record carts pulled by two oxen and carriages pulled by four donkeys or mules and, although this is unlikely to be an exhaustive list of the wheeled vehicles used, it forms a rough sketch of what may have been locally available to passing armies.[306]

A two-horse wagon is roughly eight metres long, with four metres for each subsequent rank of horses and four metres allotted to the space between each wagon.[307] The 19th-century Austrian army reduced the space taken up in the column of march by reducing the number of draught horses pulling their wagons from four to three. This change enabled the two-by-two formation to be changed to one in which the horses were three abreast. This reduced the number of animals required and the amount of forage needed by 25% and shortened the column by six paces per carriage but presumably at the cost in a reduction the maximum weight of transported materiel.[308]

Wheeled transport has the disadvantage of introducing new things to break, requiring repair. The wagons have a number of critical parts of both wood and metal and these need maintenance by specialist craftspeople. Dry weather is particularly damaging to wheeled transport.[309] If wagons were to be kept on the roads then woodworkers, blacksmiths and a plentiful supply of grease would be needed.

Humans

Using humans as porters, solely to carry supplies, is rarely explicitly dealt with in historical military logistics studies yet it has been used many times throughout history. Where human transportation is considered in the historical record, it is usually with regard to what types of food or equipment may be carried by the soldiers. That is not to say that the

[298] Dennis 2001, 139
[299] Furse 1882, 65
[300] Head 1837, 235
[301] Furse 1882, 67
[302] Furse 1882, 91

[303] Furse 1882, 67
[304] Furse 1882, 262
[305] Furse 1882, 96
[306] Belke 2017, 35
[307] Furse 1882, 103
[308] Furse 1882, 98
[309] Furse 1882, 99

categories of porter and soldier are necessarily fixed, General Wolseley employed most of his troops as carriers during his Gold Coast campaign to supplement his inadequate transport provision.[310] Humans have the benefit of being able to be ordered around with more complex orders than is the case with animals. That is not to say humans are unproblematic as pack animal substitutes, though.

The Viet Cong used human porters extensively to carry food and equipment, typically carrying 20-30kg. Avoiding the use of the large columns typical of non-guerilla warfare, they could travel around 50km per day or 30-40km if travelling at night.[311] The distributed nature of the supply locations meant that a series of runs between intermediate depots was more common than a long march along a route following a large army. One Viet Cong porter told of making a 4 hour, 12km march between two supply stations once per day carrying around 33kg of supplies, although some men carried up to 45kg.[312]

The carriers in some of the campaigns in British India in the 1870s had a set maximum load of 40 lbs (18.14 kg) in addition to their own kit which weighed 22 lbs (9.98 kg). In China and the Gold Coast the load was 50 lbs (22.68 kg) with an unknown weight of kit although the carriers frequently handled loads of lighter weight than this.[313] The distance that they could travel in a day depended on load and conditions. On good roads a carrier could travel 12 miles (19km) loaded and 12 miles back unloaded and if not having to travel back, 16 miles (26km) loaded was possible. Difficult terrain would reduce the range to 8 miles (13km) loaded and the same to return unloaded.[314] Transport by carriers was considered expensive, though sometimes not much more expensive than pack animals when aspects such as replacement of worn-out parts and animals is taken into account. The cost per ton of human transport being 4-8 times more expensive than transport by pack animals in the Zulu War of 1878.

The human component of animal transport

Merely the existence of horses, mules and donkeys in an area does not guarantee a useful baggage train, although obviously it is a pre-requisite. Animals need to be trained to be effective carriers and the trainers themselves need to be experienced. Inexperienced trainers tend to produce animals that are less productive and more prone to injuries.[315] The United States Army Artillery (Pack) has devised a 21-day

training programme for mules, to equip them with the required obedience, fitness and familiarity with common tasks and situations to enable them to be effective pack animals.[316] These animals need to be at least broken to be trained, with unbroken mules requiring months of training to become useful.[317] Furse stresses the need to keep transport structures in place during peacetime because, among other reasons, it ensures that there are officers trained in dealing with pack animal transportation, a requirement that is hard to satisfy in the short period normally given to campaign preparation.[318]

It seems clear that, if similar measures were needed for untrained animals in the Byzantine army, this training would be likely to have been done outside the main column of troops with the animals and trainers catching up and fitting in with the main body of troops once the animals were fit and trained enough to present no restriction to the good progress of the army. 'Mobility and effectiveness of the pack animal detachment depend largely on the selection and training of the pack animals.'[319]

This highlights another part of the requirements of a functioning baggage train, the human components. Competent handlers would be required at every step of the way and having competent animal trainers, who may be the same people, would also enlarge the possible number of useful animals available en route. Competent mule packers in 19th-century America needed at least three years' experience, with more being preferable.[320] Competent handlers do not just ensure the smooth operation of the pack animals on a day-to-day basis but will increase the availability of animals in the medium term. Animals hired with their owners as handlers are reported by Furse as ending a campaign in better condition that animals purchased and provided for regimental transport, as the former were looked after by people invested in their welfare while the latter were looked after by hired hands.

Constantine VII Porphyrogenitus specifies one *optimatos* per animal, who looks after its needs and is responsible for its welfare, in addition to one attendant per 10 mules or 20 horses to ensure the loads are straight.[321] The concern for keeping loads stable is also reflected in modern training in using pack animals and must have been an important, and often overlooked, part of the job. The attendant is likely to have been a servant, as Maurice states that if there are no servants then poorer soldiers should look after the baggage animals at one

---

[310] Furse 1882, 11
[311] Holliday and Gurfield 1968, 9
[312] Holliday and Gurfield 1968, 49
[313] Furse 1882, 45
[314] Furse 1882, 69
[315] U.S. Army 2004, 3–13

[316] U.S. Army 2004, 3–18
[317] Furse 1882, 81
[318] Furse 1882, 3
[319] U.S. Army 2004, 2–5
[320] Furse 1882, 92
[321] Constantine Porphyrogenitus 1990, 117

man per 3-4 animals.[322] In Sir Charles Napier's Indian army, one driver was assigned per animal.[323] Modern US training information claims that leading strings of 2-3 animals is not difficult, 4-5 is good, whereas 6-10 can be a problem.[324]

The difference between Constantine's one attendant per 10 mules and Maurice's one poor soldier per 3-4 animals may be down to experience. Inexperienced pack animal leaders are recommended to start with a small number of animals and work their way up. The Byzantine army is likely to have had more individuals familiar with handling pack animals than modern United States Special Forces so it may be reasonable to assume that the inexperience of animal handlers would not be a significant source of delay to the Mantzikert campaign. The human component to draft transport is likely to be proportionally larger, per animal, than that for pack transport. Furse recommends one driver for each two mules, ponies or draught bullock, though one for every three animals can be used if reducing the number of non-combatants is important,[325] whereas one person can look after five pack donkeys or several pack bullocks.

Human competence is not just required for handling and training. If the correct animals are not selected in the first place, time, money and effort can be wasted. As Furse drily remarks, 'transport animals were often bought by committees and condemned by fresh committees on reaching the front'.[326]

Pack animal equipment

Pack animals need some form of pad or saddle to be able to carry loads. These vary considerably in type and need to be customised to the individual animal. For this reason, animals should retain their own pack saddle where possible, and if they can be hired with a pack saddle already fitted for them then so much the better. Pack saddles in the British army of the 19th century frequently had an identifying number that was also present on the animal, ensuring the two were always matched. There is no reason to suggest that some version of this system would not have been present in the Byzantine army also.

Although an amount of pre-existing research has been published on ancient saddles, they have mainly focussed on riding saddles, for which there is a small amount of archaeological evidence.[327] No complete pack saddle from the Byzantine Empire survives, leaving artistic

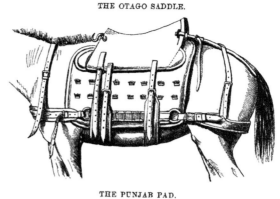

THE OTAGO SADDLE.

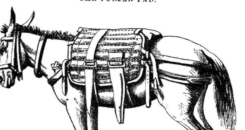

THE PUNJAB PAD.

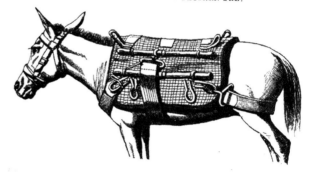

THE BOMBAY ORDNANCE PATTERN PAD.

Figure 5: Different types of pack saddle (Furse 1882, 280).

representations and historical texts as our only direct sources. Nineteenth-century data presents a much more detailed picture of the pack saddles that were available at that time, and it is not too controversial to suggest that this may be a more accurate reflection of the variety available in the 11th-century Byzantine Empire, which must surely have had many more different types and designs than have been preserved as either physical remains or textual descriptions.

Furse provides a large amount of detail on a number of different saddles and pads designed to facilitate load handling while also protecting the pack animals from chafing and strain.[328] The saddles detailed vary in weight from 18 to 48 lbs (8.16-21.77kg) and seem to be primarily geographically distinct, with names such as the Otago saddle, the Bombay ordnance pattern pad

[322] Dennis 2001, 17
[323] Furse 1882, 40
[324] U.S. Army 2004, 7–25
[325] Furse 1882, 92
[326] Furse 1882, 51
[327] Connolly 1986; Connolly and Van Driel-Murray 1991; Watson 2022

[328] Furse 1882, 82, 275–299

and the Punjab mule pad (Figure 5). This raises the possibility that the Byzantine army may have contained a more restricted range of pack saddle than the British army, which sourced and operated pack animals from all over the world. There were still a variety of different nationalities within the army and these may also have contributed to the variety of pack saddles although that would primarily have affected the baggage capacity at the unit rather than at the army level. Geographical origin is only one source of difference, however, and some variation may still have occurred due to the fact that different type of pack saddles could have been more associated with different functions rather than different origins within the Byzantine Empire.

Feeding the animals

Feeding the animals of the army is rarely dealt with in any significant way in Byzantine sources. Maurice records that one highly convenient way for pack animals to eat is by forage and that animals can be sent out to graze if the enemy is not nearby or the army needs to spend some time in one location.[329] If we require more detail we have to consult other sources, though thankfully this is a topic that is widely dealt with in sources from the 19th century onwards.

The amount and type of feed required for a pack animal depends on the amount and type of work to be done. There are three main types of animal food: forage, hay and grain. Forage has obvious advantages in that it is free, and animals can be left to feed freely while their humans can be elsewhere. Hay has to be provided and is bulky but can be easily procured in areas which contain large numbers of animals. Grain is likely to be a more expensive option but is more convenient to transport than hay and is highly nutritious.

Working animals need more proteins and minerals and will have less time to forage and so will need more human-provided food.[330] On the other hand grazing alone can provide idle animals with all the food and exercise they need.[331] Furse records that at one point during the China War of 1860, up to 4000 animals subsisted only on forage for 14 days.[332] Modern US army information states that hay is the basic component of any feed and a ration of hay alone will be healthier than one of solely grain.[333] So grain, for all its convenience and nutritional content, is largely an optional additive to forage or hay for animals that have work to do. This, however, describes all animals on the march and so, except maybe for rest days, grain would have been a necessary part of every animal's diet.

The US army recommends one pound of high-quality grain for each hour worked, up to 40% grain in a total ration. As over 40% grain can cause lameness or colic, oil is added to the grain if more energy is required.[334] If this recommendation was applied to the march to Mantzikert it would have implications for the supplies of the army as some marches would have taken more than four hours, requiring supplemental oil which would otherwise have been consumed by the soldiers.

There are several types of grains available for use as animal feed. Modern US information states that oats are the safest grain for pack animals, preferably crushed.[335] Barley is also good, but wheat should only be used when mixed in with other grains and any change in food should be done gradually over time.[336] The need for a stable (no pun intended) diet was acknowledged by the US Army in the 19th century, with Furse noting that 'Veterinary Surgeon B. L. Glover, R.A., who assisted in the purchase of mules for the Army Service Corps effected in the United States in 1880, says: "With reference to the feeding of mules in the United States, I may mention that they generally in towns receive a mixture of maize and oats in the proportion of 1 to 1½, the quality of this mixture varying, according to the size of the animals, from 4 lbs to 10 lbs per day. Together with this grain ration from 6 lbs to 12 lbs of hay is given, and with small mules it is very often the case that they are only fed twice daily, viz., morning and evening."'[337] This indicates that problems can be caused by altering the diet which animals are used to, which is a potential concern for any animals travelling the whole route with the army, from Constantinople to Mantzikert. Animals which are only hired for transport of goods in their home area are likely to be unaffected.

A related concern can affect forage, with different animals favouring different kinds. Furse notes that the Bolan Pass in 1879 contained plenty of forage for bullocks, mules and ponies but none for camels.[338] Salt is also essential for pack animals, preferably in the form of a salt block that the animal has free access to,[339] though total quantities are unspecified in either ancient or modern sources and are likely to be low.

Quantitative data

With all this in mind, where does our lack of quantitative Byzantine data get us? Some tables are included below, summarising the data from different sources (Table 2, Table 3, Table 4). One thing that should be apparent from both the tables below and the discussion above

---

[329] Dennis 2001, 99
[330] U.S. Army 2004, 2–13
[331] U.S. Army 2004, 2–22
[332] Furse 1882, 42
[333] U.S. Army 2004, 2–21

[334] U.S. Army 2004, 2–17
[335] U.S. Army 2004, 2–19
[336] U.S. Army 2004, 2–20
[337] Furse 1882, 84
[338] Furse 1882, 58
[339] U.S. Army 2004, 2–20

Table 2: A summary of the maximum loads of various pack animals

	Carrying capacity (Engels)	Carrying capacity (Haldon)[*]	Carrying capacity (Furse, Art of Marching)	Carrying capacity (Roth)	Carrying capacity (Furse, MT 'a fair average load')
Horse	91kg	104.5kg	-	180kg	91kg
Mule	91kg	104.5kg	-	-	91kg
Donkey	-	76kg	-	-	45kg
Ox	-	-	73kg	-	73kg
Camel	136kg	-	181kg	-	145-181kg

[*]Haldon 2006c, 146

Table 3: A summary of water requirements for pack animals

	Water requirement (modern US Army) (l/day)[*]	Water requirement (Engels)(l/day)[**]	Water requirement (Roth and Haldon) (l/day)	Water requirement (Furse) (l/day)
Horse	30-50	22.7-68.1 (av 36.4)	30	-
Mule	15-30	same as horse	20	-
Donkey	10-20	-	20	-
Ox	20-35	-	30	22.5
Camel	20-30	45.5	-	-

[*]U.S. Army 2004, 2–22
[**]Engels 1978, 127

Table 4: A summary of food requirements for pack animals

	Food kg (Engels)	Food kg (Roth and Haldon)	Food (Furse)
Horse	9kg-14.5kg (half grain) although uses low bound for calcs	2.5kg grain 7kg hay	-
Mule	Same as horse	2kg grain 6kg hay	-
Donkey	-	1.5kg grain 5kg hay	-
Ox	-	7kg grain 11kg hay	-
Camel	4.5 grain 11.3 straw	-	3 lbs meal and 3 oz salt

is the complexity and heterogeneity inherent in the populations of animals that were likely to have been available to the Byzantine army. The uniform loads used by modellers of military logistics such as Engels and Roth are necessary and useful within the context that they operate, simple models calculating logistical requirements using relatively straightforward maths. The historical detail paints a more nuanced picture of a disparate selection of species, sizes, conditions and contexts which is impossible to investigate with simple, top-down calculations.

Equipment

The amount of equipment carried by each member of the column is significant in that it all requires transportation by either human or animal power. This equipment includes weapons, clothes and cooking equipment for the common soldiers, feeding bags, saddles and tack for cavalry, tents for each small unit, specialist equipment for support staff and an entire luxurious mini baggage train for the emperor's accoutrements. The most significant aspect of the equipment carried by the army, for the purposes of creating our computer simulations, is the weight. This is not only because it would have been an important consideration to those in charge of logistics on the march during the Mantzikert, or any other, campaign but also because it is relatively easy to quantify. Factors such as space and packaging, along with ease of stacking, loading and unloading would all have been important, but they are much harder to model and therefore have to be accounted for in considerations outside the simulation. Quantifying weight requires a large element of supposition due to the lack of specific detail from accounts of the Mantzikert campaign and the disputed nature of the quantitative data,[340] but there are enough sources from the Byzantine period, and also from before and afterwards, to enable us to produce plausible parameters for the army's equipment needs.

Byzantine sources

There are a few Byzantine sources which contain recommendations on the amount and type of equipment to be carried by both individuals and units. Maurice's *Strategikon* has descriptions of equipment for both infantry[341] and cavalry,[342] as does the *Praecepta* of Nikephoros Phokas.[343] Although there is over 300 years between the two works, there is no reason to believe that the difference between the equipment described in each is more significant than the difference within each arm of the army. It is likely that the kit of an infantryman in Romanos IV Diogenes' army varied more within the army than it did from either Maurice or Nikephoros' idealised description.

Every soldier in the army would have had his own weapons. These would have varied depending on the wealth of the individual and what his role was within the army. Although Imperial arms manufactories existed and would have supplied a lot of equipment, there would have been some that would be created by local craftsmen and therefore equipment may have been heterogeneous within a unit and across units.[344] Most infantry would have possessed some combination of spear, javelin, bow, sword and sling. Some of the spears could have reached up to 5m in length and the stocky *menavlion*, though fairly short at 2.7-3.6m, was thick enough to have been required to be made from a whole sapling.[345] Spare weapons were also needed to cover wear and tear, loss and to add a degree of tactical flexibility. As these would have been relatively little used, they could have been carried in the main baggage train.[346] Byzantine sources mention certain items that would have constituted both the personal kit of an individual soldier and the more general kit of the army as a whole. Unfortunately, there is often no way of plausibly reconstructing the weights of each individual item except by bringing in data from other sources.

In an army with a large number of troops armed with missile weapons, the supply and transport of ammunition becomes significant. In a rare example of Byzantine quantitative data, Nikephoros Ouranos recommends a total of 180,000-200,000 arrows for an army, preferably 400,000 if possible. These are to be kept in cases of 50.[347] Without knowing the size of the army that this seemingly large number is recommended for, it is less helpful that it first appears, beyond indicating that the army routinely dealt with such large amounts of ammunition. Maurice's *Strategikon* recommends 30-40 arrows per cavalryman,[348] which means that Ouranos' 400,000 would equip an army incorporating up to 13,333 cavalry at 30 arrows per cavalryman, if they were the only troops with bows. This would create an awkward practical problem if the arrows were kept in cases of 50, however. The number of 50 arrows per case implies either 25 or 50 arrows per person, although it does not preclude a situation in which there was no single regular number and various troop types, or individual troops, had differing numbers of arrows. We also cannot know for certain what percentage of cavalry, or infantry, had bows, but if we assume that the number of bow-armed infantry cancel out the number of cavalry without bows we can see that Maurice's recommendation maps fairly well onto Nikephoros', implying as it does a cavalry force of 4,500-13,333 cavalry in an army (Table 5).

Table 5: The implications of Nikephoros Ouranos' recommended total of arrows on cavalry size

	180,000 arrows	200,000 arrows	400,000 arrows
25 arrows per cavalry	7,200 cavalry	8,000 cavalry	16,000 cavalry
30 arrows per cavalry	6,000 cavalry	6,667 cavalry	13,333 cavalry
40 arrows per cavalry	4,500 cavalry	5,000 cavalry	10,000 cavalry
50 arrows per cavalry	3,600 cavalry	4,000 cavalry	8,000 cavalry

But some infantry clearly did have bows as Ouranos also says that infantry archers should have two quivers, one with 40 arrows and one with 60.[349] If these figures are also applied to cavalry instead of Maurice's 30-40 per soldier then we have a much easier task of equating

---

[340] e.g. Dawson 2007
[341] Dennis 2001, 139
[342] Dennis 2001, 12–13
[343] McGeer 1995, 202
[344] Haldon 1999, 131
[345] McGeer 1995, 19
[346] Dennis 2001, 14

[347] McGeer 1995, 97
[348] Dennis 2001, 12
[349] McGeer 1995, 15

Ouranos' total arrow numbers to 1,800, 2,000 or 4,000 bow-armed troops respectively.

If we somewhat arbitrarily assume a weight of 35g per arrow with every 50 being kept in a case weighing 150g, 400,000 arrows represent a requirement for the capacity to transport 152,000 kg, either along the whole route or in ever increasing amounts up to that maximum. Engels specified 91kg as a typical load for a mule so Ouranos' army would have needed 1,653 of Engels' mules just to carry arrows. It is likely that some of these arrows were carried by the soldier themselves, particularly in the case of cavalry, but this in turn would take up capacity that could otherwise be used for other equipment, food or water.

Although the majority of the weight of an average soldier's equipment was probably made up of items of food, clothes, weapons, armour and cooking utensils, there are likely to be other items of equipment that we commonly overlook that would have been used on campaign. Items such as inflatable skins to aid the crossing of rivers,[350] leather or wicker cases for coats of mail,[351] or stakes and caltrops for fortifying the nightly camp[352] could have formed a small but non-negligible part of the army's equipment.

In some texts we find clues to how equipment may have been transported. The *Sylloge Tacticorum* recommends soldiers have pennons on their spears on the march in order to create an impressive spectacle.[353] This implies spears being carried upright by the soldiers rather than transported in carts. Whether this applies to all spear-armed soldiers and whether it only applies to times when other people, maybe even the enemy, were watching or not is unknown.

The *Sylloge Tacticorum* also recommends each *dekarchia* should have a wagon which contains 'a hand-mill, an axe, a hatchet, two picks and two shovels, a goat-hair mat and a basket, as well as an adze and other [tools] of that sort. Besides, a battle-axe, a scythe, and iron caltrops which are attached to wire by iron nails, in order to be easily thrown and in turn easily collected. Each wagon should also have extra bows and arrows, hardtack and flour, and all the other [things] which are necessary and have been omitted by us.'[354]

The needs of the emperor are perhaps the least precisely defined of all the possible members of the army column. The emperor would have had to receive and entertain important guests and fulfil a number of roles that were non-essential from a logistics point of view

but very essential from a ceremonial and governmental point of view. He would also have been able to insist that he travel in as comfortable a manner as he felt he had a right to expect, without anyone possessing the authority to countermand him. The sum total of the emperor's equipment could therefore amount to anything from not much more than that of the higher-ranking officers all the way up to a highly significant amount requiring a dedicated baggage train of his own.

Constantine VII Porphyrogenitus goes into great detail regarding the pack animal requirements of the Imperial household and associated personnel.[355] He describes a household with requirements for 1086 mules and packhorses, with an extra 30 saddled horses. This includes 100 spare mules to cover for any which were unable to work through fatigue or illness. The emperor would need extra horses to give as gifts along the way, but he may also receive horses in like manner. Clearly gifts were an important part of the emperor's progress on campaign, in the eyes of Constantine, as a substantial number of pack animals were dedicated to carrying gold and clothing to be given to notables and helpful people along the way.

Ancient comparators

Quantitative data about the loads of ancient soldiers can be even harder to come by than that for the Byzantine army. Often, we rely on modern estimates of ancient equipment loads rather than primary evidence. Estimates have been made of 27.5-36.5kg for the equipment of an Assyrian spearman and 22.5-32kg for that of a Greek hoplite.[356]

Jonathan Roth, in his *Logistics of the Roman Army at War*,[357] gives a summary of the Roman legionary's personal equipment along with that belonging to his squad, as listed in ancient sources and modern research. As with Byzantine sources, Roman sources are fragmentary and often lacking in quantitative detail. The list of equipment attributed to a squad reads very similar to that noted for Byzantine units: clothes, weapons, a tent, a hand mill, cooking equipment and tools for creating the camp such as digging tools and the sharpened stakes that would have topped the bank. Josephus listed a soldier's equipment as an axe, a basket, a spade, a rope, a chain, a saw and a sickle, although Roth plausibly speculates that not every soldier would have had every item on the list. Estimates of the load carried by Roman legionaries vary but 36.5kg is considered a reasonable figure towards the upper end of normal.[358]

---

350 Constantine Porphyrogenitus 1990, 137
351 Dennis 2001, 14
352 Chatzelis and Harris 2017, 54
353 Chatzelis and Harris 2017, 37
354 Chatzelis and Harris 2017, 54

---

355 Constantine Porphyrogenitus 1990, 101–121
356 Orr 2010, 68
357 Roth 1999, 68–77
358 Orr 2010, 71

Examples from later periods

A pikeman of the English Civil War has been estimated to carry at least 29.5kg, including pike, armour, clothes and food.[359] This is a similar weight to the standard kit of a British soldier in the American War of Independence, which was 63lbs and 10oz, almost 29kg.[360] Whether as a result of an increase in body size and power due to an improved diet, or as an artefact of more accurate and complete data, soldiers of the 20th century have been recorded with heavier loads than those estimated for antiquity. Australian troops in Vietnam could end up carrying over 50kg and the Marines involved in the three-day, 129km yomp during the Falklands Conflict in 1982 carried between 54.5-66kg each.[361] Yet both Field Marshal Montgomery and a 2001 report by the US Army Science Board agree in recommending a maximum load of around 22.5kg for effective continuous operations.[362]

In a memorandum during the Second Afghan War, there are five categories of equipment that should be near each soldier and that he should have easy access to.[363] These were:

- Ammunition
- Entrenching tools
- Kits
- Tents
- Cooking pots

These correspond very nicely to those items listed by Josephus as being required for Roman soldiers, and although there are historical variations, they represent a fairly constant set of staples in the soldier's pack throughout the ages.

Variation

The amount of equipment carried by soldiers from a particular army or time period, as expressed by a single weight, is of limited use. Firstly, different types of troops will have had different types of equipment. Secondly, different individuals will have had different loads and capabilities. Thirdly, loads could vary based on environmental considerations. It was possible for a First World War British soldier's 27.5kg load to be increased by over 50% once saturated water and mud were taken into account.[364] Within this context, a technique such as computer simulation has a role to play in examining this heterogeneous, and sometimes dynamic, situation which contains more complexity

than that captured by simpler tools such as those used by Engels.

Camps

At the end of each day the army would have needed a place to camp. Unlike some other aspects of campaigning, the locating and setting up of camp attracts a significant amount of commentary from Byzantine military writers. The information mainly comes from treatises, with isolated details specific to a particular campaign being recorded in more personal works. The regularity with which it is dealt with in military treatises from all periods indicates that the most significant factors are both important and not necessarily obvious. Failures in locating and setting up secure camps are usually looked upon harshly by military writers.

The two main points emphasised by Byzantine writers are that camps should be set up in a suitable location and that a defensive cordon should always be erected, regardless of perceived threat. As Maurice records in his *Strategikon*, a general should never have to say, 'I did not expect it'.[365] The main criteria for camping locations are that they should be defensible and have access to water and firewood. Access to water is a debated point, as a river running through a camp will hamper its defence if it is attacked and create problems when people and animals need to be watered. Maurice also suggests not camping too close to rivers in case the horses drink too much.[366] The *Sylloge Tacticorum* recommends that the camp site should neither be rocky nor swampy and not too near water or the horses will get used to the easy access and suffer when it is more scarce.[367] Nevertheless, Nikephoros Phokas warns of ruin if the camp is not set up at least somewhat close to a water source.[368]

Byzantine camp locations are recommended to be selected in advance, with quartering parties going ahead of the army to look for good places to camp, along with possible sources of water and forage. Surveyors then set out the camp, marking out where the surrounding bank and ditch are to be, along with the entries and interior roads.[369] Thus when the first units of the army arrive at a camping location at the end of their march, they should be able to easily find their allotted camping location. The layout is supposed to be the same each day although that obviously does not take into account the fact that units may join and leave along the route. It's not explicitly recorded in any Byzantine work, but it seems likely that the first few times that camp is set up on a particular campaign there is likely to be a certain

359 Orr 2010, 72
360 Huston 1966, 26
361 Orr 2010, 76
362 Orr 2010, 75
363 Furse 1882, 255
364 Orr 2010, 68

365 Dennis 2001, 82
366 Dennis 2001, 78
367 Chatzelis and Harris 2017, 39
368 McGeer 1995, 23
369 Dennis 2001, 15

amount of confusion as soldiers become accustomed to the layout of the camp and their place within it.

Maurice recommends that camps should always be set up, even if only being occupied for a day.[370] This implies that longer stays were not uncommon, although there may have been strategic reasons for an army to linger in an area for a short while. Romanos IV Diogenes seems to have had a professional approach to camp construction and it is likely that he followed the wisdom of his predecessors in setting up camp, with bank, ditch and defences, each day. Attaleiates records that he erects a proper camp outside Hierapolis in 1068[371] and is mentioned doing so several times afterwards.

Aplekta were military camps that could act as mustering points for elements of the army to gather together. The extent to which they were used during the Mantzikert campaign is unknown, but they were largely sited with regard to common sense criteria such as transport links and availability of food, so it seems likely that they would have provided attractive options as mustering points and resupply bases. A very short military treatise associated with Constantine VII Porphyrogenitus provides a list of locations, along with the *themes* which would muster at those points for a military expedition to Eastern Anatolia or beyond.[372] This advice is also given in Leo Katakylas' treatise on expeditions, although it is a straightforwardly common-sense piece of organisation.[373]

Health and hygiene

Hygiene and the health of the humans and animals in the army were both significant factors in the location of camps. Maurices states that, 'healthy, clean places should be chosen for camps, and we should not stay too long in one spot, unless the air and the availability of supplies are more advantageous. Otherwise, disease can spread among the troops. It is very important that sanitary needs not be taken care of inside the camp, but outside because of the disagreeable odor, especially if there is some reason for the army to remain in one place.'[374]

The close association of many people from around the empire and beyond must have facilitated exposure to diseases that some of the human and animal members of the army had not been exposed to before. Furse records that 'an army no sooner commences to move than its numerical strength undergoes a sensible reduction by a number of men falling sick'.[375]

Regardless of the possibility of becoming sick along the way, some people will have started the campaign in poor health. This may then be exacerbated by the strains of marching, until they drop out through illness. There were many campaigns in which the casualties through sickness and disease were much greater than those through enemy action; the First Crusade lost over 100,000 people due to a variety of pestilences between 1097-1100.[376] Furse blames 'considerable difference of temperature between day and night, drinking impure water, monotony of food, want of rest, exposure to the rays of the sun by day or to heavy dews by night, lying on damp ground, breathing pestilential air etc' for this inevitable decrease in manpower.[377]

Nevertheless, the Mantzikert campaign possessed several characteristics which may have limited the problems caused by poor health. Significant factors in pre-modern military campaign health include dysentery through poor water and waste-handling procedures, malaria, and problems caused by poor provision of food and footwear.[378] Of these, the threat from malaria would have been mitigated by avoidance of wet, low-lying areas, the provision of decent food and footwear should have been helped by the majority of the route being through well-settled areas and, if the advice in the treatises were followed, the threat of dysentery would be minimised by sensible access arrangements to water sources and the fact that the army is likely not to have stayed in one location for any extended period.

Routine on the march

The daily routine of marching will have been required to have some structure around it to facilitate organisation. It would be essential for each unit to know when they need to get their equipment packed away and be ready to march as the gap between the troops at the front of the column and those at the rear could have been many hours. Both humans and pack animals become fatigued by standing under load for an extended period of time. If the same march order was used each day, units would become accustomed to watching out for units further up the column setting off, providing an early warning for their own departure. Maurice states that marches can be commenced by either the sound of bugles or the movement of banners.[379] To aid in timing, clocks were used in Roman armies, sundials by day and water clocks by night.[380]

The order of march of the army as a whole would start with the quartering parties, surveyors and teams who

---

[370] Dennis 2001, 59
[371] Attaleiates 2012, 199
[372] Constantine Porphyrogenitus 1990, 81
[373] Constantine Porphyrogenitus 1990, 89
[374] Dennis 2001, 160
[375] Furse 1882, 179
[376] Prinzing 1916, 13
[377] Furse 1882, 180
[378] Haldon 2014, 240–242
[379] Chatzelis and Harris 2017, 37
[380] Haynes 2015, 117

would repair and clear the road out ahead, who were probably a day or more in advance of the main body of the army in friendly territory. Of the main column, the emperor would go at the head of the army, although some officials and possibly a small number of troops would go on ahead of him.[381] Then the units of the army would follow, then the baggage train and a rear guard to cope with stragglers, which would include both people and animals with issues that affect their mobility, along with the inevitable malingerers and would-be deserters.

Once arrived in camp at the end of the day's march, animals would need to be fed and groomed, preferably being groomed at the start of the day as well.[382] Cavalry troops would have the logistically complex task of watering and feeding their horses while the infantry are likely to be the ones on whom the majority of the work of digging the camp defences fell.

Maurice's *Strategikon* has various pieces of advice and information regarding the practicalities of how the march is organised. These do not form a comprehensive description of how an army moves itself, but they are very useful snippets that can help the construction of a simulation of the march of a Byzantine army. These include:

- Soldiers should not march amongst the baggage trains, especially if contact with the enemy is expected.[383]
- Allies should camp and march separately so that they have less knowledge of the army's composition should they ever rebel.[384]
- The troops at the head should place signs at forks in the road so that those following behind will not get lost. These could be written on trees or could be piles of rock or earth.[385]
- The rear guard should travel 15-20 miles to the rear of the army to pick up stragglers although it is debatable as to whether this only applies when the enemy are in the area.[386] It does imply that this rear guard may travel a whole day behind the army, although if the rear guard consisted of only a small cavalry force then it could catch up with the rest of the army in the evening.
- Marching in scattered groups makes the army look bigger than if they were in a regular formation, 'all the more so if they are marching on sloping or hilly ground'[387], presumably because this spreads them out even further.

- Scythians travel with a huge herd of horses and do not camp within encampments.[388]
- A formation two, three or four men wide is used for passing through 'defiles, rough terrain and thickly wooded country'.[389]
- A formation suitable for hunting can be used on the march but says that it has to be practiced or it will cause fatigue.[390]

To these can be added the advice of Nikephoros Phokas that spare mules should be brought along by those at the rear to assist stragglers.[391] Nikephoros Ouranos paints a vivid picture of life on campaign with Basil II in 999 in a letter to the metropolitan of Nicomedia:

Let others speak of the gains and the luxuries if they wish. The costs, the toils, the sleepless nights, the days without wine or sustenance, the night marches, and 'the noise of flutes and pipes and the din of men' even during sleep; but also the bread we eat, or rather the stone made into bread on which we break our teeth and nearly destroy our entire body – for grinding it without sparing the stones in it and swallowing it not when it is more readily digestible, but downing it half baked in one gulp like Kronos, so to speak, we suffer greatly from indigestion and put our very lives at risk – I forego mention of the swarm of cares and the multitude of tasks, the disputes, the jealousies and the enmities, or the terrors and the dangers, the windings hither and thither, the tumult and the confusion. All these things I had best leave aside.[392]

Non-combatants

You will not find in a gallant army of 50,000 men a single fat man, unless it be a quarter-master, or a quarter-master-serjeant[393]

The number and nature of non-combatants in the Byzantine army is largely a matter of speculation, and it is here that data from other periods and situations may be least helpful. Official non-combatants such as slaves, or servants for soldiers who could afford them, are likely to have been present, although their numbers are hard to quantify. Maurice recommends slaves or servants for the soldiers in the cavalryman's equipment section. Considering that he also recommends a spare horse, presumably they would ride this when present.[394] Other official non-combatants include those at the top of the army's hierarchy such as Attaleiates, a military judge who had no military background and was therefore unlikely to have played a direct role in

---

[381] Constantine Porphyrogenitus 1990, 89
[382] Furse 1882, 251
[383] Dennis 2001, 78
[384] Dennis 2001, 89
[385] Dennis 2001, 97
[386] Dennis 2001, 100
[387] Dennis 2001, 102

[388] Dennis 2001, 116
[389] Dennis 2001, 132
[390] Dennis 2001, 167
[391] McGeer 1995, 23
[392] McGeer 1995, 340
[393] Grose et al. 1867
[394] Dennis 2001, 14

the battle of Mantzikert. There would have been other court functionaries and enablers within the emperor's household. Lower down the social order, certain specialised trades and roles would have been filled by non-combatants, although some may have been covered by soldiers who pursued that particular trade in their normal daily life. The carpenters and blacksmiths required for mending carts could have been found in the usual ranks of the soldiers, though they would also have needed equipment and tools to be useful. Whether this was practical or not remains an unknown, as it may have been easier for broken equipment to be kept until the next settlement, to be attended to by the relevant local professionals. Some specialists are mentioned

directly, such as the medical corpsmen whose job was to follow behind the line to rescue and take care of those wounded in battle, and who presumably provided other assistance during the march.[395]

Officially sanctioned merchants have already been mentioned and there would have been traders following the army for a short while as it passed through their home territories, hawking their wares to soldiers. The tolerance for any further attending non-combatants is unrecorded and as the situation varies so widely from case to case it is difficult to even speculate how much the Byzantine army on the march to Mantzikert was swelled by non-official hangers-on.

---

[395] Dennis 2001, 15

Chapter 5 – 19th-Century Military Writing

Introduction

History sometimes yields lessons of direct applicability which too often go unrecognized and unheeded, and sometimes are deliberately ignored – presumably on the naïve assumption that 'this time everything is different.'[396]

Sometimes a productive avenue of research only opens by chance. Such a fortunate coincidence occurred on a stairway at the University of Birmingham in 2009. The ABM's technical infrastructure had been created and the question had turned to how exactly you would move an army, simulated or otherwise.

One of the benefits of computer simulation is that computers work with actual numbers. You cannot start a simulation of an army on the march with 'around 10,000' agents as variables require precise, though not necessarily accurate, values. They may change across different runs of the simulation and even within a single run of a simulation, but any variable '*x*' must equal a value, regardless of what '*x*' may represent. '*X = probably somewhere between 5000 and 10000*' is not valid computer code. The same is true of mechanisms of order and movement, which must be described completely, incorporating every detail required for them to function. Code is specific, digital and precise (though not necessarily accurate) whereas, as we have seen, historical detail is usually vague and untrustworthy, and more often than not it is entirely absent of quantified data. Within an ABM, there have to be rules regulating the behaviours of the agents. If we relied solely upon the Byzantine military treatises and historical accounts, we would be starting with an almost blank page regarding these rules.

Returning to the Birmingham stairway, project members had been discussing over a mid-morning coffee how these rules might be created. It seemed there was nothing in the commonly available literature that might help formulate the rules and mechanisms by which an army might organise itself for a day's march. 'If only there was a book called "Marching for Dummies"', they gloomily concurred. On the way back to his office, Vince Gaffney ran into Gary Sheffield on the aforementioned stairway. At the time, Gary was a Professor in the Centre for War Studies at Birmingham. 'Do you know where we can find details on how you'd

march an army?', asked Vince. 'Ah, you'll need *The Art of Marching*', replied Gary.

The Art of Marching was published in 1901 and was written by George Armand Furse, a military veteran of many 19th-century campaigns. It is indeed essentially 'Marching for Dummies', and provided exactly the practical base upon which a plausible ABM could be created. It also opened up a whole new range of sources often ignored within modern research into pre-modern military logistics.

The problem with prior work

Donald Engels attempted to calculate the supply requirements of the army of Alexander the Great[397] and, while it was a pioneering and insightful piece of research, several aspects were criticised.[398] He used a recommended daily calorie amount for a modern 19-year-old of 175.2cm in height as the calorie requirement of an ancient Greek soldier, overestimated the amount of wheat required to generate a required amount of bread and ignored sources of calories other than bread in his calculations. Alternative approaches to similar problems have been suggested, and although it is impossible to arrive at the 'correct' figures for variables such as how much bread could be made from a particular volume of wheat or what the average energy expenditure of a soldier of any particular army was, we, like Engels, will have to make an undoubtedly flawed attempt.

The need for more information

As can be seen from previous chapters, the information available from Byzantine sources is inadequate, unreliable and antiquated to varying degrees. Some of it, however, is exceptionally useful and can be part of a good framework within which to construct a model. Absent are specific procedures involved in the organisation of an army on the march and quantitative details against which to measure a model's outputs. Our simulation requires specifics and metrics while the Byzantine sources frequently deal in generalisations and vagaries. It is at this point we return to the (re) discovery of *The Art of Marching* and explain what it is, how it came to be written and why it is so important to a simulation of 11th-century military logistics.

---

[396] Huston 1966, ix

[397] Engels 1978
[398] O'Connor 2013

19th-century military writing

The Art of Marching was published in 1901 and was written by George Armand Furse K.C.B (1834-1906). Furse was a modestly prolific author and wrote 13 books between 1877 and 1905. He is described in the frontispiece of *The Art of Marching* as 'Late of the Black Watch' and this, while correct, is a trifle understated as he enjoyed a long and fairly distinguished career. He was made an Ensign, the lowest rank of commissioned officer, in 1855. This commission was purchased, a practice which was subsequently abolished in 1871, but was the cheapest commission available giving some indication of Furse's socio-economic background. Furse purchased his commission during the Crimean War at a time when the Siege of Sevastopol was underway. There was considerable domestic debate about the war and William Howard Russell's pioneering war reporting had made the public aware of some of the conflict's logistics-related disasters, so Furse's deliberate involvement at this time could be considered as demonstrating a genuine enthusiasm for military life. After Crimea he served in India and the Gold Coast, being part of the First Ashanti Expedition led by General Garnet Wolesley. In 1878 while serving as aide-de-camp to Lt-General Sir C. Staveley, Commander-in-Chief of the Bombay Army, he published his first book, *Studies on Military Transport*. By 1882 when his second book, *Military Transport*, was published, he had been made a Lieutenant-Colonel and was Deputy Assistant Quartermaster General working from Horseguards Parade in London. He was promoted to Colonel for his service as part of Garnet Wolesley's attempt to relieve General Gordon at Khartoum in 1885 and was made a Companion of the Most Honourable Order of the Bath in 1888. It is notable that Furse's output increases dramatically once he reaches 60 years old, implying that may have been when he retired from the army. Prior to 1894 he wrote five books but between 1894 and his death in 1906 he wrote eight.

The Art of Marching draws on Furse's experiences as a quartermaster, often in countries far from Britain where conditions resembled those of the march to Mantzikert to some extent. He took part in campaigns in which mixed cavalry and infantry forces travelled long distances away from modern infrastructure such as railways and paved road surfaces. Crucially for our purposes, *The Art of Marching* includes specific organisational details required to move an army, along with detailed metrics such as the speed of individual troops, the carrying capacity of beasts of burden, the amount of stretching of the column of march to be expected and much more. The fact that the conditions in which Furse collected his observations were not so far from those that were likely to have existed during the Mantzikert campaign make *The Art of Marching* even more useful.

Interestingly, *The Art of Marching* was also the title of a talk at the Royal United Services Institute in London by Colonel E.T.H. Hutton in 1893, eight years before Furse's book was published.[399] Like Furse's book, Hutton's talk focussed on large-scale movements of troops with examples containing quantitative data. Hutton, like Furse, took part in the Nile Expedition in 1885 during which he commanded the mounted infantry. At the time of Hutton's talk, March 15th, 1893, Furse was probably still working at Horseguards Parade in London. It is far from unlikely that Furse was in the audience when someone who was a likely acquaintance gave his talk on a subject that Furse had published books on, in the city in which he worked. If so, Furse may well have gained an approach, and a title, from Hutton's talk, although the talk is much briefer than Furse's book and its intention is to make the case for a systematic approach to organising strategic marches rather than to present a complete study of the topic.

Furse's *The Art of Marching* does not simply draw upon his personal experience though. He is well read on the subject of military history, especially regarding logistics, and draws in materiel from earlier in the 19th century and further back, even to antiquity. An aspect of this which had considerable significance for the *Medieval Warfare on the Grid* project is that he referenced writers which were seldom read or referenced in modern academic papers. *The Art of Marching* does not stand alone as a useful book for the purposes of modelling an army on the march. It not only served as an introduction to Furse's other books, but it also served as a gateway into an entire literary genre. Furse was far from the only author publishing on these subjects. Unbeknownst to the project's members at the start of the project, the 19th century was the scene of a veritable explosion of military writing on a variety of subjects from a plethora of viewpoints. The search for useful details on which to build our model spread out from its origin in Furse, back in time through the 19th century and into the 18th and out across space from Britain to Continental Europe and America.

19th-century publishing

The 19th century saw the publication of a large number of books on military matters from a variety of perspectives. The sheer diversity of authors, topics and approaches stands in stark contrast to the Byzantine situation in which the writing of military treatises was restricted to the very few, publishing involving copying manuscripts by hand and the readership consisting of other military leaders. Although the military memoir was a genre which already had a sizeable number of examples[400] and earlier works had also been published

---

[399] Hutton 1893
[400] Harari 2007

on military organisation, notably Grose's 1786 history of the English army,[401] within 19th-century Britain a variety of factors came together that resulted in an explosion of military writing.

Publishing technology

During the 19th century, technological changes in various areas resulted in books becoming cheaper and much more numerous. At the start of the 19th-century, paper was largely made by hand from linen rags. By the end of the century, mechanisation, first by water and then by steam, made paper much cheaper and faster to produce. Printing had also improved, with steam-driven presses, case binding and stereotyping all resulting in a much faster, and therefore cheaper, way to produce books. Partly as a result of these technological innovations the number of titles recorded with London imprints more than trebled between the 1810s and the 1860s.[402]

Distribution network

By the end of the 18th century there were at least 1000 booksellers in England and Wales,[403] but by the end of the 1860s there were more than 500 W.H. Smith's bookstalls within railway stations alone. The building of the railways changed the national situation in two major ways. It made transporting stock around the country much easier and cheaper, ensuring provincial towns could receive more stock, sooner. Railway journeys also served as a creator of demand, with booksellers opening at stations throughout the country catering to people who were embarking on often long and tedious journeys by rail, during which there was not much else to do but read.

Literacy

Elementary education was made compulsory in 1870 but even before then, literacy rates had already sharply risen during the century. Philanthropists, publishers, social improvers and religious groups had all recognised the benefit of ensuring every adult could read, and by 1900 they had almost reached that goal. This also meant that large numbers of people were also sufficiently literate to write, especially those in the officer ranks of the military. Within military logistics, literacy was indispensable for the record keeping required to supply an army, ensuring that anyone with experience of how armies moved and were fed at the highest levels was almost certainly literate enough to record what they knew.

Public interest

Reading was a popular leisure activity before music halls and organised sport started to compete for free time within Britain. The notable campaigns of the 19th century, particularly the Napoleonic Wars, the American Civil War, the Crimean War and the Boer War all, for various reasons, caught the public's imagination. Indeed, 'hardly had the guns fallen silent at Waterloo than dozens of Napoleonic War memoirs began rolling off the British printing presses'.[404] Historical non-fiction in general could sell well, as reflected in Thomas Carlyle's £2800 payment from Chapman and Hall for the rights to print 5000 copies of the first two volumes of his biography of Frederick the Great in 1858,[405] this at a time when a typical London carpenter could expect to earn around £83 per year.[406]

The great wars

The 19th century saw warfare on a scale not previously recorded. Larger populations, better roads, industrialisation and more effective food preservation enabled armies to be mobilised which dwarfed those of earlier times. The Napoleonic Wars at the beginning of the century involved millions of men across the whole of Europe. They also created an appetite for information of the armies, battles and leaders involved. The British Empire was involved not only in Europe but also in India and North America, creating simultaneously an interest in warfare and a large number of literate officers who could write about it. The successes of British involvement in the Peninsula War and at Waterloo gave way to the disaster of the Crimean War. This was the first war to be reported on in the British newspapers in something approaching real time, greatly helped by the increasing use of the telegraph. By the Boer War at the end of the century, British officers had served in a variety of different wars around the globe in glorious victory, ignominious defeat and everything in between. American authors too were motivated by their experiences in the Civil War, a conflict that, like the Crimean War, had come at a time of increasing availability of, and demand for, books.

As can be seen (Table 6), the delay between an author's personal experience and the publication of his works varies immensely. Jomini and Clausewitz both gained their experience in the Napoleonic Wars, as did Routh, Gurwood and Edgecomb, and collectively these authors kept publishing until the middle of the 19th century. Billings and Symonds both served in the American Civil War and published within a year of each other, over 20 years after the events they record. The shortest gaps

---

[401] Grose 1786
[402] Feather 2005, 98
[403] Feather 2005, 93

[404] Harari 2007, 299
[405] Feather 2005, 137
[406] Bowley 1900, 84

between experience and publication tend to be British publications following the Crimean War, motivated by a desire to correct the problems that were displayed therein. The outrage regarding this event seems to play out in the published works much more quickly than the usually more positive accounts of the Napoleonic Wars.

In one case, that of Henry Clay Symonds, he says that it had taken him a long time to mentally face up to the prospect of reliving his experiences, and this may have been the case for others. In others, the author had finished their service within the armed forces and settled down to a normal life before deciding to commit their thoughts to the page. However they arrived at the completion of their works, the uptick in publications from this admittedly non-comprehensive list after 1880 (Figure 6), is reflective of an actual increase in available books on military matters.

Some of these authors had the support of their former employers (e.g., Routh and Lippitt), others were too critical to receive backing and had to publish privately (e.g., Symonds and de Fonblanque) or even anonymously. Some were descriptive records of events while others were reactions to military defeat,

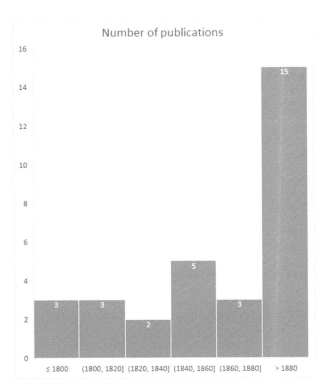

Figure 6: Number of military logistics publications in the timeline, divided by date range.

Table 6: A timeline of selected military logistics writing

Year Published	Author	Title	Notes	Military experience
1573	Whitehorne	Certaine wayes for the ordering of souldiours in battelray	British	
1777	Donkin	Military collections and remarks	British	
1786	Grose	Military Antiquities respecting a History of the English Army, from the Conquest to the present	British	
1801	Le Mesurier	The British Commissary	British	
1805	Jomini	Treatise on Grand Military Operations	Swiss	Napoleonic Wars
1820	Edgecomb	Journal of an Officer in the Commissariat Department of the Army	British	Napoleonic Wars
1832	Clausewitz	On War	German	Napoleonic Wars
1838	Jomini	The Art of War	Swiss	Napoleonic Wars
1842	Gurwood	Selections From The Dispatches And General Orders Of Field Marshal The Duke of Wellington	British	Napoleonic Wars
1845	Routh	Observations on the Commissariat Field Service and Home Defences	British	Napoleonic Wars
1855	Anon	A remedy for the evils that have caused the destruction of a large portion of the British army before Sevastopol	British	Crimean War
1856	Hodge	On the mortality arising from military operations	British	Non-military, actuary
1858	de Fonblanque	Treatise on the Administration and Organization of the British Army	British	Crimean War

Year Published	Author	Title	Notes	Military experience
1862	Marmont	The Spirit of Military Institutions; or, Essential Principles of the Art of War	French	Napoleonic Wars
1866	Hamley	The Operations of War	British	Crimean War, Egypt
1869	Lippitt	Field Service in War: Comprising Marches, Camps and Cantonments, Outposts, Convoys, Reconnaissances, Foraging, and Notes on Logistics	American	Mexican War, Bald Hills War
1882	Furse	Military transport	British	India, Gold Coast
1882	Home	A Précis of Modern Tactics	British	Gold Coast
1887	Billings	Hard Tack and Coffee	American	American Civil War
1888	Symonds	Report of a Commissary of Subsistence, 1861-1865	American	American Civil War
1893	Sharpe	The Art of Subsisting Armies in War	American	Indian Wars
1894	Furse	The Organization and Administration of the Lines of Communication in War	British	India, Gold Coast, Sudan
1895	Furse	Information in War	British	India, Gold Coast, Sudan
1896	Sharpe	The Art of Supplying Armies in the Field as Exemplified During the Civil War	American	Indian Wars
1896	von der Goltz	The Conduct of War: A Brief Study of Its Most Important Principales and Forms	German	Austro-Prussian War, Franco-Prussian War
1897	Furse	Military Expeditions Beyond the Seas	British	India, Gold Coast, Sudan
1899	Furse	Provisioning armies in the field	British	India, Gold Coast, Sudan
1901	Furse	The Art of Marching	British	India, Gold Coast, Sudan
1905	Sharpe	The Provisioning of the Modern Army in the Field	American	Indian Wars, Spanish American War, Philippine-American War
1906	von der Goltz	The Nation in Arms: A Treatise on Modern Military Systems and the Conduct of War	German	Austro-Prussian War, Franco-Prussian War

suggesting improvements in order to avoid further embarrassment.[407] Some were autobiographical (Symonds, Lippitt), while others made little mention of their own experiences (Furse) or even refrained from mentioning them altogether (Home). Nevertheless, they almost all had personal experience of organising the movement and feeding of groups of soldiers in a variety of conditions, often in conditions that were in some way similar to those in 11th-century Anatolia.

An overview of the 19th-century sources

Although all the writers on military logistics had some personal connection to the subject, these connections could vary significantly. Francis James Lippitt served in the American army during the Mexican War before becoming commander of the Humboldt Military District and then leading the United States forces in the Bald Hills War against a series of Californian Native American tribes.[408] Henry Granville Sharpe served as Quartermaster General of the United States army at their entry into World War I but had been a commissary

---

[407] Anon 1855

[408] Lippitt 1902

officer since 1883.[409] His *The Art of Subsisting Armies in War* was published in 1893 while he was still a Captain. His *The Provisioning of the Modern Army in the Field* was subsequently revised by Frank A. Cook, himself a commissariat officer, in 1908. Robert Home was a Major in the Royal Engineers and the assistant Quartermaster General.[410] He wrote his *Precis of Modern Tactics* in 1873 and it was popular enough to still be in print 9 years later. While mainly dealing with battlefield tactics, Home's experience allows over 30 pages of organisational and logistical detail along with a complete reprint of Major-General Crawford's instructions for marching the Light Division during the Peninsular War of 1808-1814. Home himself was responsible for constructing 74 miles of road to enable Garnet Wolseley's Gold Coast campaign in 1873.[411]

Lippitt mainly pulls his examples from the American Civil War but Sharpe, Home and Furse are all very widely read and use examples from across the 19th century and even from ancient writers. Furse's experience during the Boer War, where good roads were rarer than in Europe and rail transport was very limited in scope, were more comparable with medieval Anatolia than many of those from the American Civil War. Yet even the experiences of Sharpe and Lippitt contain plenty of situations where rail transport was impractical, and food and equipment had to be carried across country on wagons and pack animals. The situations described in these works differ from those in Byzantine military treatises mainly with respect to rail transport and food preservation however many of the principles remained the same, as can be seen when examining the continuity of topics and advice. This continuity gives us confidence that, with caution, 19th-century military handbooks can augment Byzantine military treatises in providing plausible fine detail that medieval sources lack.

Comparing Byzantine and modern military sources

If we can usefully take advantage of 19th-century sources which relate to troop organisation and movement then we can significantly increase the data pool that we have to draw on for our models and our hypotheses. In order to do so we first have to demonstrate that there are aspects of moving an army that are common across several eras. We also need to be careful about the context of the advice we accept from anachronistic sources. Moving an army through friendly territory is different to moving an army through unfriendly territory. Moving an army with no expectation of encountering armed resistance is done differently to moving one in circumstances where battle might be

joined at any time. The march to Mantzikert was made through friendly territory and with no expectation of encountering the enemy therefore these situations in more modern texts will be much more likely to be relevant to the Mantzikert campaign than others. In fact, marches in similar circumstances may be more comparable, despite the chronological distance, than marches of the same army in different conditions.

The differences between pre-modern and modern logistics

The relationship between the elements that make up modern warfare are themselves complex and the question of whether technological improvements fuelled rising populations and consequently army sizes or whether increasing populations drove new methods of transportation and food preservation is a bit of a 'chicken and egg' situation. Regardless of the precise nature of the underlying mechanisms and although typical army sizes fluctuate over time, during the 17th century an explosion in scale occurred. Between the Thirty Years War (1618-1648) and the War of the Spanish Succession (1702-1715), the size of an army participating in a pitched battle doubled.[412] The bloodiest battle of the War of Spanish Succession, the Battle of Malplaquet in 1709, involved a total of around 160,000 troops. Just over 100 years later, the bloodiest battle of the Napoleonic Wars at Borodino involved around twice that many. Just over 100 years after that, the bloodiest battle of the First World War at the Somme involved 3 main combatant states, Germany, France and Britain, each contributing around the same number of men on the first day as had taken part in Borodino in total. Four months later, around 4,500,000 men had been involved, with around 1,000,000 ending up as casualties.

At the strategic level, it is clear that there are differences between the logistic requirements of armies, pre-Malplaquet, to those of the First World War. However, focussing on the biggest battles ignores the mechanisms involved with moving smaller forces. Not every battle of World War I was The Somme, there were many smaller engagements requiring Mantzikert-level logistical requirements, such at the 13,000-strong force of mixed cavalry and infantry that was besieged at Kut in 1916.[413]

The similarities between pre-modern and modern logistics

Certain logistical details and recommendations are common in the experience of both the 19th-century writers and those from much earlier. These include:

[409] US Army Quartermaster Foundation
[410] Home 1882
[411] Spiers 2004, 23

[412] Perjés 1970, 1
[413] Crowley and Sheffield 2009

- Baggage trains should be kept as small as possible.
- Civilian populations should be respected.
- A combination of supply and foraging is required.
- Soldiers should be well-fed.
- March order should be rotated.
- The route needs marking with signs or people.
- Leaders who share in the soldiers' lives are more respected.
- There is a tripartite division of baggage: Army, unit and personal level.
- Parties should be sent ahead to clear the road.
- Some space should be left on one side of column for local traffic or army cavalry/messengers.
- Sensible camp locations are very important.
- In case of the column lengthening, the front should slow rather than the rear speed up.
- Local knowledge is better than relying on maps.

Baggage trains should be kept as small as possible.

The need to reduce the size of baggage trains is noted by many writers, with the *Praecepta militaria* of Nikephoros II Phokas stating that 'the host must not bring along a multitude of baggage animals or non-combatants' [414] and Furse's *Art of Marching* advising 'all that is not strictly necessary should be left behind'.[415] There is a complex feedback between the amount of baggage an army carries with it and the number of animals which that army needs to carry that baggage, which has a consequent effect on the total amount of baggage due to those animals themselves requiring food and water. This applies to non-combatants in the same way that it applies to baggage, and an excess of these are likewise warned against.[416] Indeed, both Furse and the Byzantine treatise on *Campaign Organisation and Tactics* contain examples of marches unnecessarily lengthened due to too much baggage. Furse gives a Boer War example of a six-day march that should have only taken two,[417] and the Byzantine text warns of a day's march being unable to be undertaken in four days due to an excess of non-combatants and baggage.[418]

Civilian populations should be respected.

Despite General Sherman's ruthless statement, 'where other people live, we can; even if they have to starve, or move away',[419] military leaders have been warned against preying upon civilian populations since antiquity. The *Strategikon* of Maurice states that if any member of the army causes injury to a taxpayer then they should repay them double.[420] It also recommends that cultivated fields should be avoided to ensure no damage comes to them from the passage of troops.[421] During the Mantzikert campaign, a unit of mercenaries was sent away from the army as a punishment for pillaging, as noted by Attaleiates. Leo VI recommends paying particular attention to making sure farmers are treated well, the army relying on their help more than anyone.[422] This does not just involve rural communities as a source of foodstuffs, which will be much easier to procure from a willing population, but also as a source of transportation. Furse recommends avoiding requisitions of transport and instead paying the market value for either purchases or the employment of animals and their handlers as this is less likely to result in poor quality animals and equipment.[423] He also states that looting and pillaging should not be tolerated.[424]

A combination of supply and foraging is required.

The usual Byzantine system of supplying an army on the march within its own territory was to require settlements along the route to provide foodstuffs and equipment in lieu of taxes.[425] That said, foraging for supplies in between supply points was done on numerous occasions[426] and Leo VI advises generals to both forage and carry supplies.[427] Transport and storage problems will defeat any attempt to supply an army wholly from supply depots and the uncertainty of foraging makes it also dangerous to rely on as the sole means of supply. Although 'subsistence from depots alone is impracticable in modern war',[428] they are essential, especially in barren areas.[429] General Sherman's march through Georgia had a very well organised foraging component and lacked nothing.[430] The degree to which a combination of supply and foraging has been used in the past and the circumstances in which each option is favoured are questions that have been debated within military logistics studies.[431] Broadly speaking, however, quantitative studies that try and model the practicalities of supply tend to regard some combination of supply and foraging as the most sensible option and it is probably not surprising that the debate has shifted this way in tandem with the introduction of quantitative modelling.

[414] McGeer 1995, 23
[415] 1901, 139
[416] Furse 1901, 134
[417] Furse 1901, 115
[418] Dennis 1985, 289
[419] Lippitt 1869, 130

[420] Dennis 2001, 18
[421] Dennis 2001, 21
[422] Dennis 2010, 197
[423] Furse 1882, 27
[424] Furse 1882, 253
[425] Constantine Porphyrogenitus 1990, 89
[426] Haldon 1999, 171
[427] Haldon 1999, 145
[428] Sharpe 1905, 35
[429] Lippitt 1869, 140
[430] Lippitt 1869, 138
[431] Harari 2000

Soldiers should be well-fed.

Wellington believed that his soldiers could accomplish anything provided they were well fed, prevented from straggling and kept off wine.[432] Furse wholeheartedly agrees, stating that 'in a fight, one fresh man is worth four fagged with weariness' and pointing out Suchet's late arrival at Marengo being due to the poor provisioning of his troops.[433] This also has a knock-on effect on the levels of sickness within the army.[434] Vegetius' *De Re Militari* contains a section on the importance of ensuring the army is well fed, emphasising the hopelessness of the situation if this is not so. 'Time and opportunity may help to retrieve other misfortunes, but where forage and provisions have not been carefully provided, the evil is without remedy.' Leo VI recommends 'plenty of provisions of various kinds'[435] both on the march and in camp but this is typical of the lack of detail given to the provisioning situation by Byzantine sources. Having enough food is important, but it is not given the same levels of detail that other aspects of logistics such as setting up camp.

March order should be rotated.

Rotating the vanguard and rear guard is something recommended in various sources over various time periods. From Ancient Rome,[436] through the Byzantine period[437] to the Western Middle Ages,[438] a variety of benefits are claimed. Troops at the front get access to the cleanest water, before humans and animals have stirred up the mud at the bottom of streams. They also have to contend with less airborne dust, kicked up by preceding troops. Fallot & Lagrange point out that the rear guard also get bogged down with stragglers, badly-horsed carriages and other detritus of the march.[439] Lippitt also adds that the rear guard are forever having to rescue stuck wagons and as such their job is made more bearable by being rotated with the advance guard.[440] It goes without saying, however, that there are likely to be certain units deemed too important to share in the disadvantages of bringing up the rear. In the Byzantine marching camp, the emperor's tent went up, and came down, first[441] and the elite units of the army would accompany him.

The route needs marking with signs or people.

Signposts, 'marshals' or connecting patrols prevent units from straying from the route, according to Furse.[442] Maurice agrees, stating 'the vanguard should place some signs at forks in the road and other places where mistakes can be made. If it is a wooded area, they can be put on the trees; if barren, piles of rocks or mounds of earth will do. These will be recognised by the troops marching behind, and the army will not get lost.'[443] The implication is that, regardless of how compact the line of march is intended to be, gaps large enough to lose sight of the unit ahead commonly develop. The mechanism by which these signs are placed usually goes unspecified. If surveyors are selecting camp locations at least one day ahead of the rest of the army then it would not be beyond the bounds of practicality for the surveyors to send a small unit back down the route towards the army to place the signs and also travel back up with the army providing advice on difficult sections and resting spots to the lead units.

Leaders who share in the soldiers' lives are more respected.

That a leader will be more respected if he shares the lifestyle of the common soldiers on campaign is a running theme through 3rd-century Chinese strategist Zhuge Liang's work *The Way of the General*.[444] Being considerate of soldiers' conditions, feeding them well and treating them courteously are all presented as essential traits for a successful general. 'Generals do not say they are thirsty before the soldiers have drawn from the well; generals do not say they are hungry before the soldiers' food is cooked … Generals do not use fans in summer, do not wear leather in winter, do not use umbrellas in the rain. They do as everyone else does.'[445] Maurice recommends that the general should work hard in order to set an example for the troops and that he should live a plain and simple life like they do.[446] He should do more than his share of work and take less than his share of grain in order to enhance his standing with his soldiers.[447] 'A general who loves luxury can destroy the whole army'.[448] Prudence and a lack of self-indulgence are listed as essential characteristics for a general in the *Sylloge Tacticorum*.[449] By the 19th century, the notion of an emperor leading his troops into battle was somewhat antiquated, and many nations had a professional, though still somewhat aristocratic, officer class. To some extent, this necessitates a narrowing of the social gap between the top and bottom of the army,

---

[432] Furse 1901, 18
[433] Furse 1901, 19
[434] Furse 1901, 22
[435] Dennis 2010, 197
[436] Roth 1999, 23:36
[437] Constantine Porphyrogenitus 1990, 131
[438] Rogers 2007, 76
[439] Home 1882, 175
[440] Lippitt 1869, 42
[441] Dennis 1985, 277

[442] Furse 1901, 212
[443] Dennis 2001, 97
[444] Zhuge Liang and Liu Ji 2005
[445] Zhuge Liang and Liu Ji 2005, 52
[446] Dennis 2001, 79
[447] Dennis 2001, 87
[448] Dennis 2001, 88
[449] Chatzelis and Harris 2017, 21

but Furse still states that leaders on campaign share in the hardships of the soldiers to an extent that would astonish the public.[450]

There is a tripartite division of baggage: Army, unit and personal level.

The overall organisational scheme of an army's equipment and food transportation seems to have changed little from the Byzantine period to the 19th century. Each army, when it was not under threat of attack, would have a baggage train following behind it which carried large, heavy or infrequently needed items. Units of smaller size would also have their own baggage train carrying more frequently needed goods, with the most frequently needed items carried at the individual or squad level.[451] The smaller units are replenished every so often by the larger, thus ensuring everyone stays supplied and control is kept over the whole process, but also that each soldier does not need to travel to the rear of the column whenever he needs something. An anonymous writer of 1855 suggests two wagons per regiment.[452] The British army during the Peninsula War had three echelons of baggage transport: the first at the regimental level, the second to transport provisions from magazines to the troops and the third to resupply the depots.[453] Sharpe claims that 'most nations fix the minimum number of rations to be carried by their armies, and allot to various units the necessary number of wagons or other transportation required to carry this minimum number, relying on the theater of operations to furnish additional transportation if circumstances render it necessary to carry more rations'.[454] He also makes it clear that although everyone agrees that soldiers should carry some rations, the amount they are required to carry varies from nation to nation.[455] Within the modern British army there still exists this hierarchical structure for logistic support, albeit using four echelons (unit, formation, force or theatre and at the strategic base) to cope with the global supply network required for a modern army.[456] Nikephoros Phokas recommends one mule for every two heavy infantrymen.[457] Going back to ancient times, Vellius Paterculus refers to both the baggage train of individual legions as well as that of the army as a whole.[458]

Parties should be sent ahead to clear the road.

In Maurice's *Strategikon*, parties are sent ahead to clear the road so that the army's march is easier,[459] something the author of *De re militari* agrees with.[460] This advice is echoed over 1000 years later by Lippitt[461] and Lt-Col Colley, Professor of Military Administration at Sandhurst.[462] These parties would have cleared obstructions, warned off slow moving local traffic, performed quick repairs to the road surface (as evidenced by the recommendation to keep their equipment wagon up front)[463] and reported back any issues which might factor into the planning of the march by the following troops. Furse also suggests they lessen slopes around fords and help create temporary corduroy roads with brushwood and grass to ease passage.[464] Having a group of soldiers march ahead of the column and repair the roads was also an activity attributed to King Cyrus by Xenophon, which at least indicates it was something familiar to Xenophon, whether Cyrus actually did it or not.[465]

Some space should be left on one side of column for local traffic or army cavalry/messengers.

Furse recommends a third of the road's width should be left clear of troops so that local traffic can go about its daily business.[466] It is also for this reason that he recommends that any units overtaken by darkness move off the road and create a temporary camping location away from the road.[467] This is echoed by Nikephoros Phokas who states that it is a necessity in order to ensure that army messengers and others who need to move up and down the column are able to do so.[468]

Sensible camp locations are very important

Although the Byzantine military treatises would have primarily been concerned with campaigning in Anatolia, the Balkans and Syria, while Victorian military literature deals with campaigns in North America, Europe and India among other places, the advice on what constitutes a sensible location for a military camp is very similar. Both stress a defensible location with easy access to water and firewood,[469] presumably due to the advantages of not having to transport either between camps. Lippitt discourages

---

450 Furse 1882, 34
451 Dennis 2001, 20–21
452 Anon 1855, 68
453 Kirby 2014, 41
454 Sharpe 1896, 21
455 Sharpe 1896, 22
456 Land Warfare Development Centre 2017, 10–4
457 McGeer 1995, 23
458 Roth 1999, 82

459 Dennis 2001, 21
460 McGeer 1995, 342
461 Lippitt 1869, 23
462 Home 1882, 168
463 Lippitt 1869, 97
464 Furse 1882, 67
465 Miller 1914, 6.2.36
466 Furse 1901, 205
467 Furse 1882, 249
468 McGeer 1995, 23
469 Dennis 1985, 249; Furse 1901, 23; McGeer 1995, 53 & 135

the digging of a camp perimeter on the grounds that it encourages cowardice [470] whereas Nikephoros II Phokas advises that it should only be done when necessary as it is tiring work,[471] though presumably not for him. The importance of selecting a good camp location is a recurring theme through Byzantine military treatises, having sections of both Maurice's *Strategikon* and the *Taktika* of Leo VI dedicated to it.[472] Leo VI recycles some advice from Maurice and Onasander but the message is consistent with others, camp in a defensible location not overlooked by high ground, with access to fresh water.

In case of the column lengthening, the front should slow rather than the rear speed up.

The column of troops will inevitably become stretched during the day's march but both Medieval and Victorian sources are clear on the solution should this become a problem. The head of the column should wait for the troops at the rear to have closed the gaps rather than requiring them to increase their pace. This advice comes from both Wellington [473] and the author of *Campaign Organization and Tactics*.[474]

Local knowledge is better than relying on maps.

Although maps are important on campaign, these are trumped by local knowledge from guides.[475] They can give detailed information on the less travelled routes in the area[476] as well as provide other useful information such as the location and timing of seasonal floods, information regarding local epidemics and details regarding the condition of the roads.[477] The Mantzikert campaign will have been reliant on local guides as, although the macro route will have been planned in advance, local conditions will have been an unknown quantity for much of the campaign, especially in the more volatile east. 'The worst guide is often worth more than the best map', claims Furse.[478] Nikephoros Ouranos considered the taking of local prisoners for information to be an essential first step to invading an enemy territory.[479] Knowing where water, wood and forage can be found are essential.[480] The treatise attributed to Leo Katakylas gives a list of preparatory steps used by Constantine the Great before setting out on an expedition, largely centred around knowing what the landscape, terrain and transport infrastructure is

like. This advice is unlikely to have anything to do with Constantine the Great but is more likely to be standard procedure when Katakylas was writing during the early 10th century.[481]

Summary

Taken together, these individual points of similarity between ancient and modern sources provide a framework within which armies are moved and fed. It is generic and to a certain extent sounds like simple common sense. Treat people well, be sensible, plan ahead, organise rigorously and all will be well. It nevertheless demonstrates a continuity of the usefulness of these elements in a military landscape which otherwise changes quite dramatically. For example, the respective importance of cavalry within a force changes significantly over time, depending on the nature of the enemy and their battle tactics, but the basic principles of moving a mixed force of cavalry and infantry remain relatively stable.

This should not come as a surprise in that there are many aspects to military logistics that do not change. The speed of human movement, the requirements of the human body, the ability of humans to be organised, the types of domesticated animals available and the length of a day are relatively constant from Gaugamela to Waterloo. The goal has also remained the same, moving humans and materiel from A to B in good shape. Battlefield tactics can change rapidly as the identity of the enemy can change, and they can in turn react to any changes themselves. The enemies of the quartermaster: time, distance, hunger and thirst, remain largely implacable throughout the ages. Only new technology such as railways and the internal combustion engine have radically altered this conflict.

Examples of marches from other works

It is not always useful to compare the marches recorded in pre-modern accounts of military campaigns against each other due to the uncertainties regarding the size and composition of forces as well as the circumstances surrounding an army's journey. Often these details are not recorded, leaving confusion regarding any conclusions than can be drawn. Yet a review of the distances recorded for the marches of certain armies may be useful in order to pick out any obvious general trends. It may also provide useful information regarding the expectations of the authors of the historical accounts, indicating which circumstances the people of the day may consider unusual.

As with a lot of other areas of military logistics, the availability of quantified data is patchy, however the

[470] Lippitt 1869, 59
[471] McGeer 1995, 55 & 139
[472] Dennis 2001, 155; 2010, 195
[473] Furse 1901, 202
[474] Dennis 1985, 281
[475] Furse 1901, 147
[476] Dennis 1985, 291
[477] Furse 1901, 137
[478] Furse 1901, 147
[479] McGeer 1995, 144
[480] Dennis 2001, 89

[481] Constantine Porphyrogenitus 1990, 83

situation is not as bad as it is in areas such as equipment weights and food supplies, and even writers as far back in time as Ancient Greece can provide useful information. Xenophon[482] records a march of Agesilaus against the Arcarnanians, noting that a march of 18 miles had surprised the enemy with its swiftness, although they had been making incredibly slow progress before that. Xenophon's *Anabasis* records a variety of distances for a day's march, although there is debate as to the exact modern equivalent of these distances due to their being recorded in parasangs, a Persian measurement of time.[483]

Large baggage trains are frequently remarked upon, even outside the more common contexts. Edward III's army took a month to travel 240km from Calais to Rheims in 1359 due to a supply train that was said to consist of 6,000-12,000 carts.[484] Livy records that one baggage train was so long that it managed only 5 miles (8km) per day.[485] Lippitt remarks that General Buell's wagon train in 1862 was 15 miles (24km) long.[486] This is clearly mentioned specifically as it was considered to be on the large side of normal.

Sir Donald Stewart's Field Force in the Second Afghan War

The march of Sir Donald Stewart's force from Kandahar to Ghazni is a well-recorded example of a march that contains dates, distances and numbers of people and animals.[487] The force departed Kandahar on the 29th, 30th and 31st of March 1880, seemingly being split up over three days using the same route. This is explained by the fact that the baggage train took up 9 miles (14.5km) of road in single file with the average march per day being around 11 miles (18km). There were 7193 combatants, 6207 followers, 2589 draft animals and 6112 transport animals, though this is a snapshot on the 8th April and these figures did not remain static throughout the whole march. Nevertheless, losses in both human and animal members of the force were supposedly light, with not a single follower lost, so the figures for the humans at least can be seen as representative of the force during the whole march.

The transport animals seem to have been mainly camels and the report highlights the scarcity of their availability, implying more camels would have been preferred. The number of followers recorded was fewer than one per pack or draft animal and so presumably, the majority of these followers had animal handling duties of some kind. Presumably they did their job

adequately as no more than 3% of the camels were lost during the march, despite a lack of forage and a generally poor cohort of camels to begin with.

The first half of the march contained no significant supply problems with food being easy to obtain. The second half was through hostile country, although forage was plentiful and hidden supplies were rooted out by local allied troops. From the 12th to the 21st of April the troops foraged for themselves and never went without, although they often had reduced rations. Enemy action meant that, although they travelled 190 miles (306km) to Karabagh in 8 days, the remaining 44 miles (71km) to Ghazni took 13 days. Whether the 190 miles to Karabagh were crossed with the army split on the same route over 2 or 3 days as it was when leaving Kandahar is uncertain but cannot be ruled out, especially as over 23 miles (37km) per day would represent good going for a force of over 13,000 people and over 8,500 animals. The report claims that General Stewart was in Karabagh on the 16th but does not mention whether all the baggage was also with him on that date.

Logistics failures

Examples of military failures due to logistical problems occur throughout history and range within the literature from large-scale general failures[488] to smaller expeditions that failed for more specific reasons.[489] The Peloponnesians invaded Attica before the corn had ripened enough to be foraged and had to retreat again after 15 days due to insufficient food.[490] Although the American Revolutionary Army in the War of Independence was often poorly supplied, it was the difficulties involved in forming a coherent administration for the supply of the American soldiers that at times threatened to undermine the cause of independence.[491] The British army landed in Crimea in 1854 with only 75 mules and a few carts. By the beginning of 1856 this had increased dramatically to 28,000 horses, mules and camels, although the war was over shortly afterwards.[492] The rapid improvement was precipitated by the complete inadequacy of the initial arrangements, and a variety of *ad hoc* attempts were made to acquire some kind of transport provision before a Land Transport Corps was raised in early 1855.

Logistics failures can have effects beyond the immediate implications of a military defeat. The loss of 26,700 camels in the First Afghan War represented a third of the beasts of burden of the province of Sindh from where they had been procured. Their loss would

---

[482] Xenophon, 4.6.6
[483] O'Connor 2015
[484] Harari 2000, 316
[485] Roth 1999, 81
[486] Lippitt 1869, 97
[487] Furse 1882, 60–61

[488] Anon 1855, 43
[489] Crowley and Sheffield 2009
[490] Lazenby 1994, 11
[491] Huston 1966, 12
[492] Furse 1882, 38

have had repercussions within the province, causing a shortage which would have affected economic activity until they could be replaced.[493]

One of the most notorious logistics failures in military history was Napoleon's invasion of Russia in 1812. Of interest primarily as an extreme outlier in the history of military marches, the campaign killed a total of around a million people from both sides, fewer than a quarter of whom died in battle. The majority of the remainder died for want of food or equipment in some form or another, some of which was insufficient at the onset of the campaign, let alone towards the end. Of particular note is the uneven distribution of resources, and therefore outcomes, throughout the invading force. Some units towards the front of the column, and therefore with first access to food supplies, returned with around 25% of their initial strength. Others, who could be up to 100km behind the head of the retreating column at times, did not even preserve 5% of their initial numbers.[494]

Modern developments

Alongside the Roman, Byzantine and 19th-century technological and sociological developments that have resulted in the production of such a large library of military writing, a uniquely 21st-century change has to be acknowledged. The scanning of many books that are now out of copyright, by such organisations as Microsoft and Google, has ensured that these publications, some of them very rare in physical form, are accessible to modern researchers. This explosion of new and often freely available materiel makes the military logistics researcher's job simultaneously easier and more difficult. It is easier, in that the majority of the 19th-century texts can be downloaded in a few short minutes from archives and online booksellers when only 20 years ago consulting them would sometimes have required a trip to an obscure collection or the British Library. It is, however, more difficult, in that it is now no longer possible to rely on the same small number of sources that find themselves referenced over and over again in modern academic writing. The amount of materiel which we need to process is much larger and old conclusions are not necessarily secure. This new resource demands a fresh look at existing research.

Conclusion – where does this leave us?

There is no finality in the art of war[495]

The amount of information and advice that is common between the logistics writing of the Byzantine period and that of the 19th century gives us confidence that the process of moving thousands of soldiers carries strong common elements between these periods. Logistics can be seen as the war against distance, hunger and thirst. These enemies are relatively static, and prior to the advent of rail travel and improved methods of food preservation, the technologies employed against them likewise stayed fairly constant. Even after new developments in transport and food preservation, there were instances in which the old principles stood firm. The last unit of the British Army using pack mules on anything other than an *ad hoc* basis was disbanded in Hong Kong in 1976, but US Special Forces still train in the use of pack animals due to their enduring utility in certain situations. In the 19th century, plenty of troop movement occurred away from the rail network, especially in Africa and India, and better food preservation reduced wastage but seems not to have significantly altered the organization needed to feed an army on the march. Even after the advent of canning, canned food took a long time to become a significant part of a soldier's diet. The troops involved in the American Civil War rarely saw canned goods, and it was only the scale of other types of food preservation which was unlike earlier wars, not the actual rations on offer.[496] With this in mind, cautious use of more modern data can provide much needed detail for computer simulations of medieval logistics, or indeed almost any pre-modern environment. A computer simulation requires detail and quantifiable variables that are largely absent from the medieval sources. These occur much more readily in the 19th-century military sources and derive from the experiences of seasoned military campaigners whose enemies: distance and hunger, remained as dedicated to trapping the unprepared as they were 1000 years before.

---

[493] Furse 1882, 52
[494] Zamoyski 2004

[495] Home 1882, 2
[496] Billings 1887

Chapter 6 – The Models

Introduction

The origin of the quote 'writing about music is like dancing about architecture' is debated. Nevertheless, the saying is apt and can quite easily be applied to either writing or talking about ABMs. ABMs excel in modelling complex systems that have a spatial dimension to them but that also change over time. Four-dimensional processes resulting from the interactions of autonomous agents are hard to describe concisely in a sequential medium such as writing. Nevertheless, documentation is essential in order to explain why the results of a model are helpful in investigating a problem. In this chapter we will describe the architecture and workflow involved with modelling the march of the Byzantine army to Mantzikert. The specific circumstances behind each individual model and the results that they produce are described in the following chapter.

Is modelling valid?

Two key concerns within computer simulation are verification and validation. Verification refers to whether the model functions as it should, whether it calculates two plus two as equalling four, for example, and not three or five. Validation concerns whether a model's results are actually useful, whether adding two and two is the correct thing to do to help solve the problem we are addressing. Verification of a computer simulation is largely a software engineering problem, and its solutions lie in robust oversight and testing of each component of the model and how it relates to the others. Validation is more philosophically complex.

A model is an abstraction of its subject, an incomplete reproduction that usually has many missing parts. Some of these parts are missing because they are not considered to have a significant impact on the system being modelled, some are absent because they are too difficult or time-consuming to be included. We have previously quoted George Box in saying that 'all models are wrong but some models are useful', and it is the 'useful' side of the equation that validation concerns itself with. The validity of a model is partly a function of which elements are chosen to be represented and which have been omitted. The absence of the processes that have been omitted and inaccuracies in those that have been included render the model 'wrong', in that it is not a perfect replica of the system to be examined. Do these factors also mean the model is not useful?

When looking at medieval military logistics, this is a difficult question to answer. We cannot build a complete reconstruction of the Byzantine army on the road to Mantzikert. If we had all the data we needed to construct a faithful replica we are likely to have few unanswered questions that we could pose of the simulation. Instead, we can simulate certain processes that were involved in ways that we hope can tell us about the Mantzikert campaign and the lands through which it travelled. Consider a model that had its individual behaviours set to theoretical human maximums, with speed set to its highest likely value, baggage set to its lowest amount and organisation set to its most efficient. This model will be 'wrong' in that it would not be a recreation of the Mantzikert campaign as it actually happened. If, in this model, the simulated army moves slower than the real-life army of Romanos IV Diogenes as recorded in the historical accounts then we know that some other aspect of the model varies from the historical reality. Maybe our simulated army is much larger than the historical version. Maybe the historical accounts are not an accurate reflection of the truth. Nevertheless, our model, stripped down and unrealistic as it is, has told us something and we have gained knowledge of the past and established a set of parameters within which we can build a new model with different assumptions.

If our model results in a simulated army which performs as closely as possible to the army as recorded in historical accounts, does this mean the historical army was made of the same numbers and types of individuals behaving in the same way as our simulated agents? Unfortunately, not necessarily. The problem of equifinality in simulation says that there may be many possible sets of circumstances, many combinations of agents and behaviours, that could lead us to the same end result. It is down to the individual researcher to determine to what extent the model replicates the historic situation, whether the model is 'wrong but useful' or merely 'wrong'.

A necessary part of demonstrating the validity of a model is to adequately describe it. If everyone understood the programming languages used in the implementation of a model, then the code could act as a description. It is after all the exact series of actions that comprise the model. However, there will be many interested people who are not sufficiently conversant with the programming languages used or who simply do not have the time or patience required to follow the installation and operation of the code from start to finish. This chapter, therefore, describes the architecture and workings of the different elements that comprise the MWGrid model in sufficient detail for the interested observer to understand the workflow involved with getting the models to produce comprehensible outputs. Although the MWGrid ABM is the core of the project, it actually requires several other pieces of software in order to constitute a complete package, able to take a set of circumstances and translate them into the useable results of a simulation process. The resulting collection of disparate pieces of software may seem inefficient but decisions were primarily made based on the expertise available to the project at the time. All software used is either bespoke or open source and therefore the entire process of specifying and running a model and then analysing the output can be done by anyone with the required software and hardware at no monetary cost. Unfortunately, the end result is not user friendly, but the whole process can be accomplished by a sufficiently technically proficient end user with no programming experience, using the description in this book and the instructions included in the downloaded software.

The complete MWGrid software suite

The complete process of running and analysing a simulation from start to finish uses several pieces of software. The software prerequisites are:

- The MWGrid ABM software, downloaded from Philip Murgatroyd's Github repository (elfdev001.github.io).
- OpenOffice, or other compatible spreadsheet software.

- Blender, downloaded from the Blender Foundation.
- Java, downloaded from Oracle.
- A Java development environment such as Eclipse (optional, but recommended).

Installation instructions are available from the source of each of these pieces of software. One of the key benefits of the Java programming language is portability, meaning that the same code can be run on many different kinds of systems. The software was developed on a system running Microsoft Windows and the installation instructions are tailored to this environment, but it can be run under other operating systems such as Linux.

The complete process of running and analysing a model comprises the following stages:

- Creation of a text initialisation file.
- Running the MWGrid ABM software.
- Loading the output dayfile into OpenOffice to examine the aggregated data for each agent.
- Processing the output tickfile.
- Loading the tickfile through the Blender Python script to visualise the movement of the agents.

The ABM

The MWGrid ABM is a standalone programme written in the Java programming language, which takes the variables to be used for a given run of the model from an initialisation file. This initialisation file is a text document consisting of the name of a variable and its value. Although the text initialisation file can be read

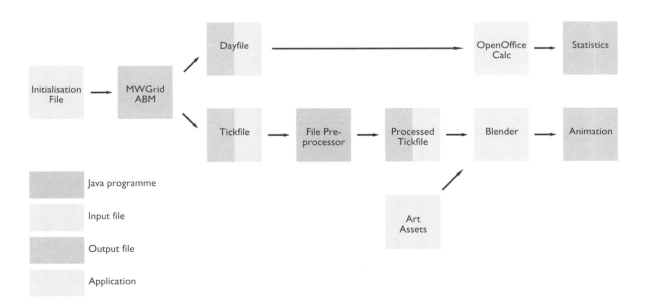

Figure 7: The software used in the MWGrid system.

and altered by anyone regardless of programming knowledge or experience, its effects are limited to specifying the values that are used by the processes within the MWGrid ABM. It cannot change the steps within those processes. For example, the initialisation file can change the number of cavalry and infantry in the army, it cannot make the army march in a different order or make the agents in a squad follow a different leader.

The ABM searches the initialisation file for a specific text string associated with a variable and loads in the subsequent value if it finds it. The use of a standard text format for this file means that it can be read, edited and saved in a standard text editor and it is comprehensible without reference to tables of codes. This data could be contained within the Java code but that would require recompiling the code whenever a value is changed, whereas running multiple models one after another is easily accomplished simply by changing the initialisation file between runs and resaving it. The only argument that is passed to the Java ABM programme is the location of the initfile. Output files are automatically saved in the same directory.

The Java ABM programme constitutes around 6000 lines of code and was developed within the Eclipse integrated development environment (IDE). Although the use of an IDE is optional, IDEs provide a series of tools to make programming, debugging and running software easier. Even if you are not interested in learning Java or interrogating the code, you may find the use of an IDE such as Eclipse makes running the MWGrid ABM easier. Java was chosen to be the programming language in which the MWGrid ABM is implemented due to its object-oriented architecture, its portability and its ease of learning when compared to alternatives such as C++.

The function of the MWGrid ABM is to take the parameters specified in the initialisation file and to use them to set up a day's march of an army from a starting point to a destination point. The army is initially placed according to a hypothetical camp plan, and this plan is identical at the start and end of the day's march. The army will make its way to a point just outside the start camp where an agent, called the column leader, will plot a route to a similar point outside the destination camp. The column leader will set off for this point, with the rest of the army following on behind, in order, starting with the cavalry. Once the point outside the destination camp has been reached, each unit will make its own way to its allotted camping spot in the new camp.

The ABM software works in time units known as ticks. A single tick is the shortest time period within the simulation. On each tick of the simulation, the software goes through the list of all agents within the simulation and follows the agent's internal rules to decide what that agent does during that tick. Agents who are part of a squad of either cavalry or infantry are fairly unsophisticated. They will follow their squad leader as closely as possible within the constraints of speed and the space available. Other agents are slightly more sophisticated, but at the heart of all the different simulations within this book are the constraints imposed by the speed of an agent and the amount of space it takes up. These constraints are constraints important in the real world when moving large bodies of individuals and they can be easily modelled within a simulation.

The ABM software moves each individual agent at the rate specified in the initialisation file and ensures that there are no more agents within a cell of the environment than could plausibly fit inside. If delays are caused, the line of march bunches up behind. Blockages on the line of march can be created in the same manner as holdups are created on the motorway. These do not occur as part of an overall plan, managed from above, but are created due to the interactions of individuals acting according to their own internal rules.

Once a day's march has been simulated, the ABM software outputs data such as the time each agent set off on the day's march, the time it arrived at its destination, the distance travelled, the number of kilocalories consumed and exactly where each agent is on each tick of the simulation.

Data processing with OpenOffice

The model can involve tens of thousands of agents all moving via subtly different routes at different times and expending different amounts of energy. Presenting this to others poses a problem as different aspects of a model's results are of interest to different people. One of the key points of using ABM is that the idea of what an army does, how far it moves and how much energy it expends, is an abstraction covering a lot of complexity in the behaviour of individual agents. The raw data is too complex to easily interrogate and therefore, some form of data aggregation has to be conducted. A statistical summary of the simulation is needed at this point. The summary is derived from the dayfile, a text file created by the ABM which shows aggregated data for each agent from the whole run of the simulation. This includes the total distance moved, ticks spent resting and energy expended in kilocalories. An OpenOffice Calc spreadsheet was created which takes this data and aggregates it into a series of statistics in table format (Table 7), illustrating the average, highest and lowest values for a range of values. It also shows the number of agents and the time used to complete the march. The tick on which the final agent arrives in camp provides an indication of the total amount of time taken by the army.

Table 7: Aggregated statistical output of a day's march

	1 column	3 columns
Average arrival time (ticks)	7792.20	6446.21
Average distance covered (m)	24823.62	27009.46
Average arrival time (Officers only) (ticks)	7166.73	6156.22
Last arrival tick	10877	8197
Squads	1260	1260
Agents	7061	7061
Column Leaders	1	1
Cavalry Officers	1060	1060
Infantry Officers	200	200
Cavalry Soldiers	4000	4000
Infantry Soldiers	1800	1800
Average Kilocalories Expended	1423.32	1480.98
Average travel time (ticks)	4038.72	4876.69
Column Leader kcals	1225	1037.36038
Cavalry Officer average kcals	1354.10	1252.10
Cavalry Officer high kcals	1508.00	1467.06
Cavalry Officer low kcals	1193.00	1056.64
Cavalry Soldier average kcals	1404.23	1288.15
Cavalry Soldier high kcals	1598.00	1447.48
Cavalry Soldier low kcals	1191.00	1087.22
Infantry Officer average kcals	1496.13	1983.80
Infantry Officer high kcals	1749.00	2041.00
Infantry Officer low kcals	1260.00	1948.00
Infantry Soldier average kcals	1498.53	1988.64
Infantry Soldier high kcals	1750.00	2110.00
Infantry Soldier low kcals	1271.00	1956.00
# of agents on last arrival tick	1287	9

Data Processing with Blender

The processed tickfile is imported into Blender via a bespoke Python script. The Python programming language was chosen as it is the default scripting language for Blender and is heavily integrated within the application. The script creates an object for each agent based on its type and moves this object on a tick-by-tick basis depending on the location specified in the tickfile. The object it creates can either be a simple geometric shape or a rigged, animated character depending on the requirements of the visualisation.

An initial version of the ABM focussed on individual agents performing complex behaviours involving item manipulation. It used, as a case study, the setting up of the army's camp at the end of a day's march and included such behaviours as setting up each squad's tent and setting fires to cook food. As this involved behaviours that require multiple steps performed by multiple agents, a visualisation system was implemented to show the agents' behaviours in more detail, such as the tasks the agents are performing and the tasks they intended to perform in the future. The Python script used for reading the data into Blender inserts fully animated, humanlike models into the virtual scene to represent each agent. These humanlike models contained the mesh data for the agent itself and data for each animated action they could perform, along with speech and thought bubbles for tasks each agent was performing or intended to perform in the future, respectively. The Python script also imported 3D models from other Blender files for each type of item such as firewood, food and tents in both packed and erected forms.

The output worked well from a debugging point of view, as it was easy to identify each agent's behaviour at any given time. The modular nature, with the models being held in separate files, meant that it was easy to create two different types of 3D models, such as basic, low-polygon stick figures and more realistic 3D models (Figure 8). This modular nature also allows professional 3D models to be integrated within the visualisation system if required. Although the system worked well for small numbers of agents, the details involved with this visualisation resulted in computational times that were unacceptable for large scale simulations.

As the focus of modelling shifted from setting up camp to simulating large scale movement of thousands of agents, a much faster way of visualising ABM output was required. The Python script was pared down to represent each agent as a 2D geometric shape. Blender's camera can be set to orthographic projection, which removes perspective distortions that may occlude the results. The end result was a 2D representation

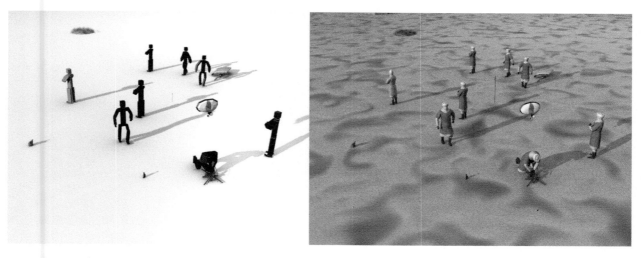

Figure 8: The same point of a simulation rendered with both lower polygon (left) and higher polygon (right) models.

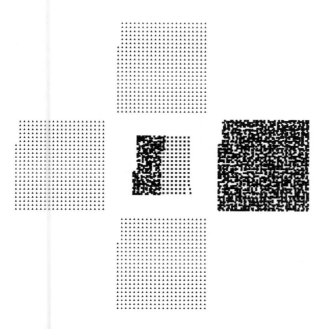

Figure 9: A 2D representation of MWGrid agents in a typical camp layout.

related to ABMs. It, however, provides no indication of the way route finding works within the model. Within the MWGrid ABM, each column of the army, by way of its behaviour, selects a route based on the terrain and creates the shortest possible route to their destination while avoiding unnecessary climbing of hills. A better way of visualising the results of the route planning algorithm is to represent the agents' movement in a 3D landscape (Figure 10). The existing Python script which had been used for producing the 2D representation of the agents' movement was modified to create 3D geometric shapes for each agent. The landscape was created in a separate script which simulated a 3D landscape of blocks representing the actual terrain data that is used in the ABM. The orthogonal camera view used in the 2D representation does not adequately show the 3D nature of the terrain so a perspective-based camera view was used. This allows freedom to create multiple visualisations from the same Blender file but requires the user to decide which behaviours in the model are most important, and from which angle they can best be visualised, introducing a degree of subjective directorial control.

Formats of visualisation

The MWGrid ABM and its associated programmes are able to generate structured and highly visual datasets via Blender and OpenOffice Calc. This allows the presentation of the data as either statistical tables and graphs, or still images and animations. Different formats have different uses. Whilst still images can give a snapshot of the model at work and can be a good way of examining spatial distribution of agents, an animation is often the most effective way to visualise behaviour over time. Tables can show large amounts of data at the same time and graphs can track individual values over time. By using Blender as a rendering

of the agents' movement which would be familiar to ABM researchers (Figure 9). This meant that tens of thousands of agents could be modelled in a reasonable timescale. At this point of the development the focus had shifted to the movement of the agents over the day's march and so the extra mechanisms used to indicate specific items or the intention of the agents were not necessary. The result shows movement well but has no way of representing the underlying terrain.

This type of output that is represented by simple geometric shapes, represented orthogonally on a plain background is commonly seen in academic publications

Figure 10: A 3D representation of MWGrid agents moving across the landscape. The two lines of yellow represent columns of infantry agents making their way to the night's camp, at which a blob of blue and purple cavalry have already arrived.

engine, still images can be made of any tick of any simulation. If the end result is to be reproduced in a printed format then, given the scale of the Mantzikert model and the number of agents used, any image that reproduces the complete army on the march will be at the wrong scale to identify individual features but it can show patterns in the movement of the army as a whole. However, there is no reason for the output to be restricted to paper publications. Publication via the Internet allows much higher resolution images in which macro-scale patterns can be seen but each individual agent's movement can be focused on by zooming in to an appropriate scale. Once the data is imported into Blender and the appropriate frame of the animation chosen, a high resolution still image can be generated.

In order to see the movement of agents within the model during its operation, animations must be created. Unlike still images, animations cannot easily be created in a way that enables the user to choose which parts to focus on; there needs to be an element of directorial control at the point of creating the animation. The virtual camera through which the animation is seen needs to be placed in appropriate locations and to have an appropriate scale to visualise the required activity. This may result in interesting behaviour in the model being missed due to the camera being elsewhere. Animations however are ideal for illustrating the actual micro-scale behaviours which make up the macro-scale results that are more often shown via statistics and graphs. Graphs can more accurately show data, but they are not good ways of illustrating what an army on the march actually looked like.

The most complete way of visualising the behaviours of complex systems is to provide access to the systems themselves and allow users to perform their own simulations. If the system is published with full featured visualisation capabilities it allows users to specifically create the information they wish to see. They may be able to see the simulation running in real time or they may produce data from which visualisations can subsequently be made. This is an ideal scenario for simulations which require minimal processing time and small numbers of complete runs of the simulation but will be impractical for models requiring parallel processing, many thousands of iterations or days or even weeks of processing time. In these cases aggregated data is usually much more practical. The modular nature of the MWGrid system enables, for instance, the tickfiles from certain simulations to be made available so that they may be visualised in different ways by different people. Others may even create their own Blender models which, as long as they adhere to certain naming conventions, can easily replace the models used in the visualisation seen here.

The production of statistics, stills and animations allows the project to present its data in traditional paper-based publications as well as via the Internet. In addition to using the outputs of the model to explain the results of the project, the art assets and initial Python script were used to produce an explanatory video in the design stages of the project. Titled 'The Road to Mantzikert', it was part of a University of Birmingham pilot scheme to provide the equipment and technical expertise to allow PhD students to present their research in a short film. The result was a useful introduction to the project and although it describes the project in an earlier form rather than as it subsequently developed, it was a useful exercise in presenting a specialised project to a lay audience.

Agents

The agents within the MWGrid ABM consist of two elements: the rules that govern their behaviours and the variables and constants that are used to describe their characteristics. Examples of the variables that each agent contains include:

- Speed
- Size
- Type (cavalry, infantry, muleteer, etc.)
- Location
- Distance travelled
- Kilocalories expended

Some of these characteristics (e.g. type, size) will never change throughout one run of a simulation while some will change often (e.g. location, distance travelled). Those that do change will be recorded, when appropriate, and written into one of the ABMs output files. The location of each agent is recorded on every tick whereas data such as distance travelled and kilocalories expended is saved for the aggregated dayfile as these are only of interest once the day's march has ended and the simulation has finished.

The rules which govern the agents' behaviour are hard coded into the ABM software. They may be slightly modified by variables contained in the initialisation file, but the core elements are fixed. Different types of agents often need to behave in uniquely individual ways and these differences are described below.

Agent type - Column Leader

There is one Column Leader agent in each simulation. The Column Leader is the agent responsible for planning the route from the starting camp to the destination camp and is always the first agent to move once a simulation starts. In some simulations the army's route is split between several columns but the simulation still only creates one agent with the type 'Column Leader', with the other columns led by regular agents who perform the same route planning tasks.

Agent type - Officers

Officers are soldiers that manage the task of following the unit in front of them in the line of march. They are often the leaders of a squad but, due to their semi-autonomous nature, can represent muleteers or other individuals who do not act as part of a squad, such as officials in the emperor's retinue. Officers can be either cavalry or infantry and travel at the appropriate speed for either. They will try to follow the unit in front where possible, given the constraints of crowding.

Agent type - Soldiers

Soldier agents represent squad members of either the infantry or cavalry. Their behaviour is largely restricted to staying as close as crowding allows to their squad leader.

Baggage train

Dedicated pack units are composed of a human Officer agent and a set number of pack animals. The animals whose characteristics are contained within the ABM are:

- Camels
- Mules
- Horses
- Donkeys
- Carts (which are classed as large pack animals for the purposes of the model)

They each have different characteristics, detailed in Table 8.

Table 8: Simulation characteristics of pack animals

	Speed (m/tick)	Size	Carrying capacity (kg)	Equipment weight (kg)
Camel	3.33	5	159	22
Mule	5	3	91	20
Horse	5	4	91	20
Donkey	3.33	3	45	18
Cart	4.16	40	386	0

The 'Size' variable is used in the sizing scheme to calculate how many agents can fit into a 5mx5m cell, with the maximum size of agents per cell being 20. This results in cart agents being spread over two cells. The equipment weight refers to the weight of the infrastructure required to enable the animal to be an effective beast of burden, such as the pack saddle. This is an essential element of enabling an animal to carry food and equipment for the army. As has been previously mentioned, these values are much more homogenous than would be the case in the real world, but they operate here as a starting point against which future models can examine variation.

The environment

Apart from the agents, the other essential part of an ABM is the environment in which those agents act. Within the MWGrid ABM, the environment consists of the terrain of Anatolia, as recorded by the ASTER Global Digital Elevation Map, version 1. The ASTER GDEM was released in 2009 by a joint American and Japanese team based on data collected by the Advanced Spacebourne Thermal Emission and Reflection Radiometer (ASTER) on NASA's Terra spacecraft. This provides the shape of the landscape, although obviously this is the landscape as it was recorded in the year 2009 rather than the landscape of 1071. Considering the scale of the landscape of Anatolia and the relatively coarse resolution of the data (approximately 50m x 50m), it is not thought that the differences between the shape of the landscape at the time of the Mantzikert campaign and that of the modern day will significantly alter the results of the simulation. The environment is kept in a zipped file of around 294Mb in size and only small sections are loaded in at a time, depending on the area being traversed.

Route planning

Planning the best route across a landscape may seem like a trivial task but it is a computationally complex endeavour that has provoked much research among computer scientists. The problems are twofold: working out what constitutes the 'best route' and devising a method to convert the calculation of this route into efficient code. Various algorithms exist and are suitable for a variety of different uses. The planning of routes within the MWGrid ABM is different to some of the uses that route planning algorithms are commonly put, however. Video games commonly use route planning to move computer-controlled characters around an environment, but this differs from the MWGrid ABM in that it usually must be done in real-time and it is rarely important that the route being planned is comprehensible and replicable based on a set of important criteria. In a video game, if characters appear to the player as if they move correctly and get to where they need to go then this is usually sufficient. Within the MWGrid ABM, we need route planning to conform to the criteria that we determine in advance, and we need this route to be more or less the same whenever the ABM is presented with the same situation. If we march two armies over the same landscape using the same

route planning variables then we should get the same route, otherwise the different runs of our simulation will not be comparable. However, we also need to produce a plausible route across a landscape in which we do not have specific knowledge of what the precise definition of 'plausible' is. The march to Mantzikert was likely to be tightly constrained by the road network but we have such an unreliable record of the Anatolian road network of 1071 that we cannot build a simulation that relies on the fragments which we do have. With this in mind, the best we can do is construct a route planning algorithm that produces routes that broadly follow the criteria used to plan roads. This involves aiming for the straightest and flattest route between two points, bearing in mind that these criteria may be at odds with one another.

A* route planning

One of the most popular algorithms used for route planning is the A* (pronounced 'A Star') algorithm. A* is a graph search algorithm that is used for route planning by representing each possible destination as nodes on a graph. The algorithm then searches through the nodes to find the route to the destination with the least 'cost'. The term 'cost' here can represent anything including distance, energy expended, time taken or any other method of differentiating between routes. At each step of its search the algorithm combines the cost to get to this node with an estimate of the cost to get from this node to the destination. If the algorithm keeps expanding the route with the least cost, it will eventually reach its destination via the least cost path without having to test all the other possible routes.

The estimated part of the equation, or heuristic, is based on the distance to the destination, and its

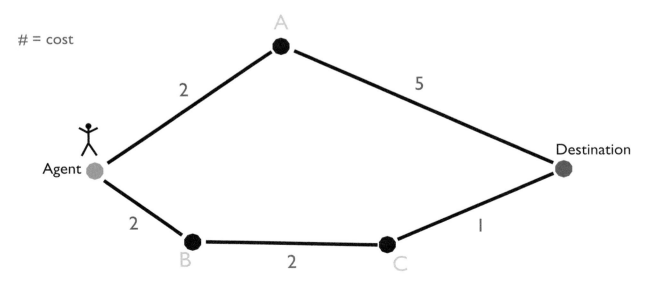

Figure 11: An example of A* in action.

presence allows us to prioritise routes that get us closer to our goal. Therefore, the nodes which are searched first are the ones that cost less energy to reach and that reduce the distance to the destination. This ensures the search procedure prioritises more likely routes in order to speed up the process.

In the example in Figure 11, the agent has two possible routes to its destination. In order to prioritise its search towards the route likely to be the most efficient it examines each node based on the cost to reach it plus an estimate of the cost to get from that node to the destination. For ease of calculation this estimate is the distance between the node and the destination, equivalent to assuming the cost of each move will be 1 from there onwards (Table 9).

Table 9: A* first planning move

Node	Cost to reach	Estimated cost to destination	Total
A	2	1	3
B	2	2	4

In this case the cost to reach nodes A and B is the same, two, however, when estimating the cost to get from each of these nodes to the destination the estimate for A is 1 whereas the estimate for B is 2, giving a total estimated cost of 3 for node A versus 4 for node B. This means that from where the agent starts, the move to node A seems the most attractive. Now the route planner expands node A and sees that the cost to move to its destination is an extra 5 making a total of 7 (Table 10).

Table 10: A* second planning move

Node	Cost to reach	Estimated cost to destination	Total
A	2 + 5 = 7	-	7
B	2	2	4

This exceeds the estimated total of moving via node B; so, with node B now looking the most attractive option; the route planner backtracks to node B and goes from there. Following the same procedure, the cost via this route will never exceed the cost via node A so the route planner will complete its plan and return to the agent a route plan of three moves; starting location to B, B to C, C to destination. In this example the route planner ended up expanding all possible nodes to return the most efficient plan; but if the cost of moving from A to

the destination had been more in line with the estimate then the best route would have been planned in 2 moves with no need to further examine nodes B or C, saving much processing time.

In order to use A*, which is a very simple, efficient and effective search algorithm when properly used, the environment must be represented in a way that can be represented in graph form. During the development of the model, two main approaches were tried.

Grid movement

Grid movement (Figure 12), moving each agent from one cell of the environment to another, has the advantage of being easy to both conceptualize and program. Each agent occupies a square of the environment, the number of agents in each cell is limited based on the size of the cell and the size of the agents (cavalry taking up more space than infantry, for example). Agents move from their cell to an adjacent cell, with each move having a cost associated with it. This cost can be used to plan routes using the A* planning algorithm. Disadvantages with this approach arise when the route being planned results in an agent visiting a large number of cells with a diverse range of costs. Short distances are resolved quickly but long distances face an ever-increasing tradeoff between lengthy processing time and sub-optimal routes. A key factor in A* planning performance is tree depth, a measure of the minimum number of nodes needed to reach any given destination. The greater the distance between the start and destination cells, the greater the tree depth. Unless the heuristic involved is very accurate, each increase in tree depth also increases the tree width, the number of nodes visited per step closer to the destination. This rapidly increases the number of nodes to be visited by the planner.

Probabilistic RoadMap movement

Probabilistic RoadMap (PRM) movement (Figure 13) relies on a series of nodes to be created over the environment. These nodes are linked by edges which are the paths that an agent can move between nodes. Therefore, an agent can move from node to node instead of from cell to cell, aggregating a whole series of movement costs into a single cost of moving from one node to another. This decreases the processing time of A* route planning because the number of steps required to traverse large numbers of cells is reduced. Disadvantages with this method arise when the nodes or edges are not created in places that would enable agents to access certain resources. This could render an agent unable to perform tasks that it would be able to do in real life simply because of the ABM's design, which is a situation that is clearly to be avoided.

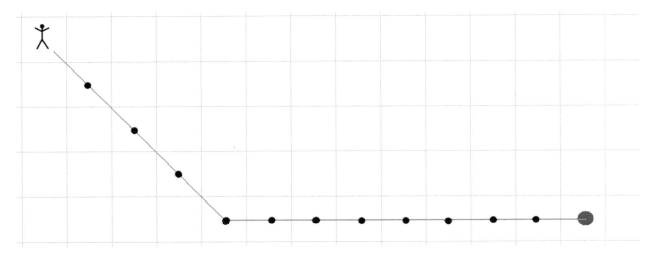

Figure 12: Grid Movement.

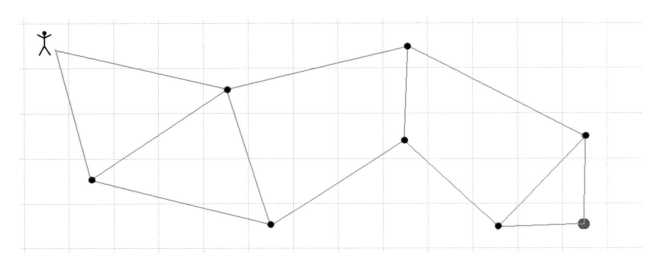

Figure 13: PRM movement.

Why not just A*

A* graph search algorithms are both admissible and complete when properly implemented. The term 'complete' means that a solution will always be found if one exists; if an algorithm is admissible then it returns the optimal solution as long as the heuristic does not overestimate the cost of reaching the goal. The closer the heuristic is to the actual cost of movement, the quicker and more optimally the algorithm will run, as seen in Table 11.

Table 11: Effects of heuristic values on the running of the A* algorithm

Comparison of heuristic to actual cost	Result
Heuristic overestimates cost of remaining moves	Algorithm runs fast but result may be sub-optimal
Heuristic estimates cost accurately	Algorithm runs fast, result is optimal
Heuristic underestimates cost of remaining moves	Result is optimal but algorithm runs inefficiently, expanding more nodes than necessary

A* route planning over an environment consisting of discrete cells works most rapidly when the distance covered is small. When the distance covered is considerable, matching the heuristic to the actual movement cost becomes more important. Using cells of 5m2, the area covered by the ABM results in a grid of 280,700 x 88,900 cells. Planning a route across large parts of this area presents an insurmountable problem for the A* algorithm unless the heuristic estimates the remaining cost precisely. Finding a plausible route, however, relies on a variety of movement costs, making any estimate inaccurate. The difference in desirability between a smooth, flat road and a hike over a hilltop is considerable. The specific movement values are not important but the relationship between them is. For a steep movement uphill to be twice as undesirable as a smooth level movement the movement cost must be twice as much. As the minimum and maximum movement values diverge, so the heuristic is more likely to be further from the actual cost of movement. So, with straight A* we're stuck in a situation with two undesirable options:

- Ensure the distances are never long by having more preset waypoints.
- Ensure the movement costs are more predictable by making the costs differ by smaller amounts.

The first option is undesirable because it reduces the autonomy of the agents, which ideally should be able to choose their own route based on our defined rules, not have it preordained from the start. The second option is likewise undesirable because the agents should make sensible route planning choices, not be more likely to select an unreasonable route because of a design decision.

What is the solution?

Even chopping the route into discrete sections, an unmodified A* route planner will not do everything needed in a reasonable timescale. One way in which performance can be improved is to have a dynamic method of calculating the heuristic modifier. The heuristic calculates how many steps it takes to reach our destination and assigns a cost of 1 per cell. If movement costs are 1 or higher per cell this means the result will be the lowest cost route. It can be assumed that the average cost of movement will be greater than 1 per cell and increase the heuristic cost accordingly. This will speed up the route planning but if the heuristic cost exceeds the actual cost then the route may not be the one with least cost.

There is clearly a trade-off to be made between performance and quality. The solution used within the MwGrid ABM is twofold. Although the ABM uses cells of 5mx5m in order to investigate the effects of crowding, the resolution of the terrain data over which

the agents move is roughly 50mx50m. Although we need the higher resolution of the environment for the effects of crowding to occur, any long distance route plans may as well ignore the 5mx5m resolution of the environment cells and only plan routes over the 50mx50m terrain data points. This cuts down the A* algorithm's tree depth by an order of magnitude without losing fine detail. Secondly, the A* algorithm in the MWGrid ABM has a dynamic method for calculating the cost that the heuristic uses to estimate the cost of moving from a given node to the destination. If this estimate is 1 and the cost of a move is never below 1 then the route ultimately calculated will always be the least cost. The higher the estimated cost of a move, the quicker the discovery of a route to the destination but the less likely it is to be the least cost route. The A* route planning algorithm within the ABM starts by calculating a route with a large estimated move cost. This returns a suboptimal route, albeit rapidly. The route is then recalculated with a smaller estimated cost of a move and this process continues until the process gets slower than a specified time. The last successfully calculated route before the process exceeds this cutoff point is used.

This dynamic method of using the heuristic trades a bit of speed in exchange for ensuring the heuristic is fairly appropriate to the circumstances of the route. The most optimal estimated cost of a move will depend on the terrain over which the route is planned. Completely flat routes can just use the same value as the cost of a move from one flat cell to another. Routes with variations in height are more complex and impossible to predict accurately in advance. The compromise used in the MWGrid ABM aims to hit the sweet spot between speed of calculation and optimality of route.

Verification and validation

Verification is the process of ensuring that the software is running as specified. This can be accomplished by a variety of different software engineering techniques, including unit testing, which is the testing of each individual element to ensure that it functions well in isolation before being added to the system as a whole. This was used extensively during the software implementation phase. The models were initially built subsystem by subsystem with verification taking place on each subsystem and then on the system as a whole once each individual subsystem had been added. The complexity inherent in the models renders it difficult to determine whether the system as a whole is functioning correctly as we cannot predict in advance what a complex system will do just by knowing how each element functions. Nevertheless, we saw no signs that the software is functioning in any way other than as designed.

Validation is a more complex subject, relating to whether the models we have created are the correct models for the job we require. Do these models reflect the movement of an army in a way that can help us understand how the Mantzikert campaign progressed? If they are reasonable, plausible models of an army on the march then they can serve as a hypothesis against which we can compare the existing knowledge of the Mantzikert campaign. Thankfully, there are plenty of examples of the progress of marching armies in the 19th-century literature and even some from further back in time. We run the risk of creating a circular argument if we rely on the same sources for the design of the model and the validation of its results but, due to the nature of ABM, we can avoid this potential pitfall. We are using data of individual elements of the army such as the speed of individuals and the maximum loads of pack animals with which to create a bottom-up model of the army. This can then be compared with top-down views of an army's behaviour such as the total distance marched in a day, without creating circular models.

Exploring the parameter space

'Parameter space' is a term that refers to all the possible permutations of variables that can be used within the model. Exploring the parameter space is the process of running simulations with different values of variables as if, in changing these variables, the modeller is searching for locations in an unknown landscape. This is an apt analogy as, just like exploring a real landscape, the smaller the area to be searched and the more clues you have to where the answer might be, the less time you are likely to spend searching. As the number of variables increases within a model, the size of the parameter space does also, exponentially. However, this can be offset by not searching the whole space; there are values of variable that, while theoretically possible, can be discounted based on the results of other simulations. For instance, we may be looking to find out whether an army with a particular organisation and size could travel six miles between two points if its constituent agents moved at four miles per hour. If the model showed that it could not, then there would probably be no point trying the same set of parameters but with agent speed set to three miles per hour. Having said that, the interaction between variables can be complex, there's nothing to say an army could not complete a march with an agent speed of three miles per hour if other variables were changed as well. For this reason, exploring the parameter space is a trade-off between time and reward. Modelling all possible combinations of variables would result in too many simulation runs to be practical. However, the more combinations that are ignored, the more chance there is of missing out on interesting complex behaviours.

Exploring the parameter space has two main purposes: to help us understand the processes involved in the system being simulated, and to produce results which can be presented to others so that they will understand those processes. These are subtly different and highlight some aspects of simulation described by George Innis in 1972.[497] Innis listed three different ways in which simulation could be useful, which he labelled Conceptual Utility, Developmental Utility and Output Utility.

Conceptual Utility describes the benefit gained from analysing a system and breaking it down into its constituent processes. This is traditionally the first step towards creating a model, but it can be useful in itself, even if no model is subsequently created. It is possible to highlight areas that had previously been ignored and suggest areas in which current data sources are deficient simply by breaking a system down and considering which data and steps would be required to build a model.

Developmental Utility describes the benefits gained by the modeller from implementing and testing the design. This involvement with the process and the ability to direct the focus of the model is an enlightening process in itself and leaves the modeller with a unique perspective on the system under consideration. It is in the design and implementation of the model that the easiest benefits are to be found, as involvement in these processes provides a form of perspective not usually encountered during traditional archaeological or historical investigation.

Output Utility describes the benefit gained from the results of the model to those who were not involved with the modelling process. This, as has already been mentioned, is the hardest to achieve as the results of the model have to be produced in a way which makes sense to people who were not involved with the process and may not have experience with simulation at all. Our method of providing Output Utility within the format of a book, which is a format sufficiently unlike the multi-dimensional nature of our models to cause an inherent amount of difficulty, is to begin by describing the operation and results of a simple model. We then increase the complexity progressively until we are examining specific instances from the Mantzikert campaign and speculating as to how sophisticated the logistic organisation could have been.

---

[497] Innis 1972

Chapter 7 – Results

Introduction

A single individual in fair health and vigour, walking unencumbered, may travel on a good road at the rate of 3.5 to 4 miles an hour with ease; but the very same man, if loaded with arms, kit, ammunition, and provisions, will not be able to maintain that pace for long. Make him march in a column of route behind others, having to pay attention not to knock against his comrades in front or on the sides, and his pace will certainly become slower. Again, let him form part of a large body of troops, exposed to frequent checks, distressed by heat and by dust, and his pace will become slower still. The more unequal the pace, the more frequent the checks, the greater becomes the fatigue to be endured.[498]

Having implemented the agent-based models, they can be used to try and answer some of the research questions described earlier. These include:

- In what ways could the army organisation have affected the overall speed?
- How would the size and composition of the army have affected the overall speed?
- How were the army's size, speed and supply arrangements related?
- What effect did the supply of the army have on the settlements through which it passed?

Given the lack of prior ABM work in the modelling of military logistics, these models also act as a test case for computer simulation as a useful tool for research into both historic and prehistoric military campaigns. A virtual sandbox in which quantitative models can be explored has the potential to be a useful addition to existing research techniques, but this needs to be demonstrated with actual results. In this chapter we describe the models and their results, along with their implications for our knowledge of the Mantzikert campaign. The models start simple and become more complex throughout the chapter. This mirrors the software development process in which simple models were tested before being expanded by new features and processes. This will hopefully also make the models more comprehensible to the reader. As previously mentioned, describing how complex models work and then presenting and explaining multiple parallel simulations is a task ill-suited for a narrative work and

care must be taken to ensure that the validity of the results is properly demonstrated.

The ABMs which deal with the march of the Byzantine army to Mantzikert in 1071 were limited in scope to a single day over the course of a simulation run. This was done for a variety of reasons:

- To simplify development and debugging of the software.
- To enable the models to be run on a single machine.
- To enable spatial resolution to stay fine enough to create a plausible movement model.

Starting at a small scale allows development and debugging of the software to progress via incremental steps. The models started small with few agents moving over short distances over the course of a day. We gradually built up the complexity and scale of the models in order to meet more ambitious goals. This also allowed elements of the model to be tested in sparser models in order to debug their behaviours, with extra functionality added a bit at a time. The modular nature of Java, an object-oriented language, actively encourages this approach.

The MWGrid ABM had to be able to be run within an acceptable time frame, especially during the development and debugging phase. While a set of scenarios may require tens of different processing runs, debugging the software in order to test that the model works as intended can require hundreds of runs. If the processing time of the model was too great, the development phase would be unacceptably long.

With this in mind, the ABM had to have suitable spatial and temporal resolutions. As the interactions between individual agents and their effect on the overall movement of the army is one of the key goals of using ABM, the spatial resolution had to stay fine enough to examine this. This means that the temporal scope needed to be reduced to ensure timely processing. Each simulation detailed within this book modelled the march of an army over the space of one day. The choice of setting the time scale at one day was driven by the fact that it represents a sensible and discrete time for marching; every attempt would have been made to arrive at the destination camp before nightfall in order to avoid the problems of marching and setting up camp in the dark.

---

[498] Furse 1901, 199

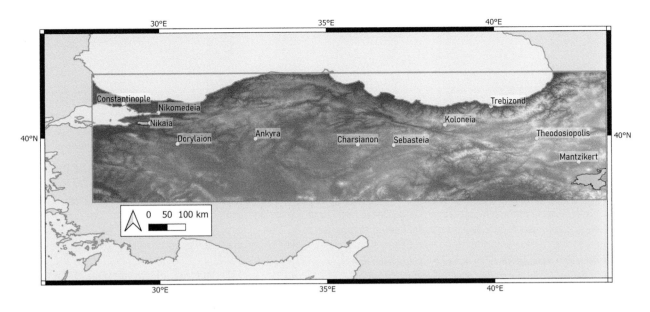

Figure 14: Anatolia with the ABM terrain extent marked in red.

Units of measurement

The ABM represents its whole environment with reference to a grid system 280,700 cells wide and 88,900 cells high (Figure 14). This covers the area between 38°-42°N and 28°-44°E. Due to the curvature of the earth this does not result in a precisely uniform cell size, nor are the cells exactly square however for the purposes of our model they can be considered as 5m x 5m squares without significant distortion of the results. This results in 200 cells to each km when measuring orthogonal distances, or around 321 cells to the mile. The length of a simulation tick was initially set to reflect the speed of the slowest common agents over the ground. By setting the length of a tick to be the amount of time needed for an average human to walk 5 metres it simplified movement calculations.

Exactly how fast a Byzantine infantryman could walk is a debatable point with few contemporary sources of information, further confounded by the fact that any heterogeneous group composed of people of different ages, sizes and levels of fitness will have slightly different usual walking speeds. *The Art of Marching* has some good quantitative data indicating how speeds are likely to vary. Furse's examples vary in their units depending on whether they are British or continental and include a baseline rate of three miles and 520 yards per hour, although there are other rates noted, including three miles and 720 yards per hour, four kilometers per 50 minutes, five kilometers per 50 minutes and 5.11 km per hour. He cites General Lewal as claiming that a realistic rate for men marching in a reasonably organised body of troops is four kilometers

per hour, although as this includes sources of delay that we model in the simulations then our base rate should be higher. [499]

It should be remembered that the examples cited by Furse will be based upon cadence marching, the method of attempting to ensure bodies of infantry keep to the same step instead of wandering along at their own rate. This is unlikely to have been the case on the march to Mantzikert, which would have had a less organised, though probably not completely laissez-faire, approach.

Taking all this into account, we have set a human marching speed of three miles per hour which, in the units used within our simulation, equates to:

4828.032 metres per hour
80.46 metres per minute
0.0124285 minutes per metre
0.0621425 minutes per 5m
3.72855 seconds per 5m

Due to the multiple speeds required by both infantry and cavalry agents and the conversion between the Imperial system commonly used in historical documents (mph for American or British publications such as *The Art of Marching*) there is no simple system that will result in round numbers for both the spatial and temporal parameters. There is no system in which the cells of the ABM, the length of a simulation tick and the speed of human movement can all be measured in

---

[499] Furse 1901, 191–2

sensible, consistent values. In this case, a regular cell size in metres and a regular human walking speed in miles per hour produce an awkward tick length.

Initial setup

For the initial models the length of a day was set to 12 hours, resulting in a total simulation time of 11,586 of our 3.72855 second ticks. This was varied in subsequent scenarios to examine the effects of the changing length between sunrise and sunset during the Mantzikert campaign. It should be bourne in mind that the apparent precision in these numbers is a function of the fact that computers require specific values. In reality, the length of a day is not practically defined by exact sunrise and sunset times, with marches possibly starting before sunup or ending after sundown. Nevertheless, a value has to be given to the software and we should make this value explicit, with any accommodation for variance being taken into account in the interpretation phase of the research process.

For both technical and modelling purposes it is advisable to start small and increase in complexity. A day's march was modelled over a variety of distances and a variety of army sizes, depending on the purpose of each individual model. Initially the models involved agents travelling over flat terrain, and consisted of march lengths of certain sample distances. Although *The Art of Marching* usually uses miles to measure distances, the early models have total distances in kilometers in order to generate round numbers of 5mx5m cells. The lengths of sample marches were intended to fall within the bounds of historical likelihood. Although marches of over 30 miles (48.2km) per day were recorded[500] these can be considered in excess of what the Byzantine army would typically have achieved considering the less professional nature of some of its combatants and the deteriorated state of the Byzantine roads. *The Art of Marching* indicates that 30 miles is far in excess of the distances usually considered to be a reasonable day's march.[501] Therefore, most simulated marches take place over distances from 10km (6.2 miles) to 30km (18.6 miles).

The impact of features such as water courses and roads were not implemented, although the way each simulated column marches ensures it is usually less than 10m wide and as such could plausibly fit on the major roads of Byzantine Anatolia.[502] Each set of day's march scenarios is presented below with an introduction and a description of the modelling and software development work required to enable the ABM to run. The results are then presented in tabular and/or graphical format

with a discussion on these results and any conclusions to be drawn. Each set of scenarios is given a different identifier, beginning with DM101. Starting at 101 distinguishes these scenarios from previous sets that were run during the course of the Medieval Warfare on the Grid project and published in Phil Murgatroyd's PhD thesis, also titled *Medieval Warfare on the Grid*.[503] The simulations presented here have been run specifically for this publication, but the software has undergone only minor modification since the end of the Medieval Warfare on the Grid project in 2011. The numbers are not sequential as it was sometimes necessary to carry out intermediate, test scenarios to clarify a particular technical or historical point which was subsequently incorporated into later scenarios, rendering the previous versions obsolete.

The Day's March scenarios

DM101 – Size and distance - Infantry forces numbering between 100 and 40,000 soldiers are marched over distances of 10,15,20,25 & 30km on flat terrain. This is a very basic model with no complicating factors, designed to provide a benchmark for a well-ordered infantry army travelling over a single route.

DM102 – Composition – These models introduce cavalry into the forces, at percentages of 10%, 25% & 50%. This allows us to start to think about how mixed forces were organised and assess the effect that the percentage of cavalry makes on the overall travel time of the army.

DM103 – Resting and squad spacing – *The Art of Marching* recommends rest periods on the march in order to give soldiers a break and allow the column to correct the natural tendency to spread out across the route.

DM106 – Splitting into columns – Both the Byzantine and Victorian writings specify that armies are sometimes split across different routes. These models allow us to examine what the benefits and disadvantages might be.

DM107 – Baggage – By calculating how much food and equipment an army could carry, we can also assess the effects on carrying capacity and speed of the use of baggage animals. This is done with simulated armies of different compositions carrying different amounts of food and equipment.

DM108 – Terrain and calories consumed – The march to Mantzikert did not take place over a flat plane but across a varied 3D terrain. These models examine the effects on marching over 3D terrain on actual distances marched, time taken, and on the route planning itself. They also add the ability to track calories consumed on the march. Carrying extra food can possibly also

[500] Furse 1901, 237
[501] Furse 1901, 217
[502] French 1981

[503] Murgatroyd 2012

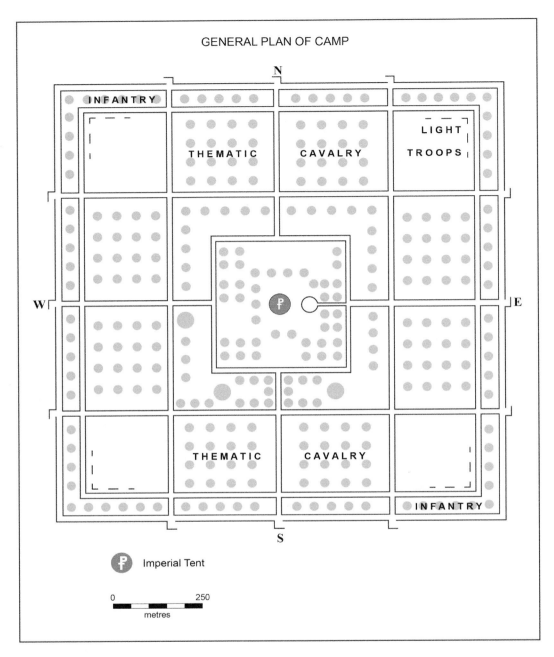

Figure 15: Layout of Byzantine camp from the Treatise on Campaign Organisation and Tactics (after Dennis, 1985) (image by Nigel Dodds).

expend more calories, creating a feedback loop. These models examine this complex relationship.

DM111 – The Mantzikert campaign – Now we have all these mechanisms in the simulation, we use it to model certain different phases of the Mantzikert campaign, piecing together a narrative that can be compared to the historical accounts, providing new insight into the march.

DM112 – Supply systems – Victorian military writing provides details of many different systems by which

armies can be supplied. These models speculatively model some of these in order to examine what the impact might be and what traces we could look for in the historical accounts to indicate that they may have been used.

DM101 – Size and distance

In this introductory scenario, armies of three different sizes are marched across a flat landscape on marches of different distances. The army sizes used are:

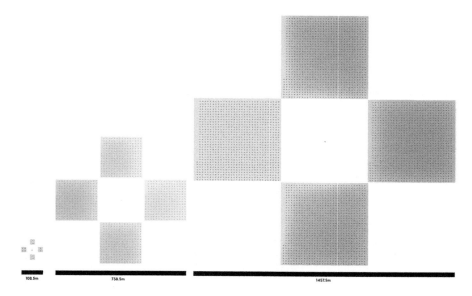

Figure 16: Example of camp layout in the DM101 scenarios, with 101 agents in red, 10,001 agents in blue and 40,001 agents in grey.

- 101
- 10,001
- 40,001

Each army consists of a number of squads of 10 infantry, with the addition of 1 Column Leader to perform route planning, hence the extra single agent in each army size. The armies consist solely of infantry, moving at 3mph which equals one 5m x 5m environment cell per tick. The distances used for the day's march are:

- 10km (6.2 miles)
- 15km (9.3 miles)
- 20km (12.4 miles)
- 25km (15.5 miles)
- 30km (18.6 miles)

These distances range from what would be considered a short day's march for a reasonably organised army to one that was on the limits of what would be commonly attempted in a non-emergency situation. The army starts out in a formation split into 5 parts, based on the information in the treatise on *Campaign Organisation and Tactics* (Figure 15).[504] The simulated approximation of this camp plan is shown in Figure 16. The centre of the camp is reserved for the emperor, his officers and selected cavalry units, which are absent in the DM101 scenarios.

In the DM101 scenarios the army heads directly south to set itself up in the same formation centred around a point that is the correct distance from the starting position. A 'Column Leader' agent calculates a route

from the starting camp to the finishing camp and the infantry squads, comprising of 10 agents each, follow in order. The terrain is completely flat so the route will be a straight line from starting point to destination. As each agent travels at exactly one cell per tick the travel time is the same for all agents and the things that determine arrival time are the position within the column and the distance to be travelled. This can clearly be seen in the arrival time of the Column Leader agent (Figure 17).

As the column leader starts its march at the start of the 12-hour period and travels at a constant three miles per hour (4828 metres per hour) then the arrival time is linear and related to the distance.

Table 12: Arrival tick and travel time of the Column Leader in marches of differing distance over flat terrain

Distance (km)	Arrival tick	Travel time (mins)
10	2001	124
15	3001	186
20	4001	249
25	5001	311
30	6001	373

As can be seen in Table 12, all travel times are reasonable for an individual day's march. This model obviously does not include many different aspects of life on the road and is more useful as an introduction to the models and as a null hypothesis against which to compare future models. It does however raise the question of how the march of the army would have looked to the emperor.

---

[504] Dennis 1985, 335

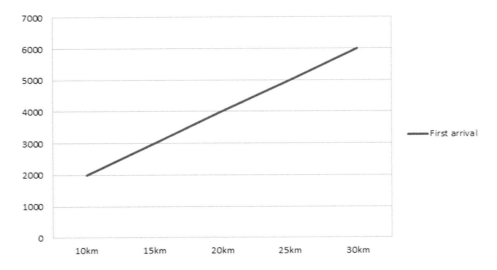

Figure 17: Arrival tick of the Column Leader in marches of differing distance over flat terrain.

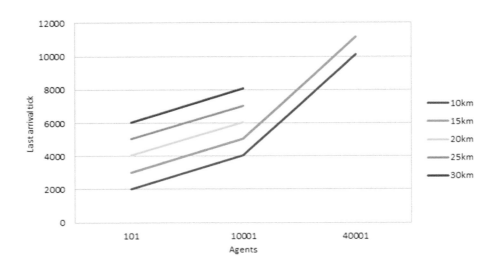

Figure 18: Arrival time of the last agent in marches of differing distance over flat terrain.

With few people in front of him on the route of march, maybe Figure 17's linear graph of arrival times is how the march would have looked to Romanos IV Diogenes on the Manzikert campaign. It would be easy to develop a blinkered attitude to organisational problems in the body of the army in such circumstances.

When looking at the time of the arrival of the last agent into its destination cell, we see similarly linear data (Figure 18).

The difference between each army size corresponds to the length of the column. As each unit cannot set off until the unit before it in the line of march has done so, those at the rear of the column set off and arrive later than those at the front. In the case of an army of 40,001 agents, the last agent has failed to arrive before the end of the 12-hour simulation. In fact, in the case of the 30km march, only 27,041 agents make it to the destination camp before the end of the simulation and almost a third of the army are still in transit. Thanks to the linear nature of the simulation we can calculate that it would take another 2646 ticks, or 164 minutes, for all 40,001 agents to arrive in the 30km simulated march. That is almost three hours after dark in a 12-hour day.

Due to the linear nature of the relationships, it is possible to extrapolate the data beyond the simulations that have been run. This is problematic in a simulation with complex behaviours but as there are no signs of complexity in this set of models we can use simple mathematics to explore the rest of the parameter space. For instance, we can say that our force of 101 agents would be able to cover a day's march of 11,556 cells, or 57.78km, in a 12-hour period, whereas 10,001 and 40,001 could cover 47.63km and 17.27km respectively. Likewise, we can work out that approximately 47,500 agents could be moved 10km in 12 hours whereas around 5,100 fewer could be moved 15km.

Table 13: Number of agents still on the march at the end of a 12 hour simulation over flat terrain

Length of march (km)	Agents arrived	Agents still on march
20	37,362	2,639
25	32,242	7,759
30	27,041	12,960

The conclusion of this set of models is not that 40,001 infantry cannot possibly march 30km in a day. Instead, what we have created is a model that states that if 40,001 infantry marched across a flat landscape at a constant three miles per hour with each squad of 10 soldiers following the squad in front and encountering no delays, uncertainties, opportunities to widen or constrict the flow of people, rest breaks or other modifications to the monotony depicted in the models then this would be the result. Of course, this situation would never exist in the real world but, as previously mentioned, simulation does not exist to recreate the past. The fact that we have modelled a set of circumstances that would never have occurred on the march to Mantzikert does not make these models without value. They are, in the words of George Box, 'wrong', but they can also be 'useful'.

DM102 – Composition

Of course, the Byzantine army did not travel entirely on foot. The exact percentage of cavalry in the army would probably have altered along the way as troops arrived and left the column of march. This was unlikely to drop much below 25% and was likely to have been higher near Constantinople. Here the emperor and elite units would have formed a proportionally much higher amount of the force, and these were much more likely to be mounted than the average soldier.

In order to examine the effects of the composition of the force upon the movement of the army as a whole, we simulated the march of a force of 10,001 agents over 20km of flat terrain, but with different percentages of cavalry compared to infantry. Within this simulation, cavalry differ from infantry in two ways: they take up more space inside a cell and they travel at a different speed. Size within the simulations is abstracted to a number which is not directly connected to any real world unit of measurement but is used to calculate how many agents can fit inside a 5mx5m cell. Infantry are assigned a size of one, whereas cavalry have a size of four, and the total of all sizes of agents in a cell is 20. Therefore, five cavalry or 20 infantry can fit inside each cell, or any combination that does not result in the total sizes of all the agents exceeding 20.

Furse advised that cavalry travel ahead of infantry as slowing horses down to the speed of infantry wearies them.[505] Allowing the cavalry to travel first means they can set their own pace without becoming stuck behind the infantry. In *The Art of Marching*[506] it is suggested that cavalry spend part of their time walking and part of their time trotting. Walking speed for cavalry is set at four miles per hour and trotting speed is described as between six and eight miles per hour.[507] It is also recommended that cavalry occasionally spend time out of the saddle leading their horses.[508] The speed at which cavalry travel while leading their horses was set at 2.5mph. As the speeds given for cavalry on the trot vary between 6-8mph we have chosen the middle value of 7mph. The agent's speed in miles per hour needs to be converted into metres per tick, the measurement used within the ABM.

Table 14: Travel speed of the different agent types

Agent Type	Speed (mph)	Speed (m/tick)
Infantry	3	5
Cavalry - Leading horses	2.5	4.16
Cavalry - Walking	4	6.66
Cavalry - Trotting	7	11.66

Within the simulation, different movement speeds are handled by giving each agent a number of 'movement points' per tick equal to the number of metres they can move in 3.72855 seconds. To move one cell in an orthogonal direction costs 5 'movement points' ensuring that infantry move one cell per tick. Any unused movement points carry over to the next tick. Diagonal movement costs the same number of movement points as the distance between the centres of the cells in metres, which is 7.07 if both cells are the same height. Therefore, if an infantry agent has to move diagonally and has no movement points carried over he will not move immediately as he has insufficient movement points (5) to move to a diagonal cell (7.07). The 5 movement points are therefore unused and get carried over to the next tick where he receives another

505 Furse 1901, 192
506 Furse 1901, 195
507 Furse 1901, 192–193
508 Furse 1901, 195

5 movement points taking his total to 10, enough for the diagonal move with 2.93 movement points carried over (10 minus 7.07). If an agent spends a tick not moving because he is resting or blocked by another agent, any carried over movement points are lost. This system ensures that agents who have insufficient speed to move at least one cell per tick still get to move at the correct rate overall. Agents can also move more than one tick per turn, for instance if a trotting cavalry agent (11.66 movement points) is moving orthogonally (5m per cell) then he will move two cells and still carry over 1.66 movement points.

A system in which there are different cavalry speeds also requires a method of determining at which speed a cavalry agent should move during any given tick. To do this, a system was developed whereby a cyclical rota could be set within which the cavalry would spend a certain amount of time walking, a certain amount trotting and a certain amount leading their horses. Once per hour the army takes a short break.[509] This break allows for answering the call of nature, adjusting equipment and the shortening of gaps between units, as only the last five minutes of this break applies to everyone, the preceding five minutes of rest is only taken if the gap between a unit and the preceding one is below a certain threshold. This rota only applies once the agent has moved out of the previous day's camp. In the DM102 scenarios a 60-minute rota is set with the cavalry trotting for 30 minutes, walking for 20 then being led for the last 10. This last 10 minutes is also sometimes used as a rest period from the DM103 scenarios onwards. There are several examples of historical records of cavalry marches which use some variant of this method in which walking, trotting and resting are alternated.[510]

One significant difference between infantry and cavalry within the simulation is that there are 10 infantry per squad whereas there are only 5 in a cavalry squad. Although these correspond to the Byzantine units known as a dekarchy and pentarchy, they are not to be taken as definitive statements of the size of either type of squad, which could have been heterogeneous, especially between units from different peoples. They are used within the simulations as convenient sizes, ensuring each squad fits within a single cell of the simulation, but they result in some discontinuity between runs of the simulation as each squad sets off two ticks after the previous one. The more squads in the army, the more inter-squad delays. Hence the arrival tick of the last soldier in the army has a tendency, all other things being equal, to get later as the percentage of cavalry increases. This may well reflect a real phenomenon as squads are likely to move off together

and maintain some sort of cohesion yet there will be a gap, albeit short, before the next squad sets off. Therefore, splitting a force into smaller units may result in a less efficient form of movement.

The differences in average arrival time are likely to represent a complex relationship between the faster speed of the cavalry, the slower setting off caused by having more squads and the greater effects of crowding caused by cavalry. As squads seek to maintain cohesion, there is more likely to be crowding with cavalry, where a squad of five are just able to fit inside a cell, than with a squad of 10 infantry who can fit in with space to spare. The army also comprises of more actual 'stuff' to fit into the same space as the number of agents remains the same whereas the average size of each agent gets larger as the percentage of cavalry increases. This probably also accounts for any slight increase in average distance covered per agent, with the shuffling caused by crowding resulting in a small but noticeable effect.

Table 15 shows this complex relationship well. The average arrival tick is earlier in the scenarios with the two extremes of 100% infantry and 50% infantry. This shows the interaction between the increasing number of squads due to increased percentage of cavalry and the more rapid movement of the cavalry. The average travel time shows a linear relationship between amount of cavalry and time spent on the march, so forces with more cavalry spend less time on the march and more time waiting for preceding squads to set off. There is also a linear relationship between percentage of cavalry and the arrival tick of the last member of the army, with more squads resulting in a later final arrival. As a well organised army would have managed this time spent in camp, this need not necessarily be a problem. It may just mean that the troops at the end of the column would get more time to relax in the mornings before commencing their march.

Table 15: DM102 aggregate data for different army compositions

	100% Infantry	90% Infantry	75% Infantry	50% Infantry
Average arrival tick	5069.05	5138.28	5181.50	5064.92
Average distance covered	20317.65	20348.94	20474.44	20523.12
Last arrival tick	6056	6280	6589	7101
Last arrival time	6:16	6:30	6:49	7:21
Squads	1000	1100	1250	1500
Average travel time	4066.36	3838.35	3522.91	3045.19

---

[509] Furse 1882, 248
[510] Furse 1901, 195–197

Arrival times

The graphs which show arrival times are split into two for clarity. The clearest way to see the difference between a homogenous force of infantry and one comprising both infantry and cavalry is Figure 19, showing both 100% infantry and 75% infantry. Here the difference can clearly be seen between a force arriving in one group (blue) and one in which the faster moving cavalry has been able to forge ahead of the slower moving infantry (green). The early arrival of the cavalry force of an army has historical precedent. Marshal Bugeaud recommended cavalry starting at 6am, and by a mixture of walking and trotting, with an hour's break for breakfast, travelling 32km and arriving at 11am.[511]

The graph (Figure 20) showing the data for 90% infantry (yellow) and 50% infantry (black) clearly shows the relationship between army composition and arrival pattern. The infantry elements arrive later in the 50% infantry scenario in which they have to wait due to the longer setting off time of the 50% of the force composed of cavalry. Nevertheless, the 50% cavalry component arrives in camp before any of the infantry in the 90% infantry scenario. When dealing with an entire army, any such considerations were likely to be a function of the composition of the army as a whole, but these dynamics would have factored into tactical planning in any situation in which a commander had to select troops to form part of a force which was split off from the main body of a larger army.

DM103 – Resting and squad spacing

In the previous models, the agents travelled without breaks and each unit set off two ticks after the one in front. These are not situations that would normally apply to an army travelling through friendly territory with no expectation of encountering the enemy, although they do provide a less complex model against which we could assess the effects of force composition and size on arrival time. In DM103 a force of 10,001 agents comprising 25% cavalry and 75% infantry, roughly the percentages from the sample mixed force detailed in the *Sylloge Tacticorum*,[512] was marched over three different distances: 10km, 20km and 30km. Two additional mechanisms were introduced into the model.

Resting

Rest periods offered a number of benefits to an army on the march. They provided a break to adjust boots or equipment, answer calls of nature, break up the

monotony of the march and created a mechanism by which the length of column could be reduced. A flexible rest period would allow the column to close up some of its gaps, with shorter rests for units that are further away from the unit in front. Furse's suggestion of 5-10 minutes rest per hour is a useful starting point,[513] with each unit having 5 minutes rest per hour and an optional extra 5 minutes depending on whether it is close to the unit ahead or not. Though this mechanism formed part of the movement scheme for cavalry in the DM102 scenarios, it is applied to the whole army in DM103 and its effects are examined.

More realistic setting off intervals

The scenarios modelled in DM101 & DM102 had an arbitrary delay between each unit setting off of two ticks, or 7.4571 seconds. Actual plausible values for the delay between units setting off will depend on the preparedness of units, how disciplined they were and how close they were to the setting off location of the unit in front. A two tick delay may be seen as unrealistically short and is definitely unrealistically uniform so a slightly more sophisticated system was used here which took into account the hierarchical nature of the Byzantine army. Each unit had a delay in setting off between the unit ahead of 3 ticks (11.18565 seconds), then every 10 units a 9 tick (33.55695 seconds) delay was introduced to reflect larger unit organisations, then each of the five sectors of the camp had a delay of 483 ticks (1800.88965 seconds) between it, these being the closest values to 10 seconds, 30 seconds and 30 minutes possible within the 3.72855 seconds per tick format.

Comparable models from literary sources are hard to come by. Furse quotes in full the march orders given by Marshal Soult for the crossing of the Belgian border in 1815 as an example of clear instructions for the movement of a force consisting of multiple units. In this, specific times are given for each unit to move out, with the earliest setting off at 2:30 am and the latest four and a half hours later.[514] Without knowing how large each unit is, it is impossible to know whether the setting off times listed give plenty of space between units or not, but they do at least demonstrate that this particular march was not a disorganised free for all.

The different scenarios modelled within DM103 are labelled with a Y (yes) or N (no) based on whether they involve resting on the march and whether they have a more detailed set of gaps between units setting off (the 3/9/483 tick system described above) or not (a uniform two ticks between each unit)(Table 16).

---

[511] Furse 1901, 193
[512] Chatzelis and Harris 2017, 75

[513] Furse 1901, 202
[514] Furse 1901, 153–155

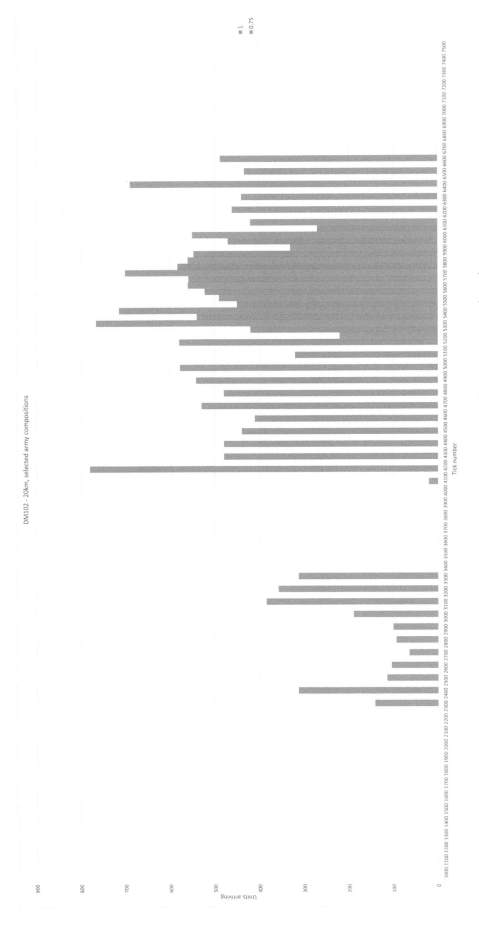

Figure 19: DM102 arrival times for 100% infantry (blue) and 75% infantry (green).

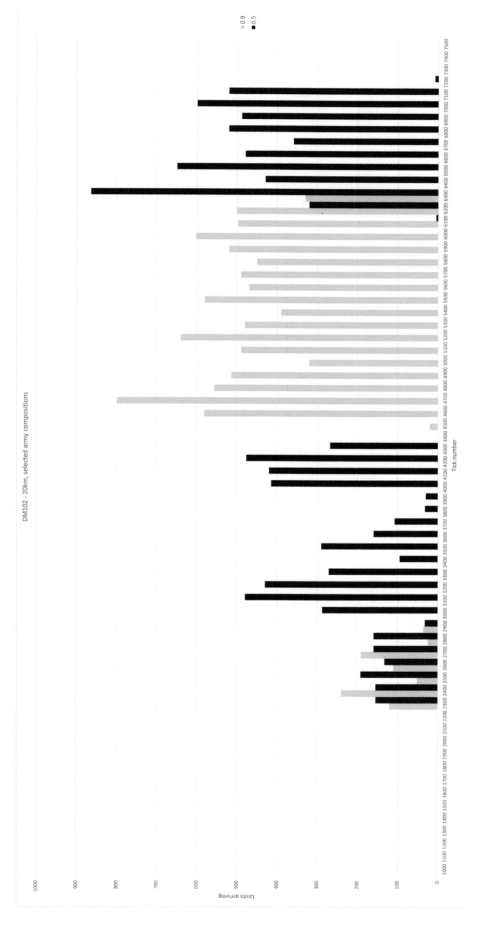

Figure 20: DM102 arrival times for 90% infantry (yellow) and 50% infantry (black).

Figure 21: DM102 arrival times for all scenarios.

Table 16: DM103 scenario labelling

Scenario label	Resting on the march	More detailed gaps between squads
Nn	No	No
Yn	Yes	No
Ny	No	Yes
Yy	Yes	Yes

Results

When comparing the results of the armies travelling over 10km, the results show a clear pattern (Table 17, Figure 22). The simulations in which the set off intervals were set at two ticks are very similar, with resting not significantly affecting the arrival times. The last arrival into camp was 81 ticks or around five minutes later with resting on than with resting off. The effect of larger setting off delays is more apparent, with the last arrival into camp being 3897 ticks after the same scenario with two ticks between units, or slightly over four hours. The graph of arrivals shows a more dispersed arrival in scenarios with larger setting off delays (red and black) compared to those without (yellow and blue), with over 1000 agents arriving at their camping location in a single tick in one of the simulations. Even without further simulation we can begin to see the differences in experience between the various scenarios.

Table 17: DM103 10km arrival and travel times

10km	Average arrival tick	Last arrival tick	Average travel time
Nn	3364.07	4589	1815.39
Yn	3440.14	4670	1882.39
Ny	5408.81	8486	1829.90
yy	5481.22	8567	1893.39

Similar patterns emerged when comparing the results over 20km, with one notable difference. As the length of the march increases, the effect of resting every hour also becomes more noticeable (Table 18, Figure 23). This is to be expected as a longer march would have resulted in more rest stops being taken. The difference between the last arrival ticks of the scenarios that have a two-tick set off delay was 242 ticks, 15 minutes compared to the five minutes of those in the 10km marches. The march from the camp to the first waypoint, and then from the second waypoint into the following day's camp are sections of the march that are excluded from the times in which rests are taken to avoid a situation in which a unit takes a rest when it is only a short distance

from its destination. The middle section of the march in which rests were taken has more than doubled, therefore the 10km march contained one five-minute rest stop whereas the 20km march involved three stops.

Table 18: DM103 20km arrival and travel times

20km	Average arrival tick	Last arrival tick	Average travel time
Nn	5181.50	6589	3522.91
Yn	5409.21	6831	3725.80
Ny	7220.97	10486	3527.47
yy	7445.82	10728	3727.12

This pattern is even more noticeable over 30km, as would be expected (Table 19, Figure 24). Here the data is slightly skewed by the fact that not all agents in the scenarios with longer setting off delays arrive at the following day's camp by the end of the 12-hour simulation time. The last arrival tick in the scenarios with the two-tick setting off delay was 403 ticks (25 minutes) later. In reality, a march of 5553 ticks (roughly 5 hours and 45 minutes) may well have involved more than 25 minutes of resting in total.

Table 19: DM103 30km arrival and travel times

30km	Average arrival tick	Last arrival tick	Average travel time
Nn	7012.66	8589	5252.35
Yn	7367	8992	5553.02
Ny	8947.34	11586	5174.68
yy	9186.23	11586	5368.84

DM106 – Splitting the army into separate columns

One way of adjusting the organisation of the day's march is to split the army over several routes. This has the advantage of enabling more people to be marching at any one time. It also speeds up the point at which the last person leaves the previous day's camp. There can only be one optimal route, however. Only one column can travel on the best route from the starting camp to the destination camp, so other columns have to take routes that are either slower, longer or harder, or perhaps all three.

Splitting an army across several, broadly parallel, routes has historical precedent, especially in the Napoleonic period when army sizes were often much too large to be moved on a single route. This was particularly critical

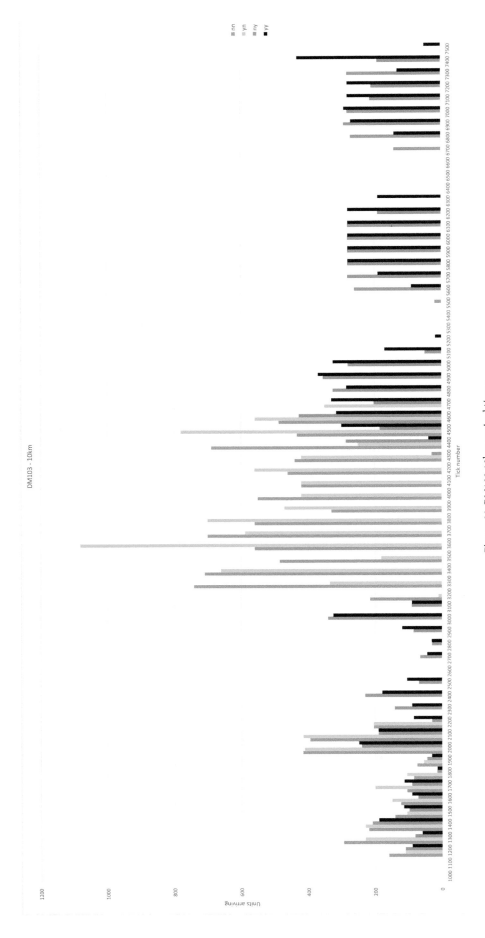

Figure 22: DM103 10km arrival times.

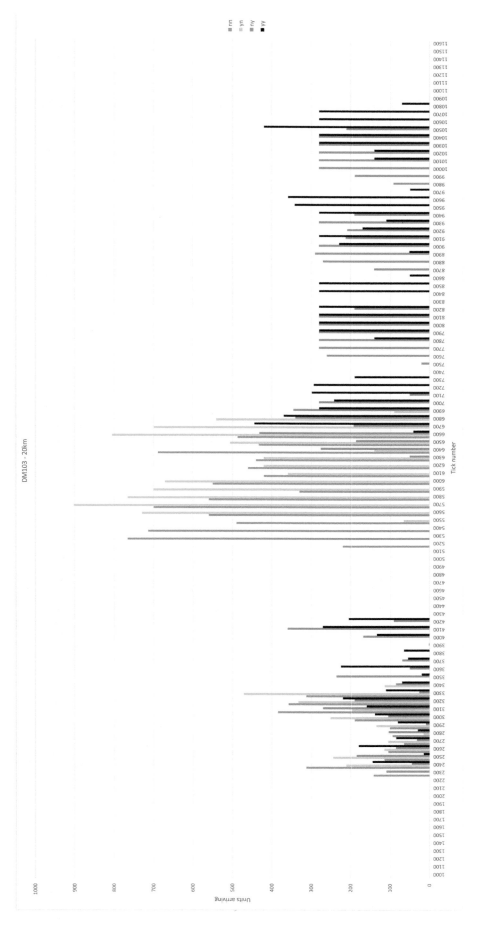

Figure 23: DM103 20km arrival times.

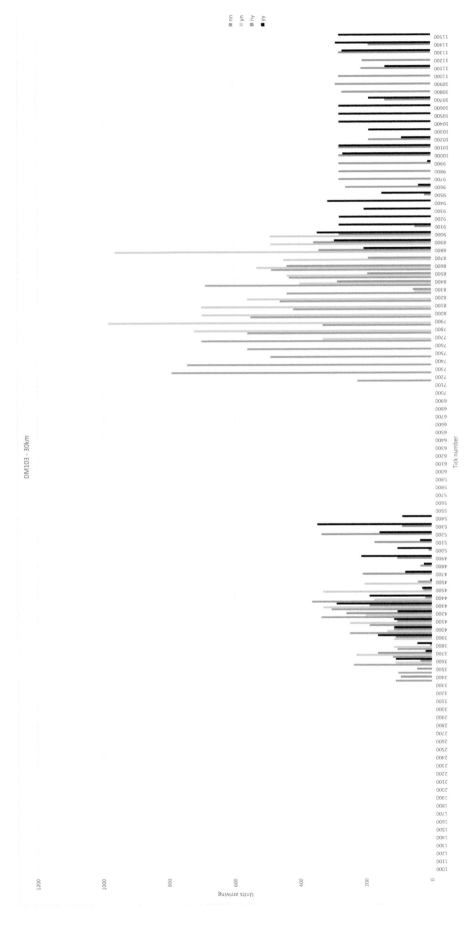

Figure 24: DM103 30km arrival times.

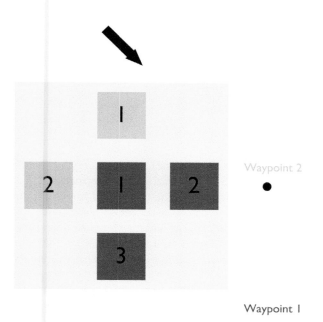

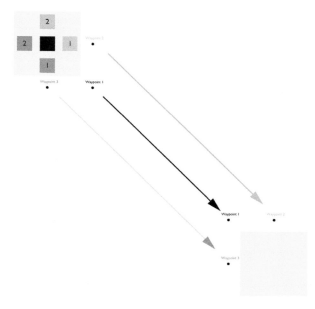

Figure 27: The three parallel columns with the corresponding waypoints outside the starting and destination camps.

Figure 25: Order of march for two columns, marching southeast. Red sections travel via waypoint 1 in numerical order and yellow sections via waypoint 2.

when a battle was likely and troops that had split apart to ensure that local resource depletion was distributed across multiple areas, came together to fight. These arrangements could become quite complex, with arrival times synchronised and routes chosen to take account of the various types of transport involved, which often involved infantry, cavalry, pack animals and wagons. Sometimes splitting an army across different routes was chosen in order to facilitate easier movement for each element rather than as a necessity to ensure the army arrived at its destination before nightfall. Marshal Soult's orders for the crossing of the Belgian frontier in 1815 emphasise the importance of sending units down different roads in order that they do not interfere with each other's movement.[515]

Within the MWGrid ABM, the software creates extra waypoints outside the starting and destination camps at 45 degrees both clockwise and anti-clockwise round the camp. This creates two or three parallel columns (Figure 25, Figure 26), although neither of the additional columns will have a route as optimal as the first.

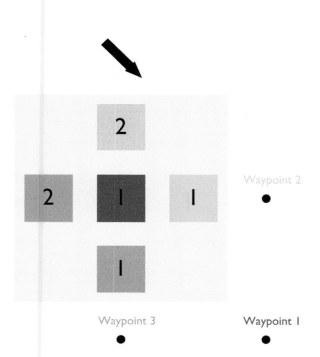

The units in each column travel, in order, towards the appropriate waypoint outside the current camp. Then the leader of each column plans a route to the corresponding waypoint outside the destination camp, as seen in Figure 27. The troops then find their own way from that waypoint to their appropriate camping location.

Figure 26: Order of march for three columns travelling southeast. Red section travels via waypoint one, yellow sections via waypoint two and grey via waypoint three.

---

[515] Furse 1901, 154

In real world examples, a significant factor in the decision to split the army across multiple columns would have been the availability of different routes, however in DM106 we are still dealing with models in which our armies march across a flat, featureless landscape and, as such, terrain or the shape of the road network are excluded from this set of simulations. In these models we would expect the first column to have the direct route between the two camps and columns two and three to have routes of equal length to each other but both longer than column one.

Armies are all composed of 25% cavalry and 75% infantry as in the previous scenarios. There are two army sizes, (10,001 & 40,001 agents) three different march distances (10km, 20km & 30km) and three different methods of marching in which the army marches in one, two or three columns. Modelling each combination of variables results in 18 different runs of the simulation.

Results

When we examine the results of the 18 scenarios of DM106 we see some clear patterns emerge. More people arrive at camp by the end of the simulation in the scenarios with three columns than in those with two or one. This is to be expected, given that splitting the army into multiple columns increases the number of marchers at any given time. We can also see from the numbers of individuals who do not make it to the destination camp in daylight that two separate mechanisms are at work.

With an army size of 10,001 agents, everyone leaves the starting camp and reaches the destination camp in all models except the one in which a single column marches 30km. With 40,001 agents, the number of agents not setting off is independent of the march distance, being a function of the number of units, the setting off delay between each unit and the length of the simulated day. Splitting the army across more columns results in fewer units ahead of any particular unit in the order of march, at least among those units in the second and third columns. As a result, all troops set off in the three column models and only around a quarter of the troops are still in camp at the end of the day in the two column models compared to the number in the scenarios with one column.

Table 20: DM106 agents not arrived by the end of the day's march

Distance (km)	Army size	Columns	Agents not set off after 12 hours	Agents set off but not arrived after 12 hours	Total agents not arrived
10	10,001	1	0	0	0
10	10,001	2	0	0	0
10	10,001	3	0	0	0
10	40,001	1	20490	5046	25536
10	40,001	2	5490	5066	10556
10	40,001	3	0	0	0
20	10,001	1	0	0	0
20	10,001	2	0	0	0
20	10,001	3	0	0	0
20	40,001	1	20490	9510	30000
20	40,001	2	5490	9510	15000
20	40,001	3	0	0	0
30	10,001	1	0	2780	2780
30	10,001	2	0	0	0
30	10,001	3	0	0	0
30	40,001	1	20490	9510	30000
30	40,001	2	5490	13509	18999
30	40,001	3	0	7470	7470

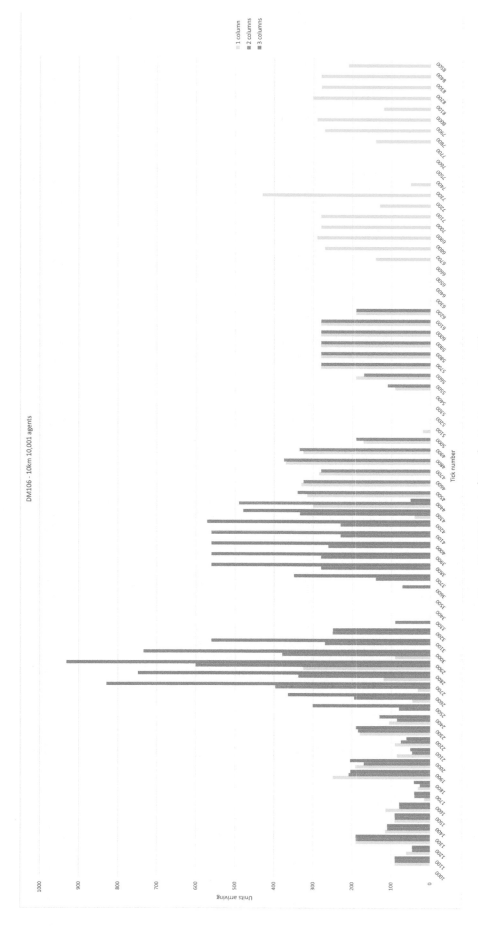

Figure 28: DM106 arrival time for 10,001 agents over 10km.

Table 21: DM106 aggregate stats for 10,001 agents over 10km

Columns	1	2	3
Average arrival time	5481.22	3952.26	3175.73
Average distance covered	10275.36	11162.01	11843.97
Average arrival time (Officers only)	4866.78	3658.68	2990.40
Last arrival tick	8567	6273	4408
Squads	1250	1250	1250
Agents	10001	10001	10001
Column Leaders	1	1	1
Cavalry Officers	500	500	500
Infantry Officers	750	750	750
Cavalry Soldiers	2000	2000	2000
Infantry Soldiers	6750	6750	6750
Average kilocalories expended	423.20	456.14	481.76
Average travel time	1893.39	2065.75	2080.01

Both the benefits and disadvantages of splitting the army into multiple columns is seen in the data for a 10km march with 10,001 agents (Table 21, Figure 28). All three armies reached their destinations before the end of the 12-hour day, however there is a clear inverse relationship between the number of columns and the arrival time of the final unit. The final unit arrives earlier when the army is split into three columns than when it is split into two, which is earlier than if a single column is used. On the other hand, the average distance covered in the models with multiple columns is higher than that in the single column model, as is the average travel time. Marching as a single column, providing there are no holdups *en route*, is easier but slower than using multiple routes. Of course, DM106 takes place over a completely flat landscape. Although it has highlighted some useful processes which would need to be taken into account by any general faced with the option of using multiple routes, it excludes other factors likely to complicate any real world equivalent.

DM107 – Baggage

It is an incontestable fact that the greater the wants of an army the less movable it becomes[516]

So far, the simulation scenarios have only used agents representing infantry and cavalry, however other categories of human participants and an assortment of animals could have also formed elements of an army on the march. The transportation of food, water, fodder and equipment is an essential aspect of military logistics and the arrangements for doing so will have affected the size and speed of the army. As Donald Engels has clearly demonstrated, there is a non-linear relationship between the number of days between points of resupply and the number of pack or draft animals required.[517] Engels did not have the tools to examine how this would affect the speed of the army though. In the DM107 scenarios we simulated the movement of an army of 10,001 agents over a 10km day's march with a rough calculation of how much baggage would be required for 1, 10 and 20 days between resupply. The simulation of only one day precludes the ability to look at how the baggage system would change over those 20 days and these scenarios did not look at how the different types of supply systems affect the number of draft or pack animals required. These will be dealt with in later scenarios.

Historical context

There are several possible approaches to calculating how many pack animals are required for an army. A set number of pack animals can be allotted per unit. This has the advantage of being very simple to calculate but it is not very flexible and has a limited ability to react to changing circumstances. It also implies that the animals needed to be available at the start of the campaign and must have been supported through to the end of the campaign. One alternative to this is to pick up and drop off animals at settlements along the way, as required. This is more flexible and helps ensure that the army was not overburdened by more animals than necessary but it also requires more organisation and forethought and presupposes that the animals required were available when and where they were needed. If this were the planned method of transport provision, it would probably have had to have been requested in advance, alongside requirements for food and equipment, by those officials whose job was to make sure the settlements along the route of march were adequately prepared. Some form of mathematical calculation would have had to have been undertaken in advance to ensure that the transport capabilities of the army matched the amount of food and equipment it needed to carry.

Within the DM107 scenarios, it is assumed that the number of baggage animals is only sufficient for the demands of the march in question. The scenarios will simulate the march of the army over 1 day with enough baggage capacity to carry supplies to feed the army's animals and people for 1 day. The 10-day scenarios will

---

[516] Furse 1882, 29

[517] Engels 1978

simulate a single day's march of an army with enough baggage capacity to carry supplies to feed the army's animals and people for 10 days. The same will be the case for the scenarios with enough supplies for 20 days. In the DM107 scenarios, a rough calculation of how much food and fodder would be required to feed the army for 1, 10 or 20 days was made and this was added to an estimate of how much equipment may have been required for an army of 10,001 combatants. An appropriate number of pack animals was added to the army to cover this requirement, with adjustments made for the requirements of the pack animals and their handlers.

As previously mentioned, it is likely that the baggage capacity would be split into at least two, if not three, levels. Individual squads may have had a cart or a mule to carry frequently used baggage, larger organisations of troops may have had their own small train and the army as a whole would have had a separate train for infrequently used items such as siege machinery and larger stores of food that would have trickled down through the system to the individual units. The emperor would have had his own baggage requirements which may also have been split between animals that were nearby and those much further back in the line of march. These factors were ignored in this set of scenarios, being introduced in the DM112 scenarios.

In the DM107 scenarios, all baggage animals follow behind the army, which moves as in previous scenarios. This is likely to have been the case with the army on the Mantzikert campaign as enemy action was not expected and therefore the baggage train would not need to be in the middle of the column for easy defence in case of attack. Organisation of march order in the column was likely to prioritise efficient movement over defence, with the unimpeded movement of the cavalry and infantry requiring the baggage to be at the rear. Marshal Soult's orders, quoted in Furse, emphasise the need to have the baggage behind the troops in order for the troops not to be delayed by the slower moving baggage train.[518]

Model setup

The army of 10,001 agents is split between infantry and cavalry at the same 75%-25% split as in the DM106 scenarios. To these will be added an appropriate number of separate units of pack animals comprising five animals and a single human handler. Armies will travel 10km and be simulated with one, two and three columns. For the purposes of this model, the assumed equipment and food needs of each soldier will be carried by the pack animals in the baggage train. In the real army on the Mantzikert campaign, the equipment

and food would be split between being carried on the soldier's own person, by the unit's pack animal (if it had one), by the larger unit's baggage handling capacity and in the army's main baggage train as dictated by the frequency of use. This complexity will be dealt with in later scenarios that explore in more detail the various different baggage organisational schemes.

The DM107 scenarios assume a pack train of homogenous mules able to carry a total of 91kg each. Each mule has a pack saddle weighing 19.5kg, based on the Otago saddle detailed in Furse's *Military Transport*.[519] Each unit has a set of equipment that needs to be carried by the mules, weighing 125kg and based on Jonathan Roth's work on the Roman army. This equipment includes a tent, hand mill for grinding grain, tools and baskets, a cooking pot and some stakes for the bank of the defensive camp built every night.[520] Any personal items, including clothes, weapons and armour was counted here as being carried by the individual soldier. This all represents a drastic oversimplification of a much more complex reality but the purpose of the DM107 scenarios is to isolate the effects of adding a simplified baggage train onto the previously modelled army and therefore simplicity is a benefit in this case.

In addition to equipment, the baggage train also needs to carry food for both humans and animals. A daily human food ration is given a weight of 1.3kg, following John Haldon's figures, along with 2 kg for mules and 2.5kg for horses.[521] Putting these figures together, the number of mules required by the army is (125kg x number of units) + (1.3kg x number of people) + (2.5kg x number of horses) x number of days, all divided by (mule load – (pack harness – (2.26kg x number of days)), where 2.26kg is arrived at by adding 20% of the muleteers 1.3kg/day to each of his five mules.

Therefore, with an army size of 10,001 agents (500 squads of five cavalry + 750 squads of ten infantry + 1 Column Leader) requires the following number of five-mule squads:

To carry 1 day of rations: ((125 x 1251) + (1.3 x 10,001) + (2.5 x 2501)) / (91 – 19.5 – 2.26) = 508 mule squads

To carry 10 days of rations: ((125 x 1251) + ((1.3 x 10,001) + (2.5 x 2501) * 10)) / (91 – 19.5 – (2.26 * 10)) = 1428 squads

To carry 20 day of rations: ((125 x 1251) + ((1.3 x 10,001) + (2.5 x 2501) * 20)) / (91 – 19.5 – (2.26 * 20)) = 4118 squads

---

[518] Furse 1901, 153–155

[519] Furse 1882, 82
[520] Roth 1999, 77
[521] Haldon 2006b, 5

As can be seen, the transport requirement for ten days is only around three times the amount as for one day, and not ten times as might be simplistically calculated. Similarly, the requirement for twenty days is nearly three times that for ten, and not twice as much. The non-linear nature of the number of squads is explained by the fact that the equipment element of the total weight to be carried remains static across all scenarios whereas the food element follows the pattern of increasing requirement and decreasing capacity so clearly demonstrated in Engels' work. The emperor, represented by the Column Leader agent, was treated as a squad in himself although this drastically underestimates his requirements, something that will be dealt with in the DM112 scenarios.

Water was assumed to be available at the start and end of the march and therefore also available *en route* via the personal waterskins of the individual soldier or muleteer. The army contains enough baggage carrying capacity to move the supplies required at the start of the march but in reality, these supplies would have been reduced as the march progresses. This was not modelled in the DM107 scenarios as the purpose was solely to examine the effects of a baggage train of variable lengths on the progress of the army as a whole. The possibility of hiring local pack animals and their handlers to carry some foodstuffs that will be exhausted before the end of the march, enabling those animals to be sent back, was not explicitly modelled but if such a circumstance did occur it would obviously result in the baggage train reducing in size as the march went on.

Results

The results of the DM107 simulations show a largely expected pattern, with some interesting detail (Table 22). Marching a distance of 10km, the smallest baggage train modelled here, consisting of 2540 mules led by 508 handlers, does not complete the march within the 12-hour time limit when marching in one column. A quarter of the baggage train, one entire section of the four that it is split into, fails to make it during the simulated day. It seems likely that this could be considered a success if this result was transplanted to the real world as the emperor could make a small organisational change such as reducing the delay between each section setting off or he could simply not care whether some of the baggage train arrives after dark. If the lesser used items were positioned at the rear of the train, any late arrival would have minimal impact on the army as a whole.

The graph of arrival time (Figure 29) shows that when split into two or three columns, the whole army, complete with baggage, arrives well before the end of the day. In the case of three column marching, the final arrival tick is just over 6 hours after the start of the day.

Carrying enough food for 10 days in the DM107 simulations involves almost trebling the number of mules and handlers. Within the organisational setup used here, this still results in the two and three column marches arriving in plenty of time before the end of the day (Figure 30) however, the single column army has major problems. Over half the baggage train has not arrived by the start of the day and over a quarter has not even set off, represented by the spikes in the 1-column data at the end and start of the graph respectively. This seems to be a more significant situation than could be dealt with by bunching up or pretending it is not happening and under these conditions, if only one route of march was practical, the most sensible alternative would be to march the baggage train a day behind the main force of the army.

Table 22: DM107 aggregate stats

Average arrival time	6681	4583	3634	6634	5656	4424	3774	7525	6413
Average distance covered	10087	11221	11706	8131	11336	11619	4721	10388	11522
Last arrival tick	11586	8159	5853	11586	9794	7484	11586	11586	11586
Squads	1250	1250	1250	1250	1250	1250	1250	1250	1250
Agents	13049	13049	13049	18569	18569	18569	34709	34709	34709
Columns	1	2	3	1	2	3	1	2	3
Mules	2540	2540	2540	7140	7140	7140	20590	20590	20590
Baggage Handlers	508	508	508	1428	1428	1428	4118	4118	4118
Agents still in transit	762	0	0	2904	0	0	3030	6046	1422
Agents not set off	0	0	0	2382	0	0	17718	1494	0

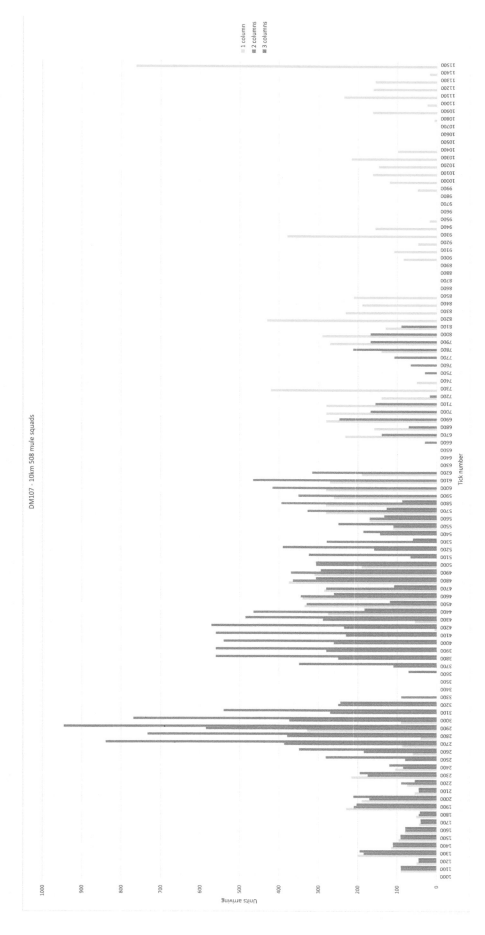

Figure 29: DM107 arrival times for armies with 508 mule squads over 10km.

97

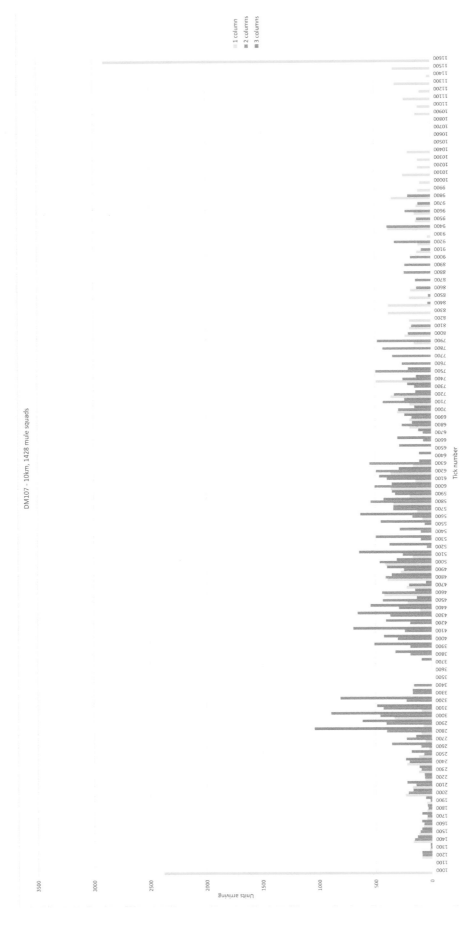

Figure 30: DM107 arrival times for armies with 1428 mule squads over 10km.

With 20 days of food (Figure 31), the results for a single column are even more stark. Less than a fifth of the baggage train arrives within 12 hours and the majority of it never leaves camp. Even split into two columns, some agents never leave the previous day's camp. With three columns, the number of agents not yet in camp at the end of the 12-hour period is probably enough for it to be considered a successful march, especially if you're at the front!

Of course, splitting the army into columns ensures that some columns travel on suboptimal routes, requiring more foodstuffs to replace calories expended by both man and beast. This will be dealt with in the next set of simulations, DM108.

DM107 has demonstrated some useful points. Equipment is important and can require a considerable amount of transportation capacity to deal with. However, the transportation requirement for equipment is not as volatile as the requirement for food transportation as it does not fluctuate quite as wildly from day to day. This means that it is likely to be prioritised for baggage animals that are permanent fixtures in the train. As the food requirement depends partly on the distance between resupply and is constantly being depleted, this would be more suitable for hired transport, preferably from the same locations that the food would be sourced from. Although we have modelled an army carrying 20 days of food, it would only carry this for one day. On the second day it would only be carrying 19 days of food and therefore some mules and handlers could be dispensed with. By the time the army was a day away from resupply, the required number of mules would have reduced by 18,050, ensuring speedier progress. Practical considerations such as how many mules were available and where they were based would disrupt this idealised model of transportation but the ability to model an army with no temporary transportation and compare it with one in which it could be used optimally allows us to set boundaries of the possible, within which the historical reality is likely to occur.

Longer marches than the 10km modelled here become more practical with the more efficient configurations. The last unit in a three-column march with 1428 mule squads over 10km is on tick 7484, around seven and three quarter hours after setting off. This suggests that longer marches are viable.

Of course, a homogenous group of mule squads positioned at the rear of the column is not how the Byzantine army would have organised its baggage on the march to Mantzikert. Availability of animals and the state of the roads would have contributed to a more complex arrangement, as would the division of animals into the three levels previously detailed.

Adding one mule to each infantry unit would reduce the baggage train by 150 squads, albeit at a cost of squeezing the mules into the main column. If all the mules were replaced by carts, assuming homogenous carts carrying 998kg and being pulled by ten mules as detailed in *Military Transport*, the 508 squads of mules carrying the equipment and one day's worth of food could be replaced by 181 wagons. This would cut the total number of mules down from 2,540 to 1,810 and reduce the time spent at the start and end of the day loading and unloading the pack mules. Conversely, it would also make the train more vulnerable to the state of the Anatolian road system.

This highlights a problem regarding the number of variables and the complexity of the models which will become ever more apparent as we move away from the previous, simpler models. The permutations with which the different means of transportation could be combined are almost endless. In reality, the Byzantine army is likely to have a heterogenous collection of horses, mules, donkeys, carts and possibly camels, all with different personal traits and abilities, all handled by handlers of different competencies. This all contributes to the complexity of the complex system that is the army on the march. One could spend a lifetime exploring the many different parameters of the DM107 scenarios, especially if marching over different types of terrain is included. At this point our parameter space becomes too large to fully explore and we therefore risk missing out on important relationships between variables because we can only model a tiny percentage of the many possible combinations of variables. We can however model what we hope is an appropriate sample in order to research the main factors regarding the march, and use the results to indicate further directions of interest in which we can head out into the uncharted areas of the parameter space.

DM108 – Terrain and calories consumed

It is the scope of every march to obtain for the troops the greatest velocity of movement with the least consumption of energy.[522]

In order to isolate the effects of army composition and organisation from extraneous factors, the scenarios modelled up to this point have used a completely flat environment. However, terrain is a critical factor in military logistics, determining which routes are taken and influencing the effects of travelling across those routes. The army marching to Mantzikert will never have traversed a completely flat landscape and the DM108 scenarios look at the effect of terrain on the overall speed of the army and the number of calories that would have been expended along the way. These

---

[522] Furse 1901, 191

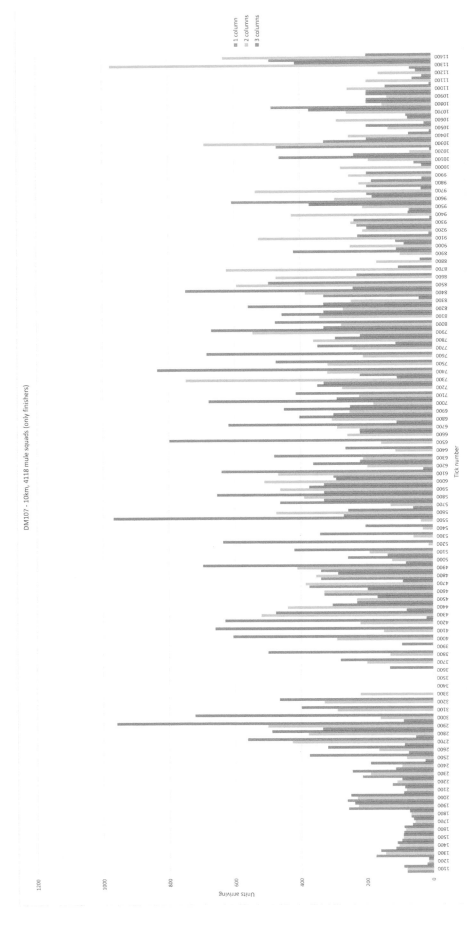

Figure 31: DM107 arrival times for only agents who completed the day's march, with 4118 mule squads over 10km.

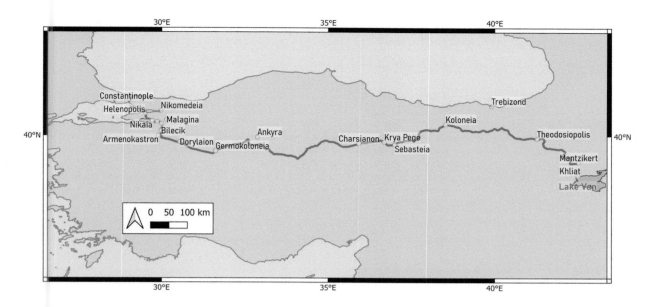

Figure 32: The hypothetical route of the Byzantine army to Mantzikert.

scenarios recorded the distance travelled, time taken and calories expended by marching an army of 10,001 agents over the terrain that would have formed part of the campaign route and compared this to the flat landscape that we have previously been using. Two different areas of Anatolia have been chosen to march over: one relatively flat and one that is more rugged.

Model setup

The scenarios modelled in DM108 use the same movement and organisation mechanisms as those of DM107 but they add the ability to move over the terrain of Anatolia and are also able to track the calories consumed by each agent.

Route

A hypothetical route for the Mantzikert campaign based on the fragments of information contained in historical accounts, the *Tabula Imperii Byzantini* maps and other relevant sources has already been created and published.[523] The route used for the purposes of our model is a slight variation on this. It starts at Helenopolis based on the account of Attaleiates, who states that sea travel was used from Constantinople up until that point. It then passes through Nikaia, past Malagina via Leukai, then through Dorylaion, Ankyra, Charsianon, Sebastea and Theodosiopolis before arriving at Mantzikert (Figure 32). This route totals almost 1,500 km in length and encompasses a wide variety of elevations (Table 23).

Table 23: The location of settlements along the route to Mantzikert within the ABMs co-ordinate system

Location	ABM Environment Co-ordinates	Elevation (m above sea level)
Helenopolis	25600,29000	1
Nikaia	30000,34500	74
Leukai	35010,36130	91
Dorylaion	44200,49400	799
Ankyra	85400,45600	964
Charsianon	139000,49900	1166
Sebastea	155800,50500	1244
Theodosiopolis	232900,46400	1885
Mantzikert	250000,63900	1478

For the purposes of the DM108 scenarios, three sample marches were used and each one was modelled with the army of 10,001 agents split into one, two and three columns. The first set took place across the same flat terrain used in the previous scenarios in order to serve as a null hypothesis against which we can compare our other routes. The second route starts in the town of Leukai and ends at a point 20km south, on the road to Dorylaion. The third starts near Dorylaion and ends at a point roughly 20km ESE of the town, on the road to Ankyra (Figure 33).

As can be seen when looking at the elevations of each town, the journey from Leukai (91m above sea level) to Dorylaion (799m above sea level) involves a larger change in height than the much longer journey from

---
[523] Haldon 2006b, 9

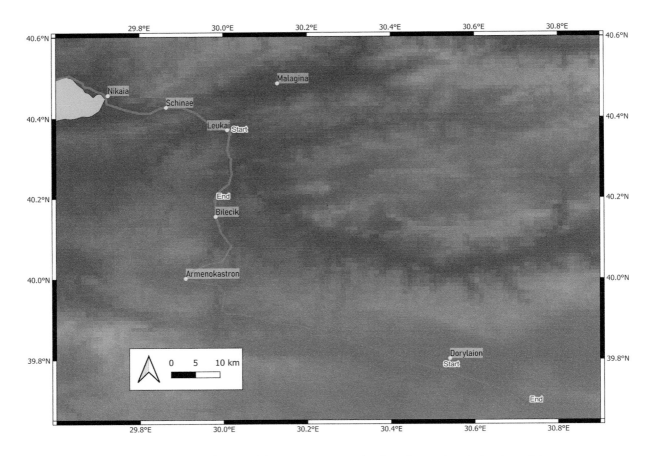

Figure 33: Start and end point of the two DM108 marches based around Leukai and Dorylaion.

Dorylaion to Ankyra (964m above sea level) due to the flatter nature of the terrain on the Central Anatolian Plateau. As a result, the route used in DM108 leading out from Leukai involves more rugged terrain and a larger change in elevation than the one leading out from Dorylaion. The scenarios are referenced by the route they take, either 'Flat', 'Leu' or 'Dor', and the number of columns that the army is split into, giving nine different scenarios, Flat1-3, Leu1-3 and Dor1-3.

Movement costs

In previous scenarios the cost of each move was the same as the 2D distance between its start and end points as the landscape has been a completely flat plane. This, combined with the length of a tick and speed of a human marching on foot, gave a speed of one environment cell per tick for a non-mounted human moving orthogonally. From the DM108 scenarios onwards, distances are calculated in three dimensions and therefore moving orthogonally from the centre of one cell to the centre of an adjacent cell is only 5m if the height of both cells is the same. In the case of uphill or downhill movement, the distance travelled is greater, taking more time.

Calorie Expenditure

Being able to determine the calorie expenditure of each agent has obvious modelling benefits. Previous works such as those by Pryor and Engels have assumed a static figure for food requirements per person per day. The resolution of the MWGrid ABM allows a more accurate calculation of the energy expended for each agent. Not all activity by every agent can be modelled, only those directly involved with the march, but the estimates provided by the MWGrid ABM provide some extra information that is beyond the scope of previous top-down approaches. As the ABM is able to record the location and activity of every agent throughout the run of the simulation, equations from exercise and sports science are used to calculate how many calories an agent would use in any given situation. The following scheme is taken from the American College of Sports Medicine's Guidelines for Exercise Testing and Prescription.[524]

In order to calculate the calories expended while walking, we first calculate the volume of oxygen consumed (VO_2). This is then used to calculate the

---

[524] Balado 1995, 276

calories burnt compared to the amount of carbohydrates and fat consumed.

$$VO_2 = R + H + V$$

R = 3.5ml per kg per minute
H = 0.1 x walking speed (in m/min)
V = 1.8 x speed (in m/min) x grade (as a decimal)

There are acknowledged flaws in this equation, but these relate to people under the age of 18 or for walking on level ground. As almost all participants in the campaign will have been over 18 and each agent would not be walking on the level for very long due to the undulating nature of the Anatolian terrain then any inaccuracy derived from these flaws should be minimal.

For example, an agent walks for an hour at 3mph up a slope of grade 0.05, or 1 metre up for every 20 metres across. This would give us:

3.5 + 8.047 + 7.2423 = 18.7893 ml per kg per minute

This value is in ml of O_2 per kg of body weight (plus any weight carried) per minute. This provides a good value against which to calibrate our data as values of over 50 can only be accomplished by a fit individual and values of 80+ are probably unreasonable for anyone likely to be in the Byzantine army. If this result is multiplied by a plausible weight for an individual plus clothing, 70kg, we get:

18.7893 x 70 = 1315.251 ml per min or 1.315251 litres per minute

Any carried items can be added onto the weight of the individual, allowing a calculation of how energy expenditure is affected by increased load. Using Table 13 of Carpenter's Tables, Factors and Formulas for Computing Respiratory Exchange and Biological Transformations of Energy[525] we can find a figure which, when multiplied with our result for litres of O_2 per minute, gives us the value of kilocalories (kcals) burnt per minute. The multiplier depends on the amount of carbohydrate or fat consumed, as they are transformed into energy differently. For this example, we will assume 100% carbohydrate consumption, this gives us a figure of:

1.315251 x 5.047 = 6.638071797 kcals per min

In our example of an agent walking for an hour they would burn about 398.28 kilocalories. Several points can be noted from these calculations.

- There are standard ways of calculating calorie expenditure that can easily be calculated by the MWGrid ABM.
- These can give a coarse indication of the amount of energy expended by each agent which will in turn relate to the amount of food required.
- This could be affected by how much equipment or supplies each agent was being asked to carry.
- There is also a feedback between the types of food eaten and the amount of calories required. Although the differences are not extreme, resulting in roughly a 7% difference between 100% carbohydrates and 100% fat, they may become significant when multiplied by the number of agents and over the length of the campaign.

Not all of our agents are infantry so the ability to determine the energy expenditure of riding a horse is essential in order to calculate energy expenditure for the whole army. A small study was carried out by Devienne and Guezennec[526] in which oxygen consumption was measured for 5 different riders and 4 different horses during dressage. Oxygen consumption varied depending on the person and on the type of movement, as seen in Table 24.

These values are in litres per minute and already have the weight of the rider taken into account. The only further calculation that would need to be performed is multiplication by the modifier used above from Carpenter's Tables. This still only allows a coarse measurement of calories expended when riding. However, if we assume all other activities remain the same, we can estimate the difference between different types of activity and how this relates to supply consumption. This in turn allows us to more accurately estimate the effects on the settlements on whom the supply burden fell.

The number of kilocalories expended by movement during the DM108 scenarios was calculated and recorded for each agent. This was then updated every minute of simulation time as the equations used to calculate this are based on millilitres of O_2 per kilogram of body weight per minute. During each simulated minute the ABM calculated the distance travelled within that minute. It also compared the current height with the previous height. A further step was required to remove a source of variability in the data for riding horses.

These values are in litres of O_2 per minute and already have the weight of the rider taken into account. The weight of the rider does make a difference though. As can be seen in Table 24, considerable variability

---

[525] Carpenter 1921

[526] Devienne and Guezennec 2000

Table 24: Kilocalories consumed while horse riding (after Devienne and Guezennec, 2000)

Rider	Walk - VO$_2$ (litres per minute)	Trot - VO$_2$ (litres per minute)	Weight (kg)	Walk (ml per kg per min)	Trot (ml per kg per min)
1	1	1.85	77	12.99	24.03
2	0.56	1.4	54	10.37	25.93
3	0.72	1.55	58	12.41	26.72
4	0.6	1.17	48	12.5	24.38
5	0.64	1.43	54	11.85	26.48
Mean	0.7	1.48	58.2	12.02	25.51

Table 25: DM108 aggregate stats

Terrain	Flat	Flat	Flat	Leu	Leu	Leu	Dor	Dor	Dor
Columns	1	2	3	1	2	3	1	2	3
Average arrival time	7859	6034	5416	7805	6178	5458	8020	6283	5507
Average distance covered	21820	21751	22918	22625	23269	23954	22153	22043	23241
Average kilocalories expended	896	892	937	1868	1808	1780	1217	1197	1253

exists between riders. We have added the weights of the individual riders and from this, calculated VO$_2$ in millilitres per kilogramme of rider weight per minute. By extracting ml/kg/min figures from the l/min averages given in the paper, it is possible to remove the variability caused by the rider's weight. For this reason, the mean of the ml/kg/min figures will be used instead of the mean of litres per minute.

Within the source data there also exists considerable variability between horses with some requiring more energy to be expended by the rider than others.[527] As there is no study which allows us to estimate the implications of this to the MWGrid ABM it has been omitted but is noted here as a possible avenue for future study.

Results

Figure 34 shows the profile of the routes taken by each column. This allows us to easily compare the difficulty and length of each route. The first thing to note is that there is not much difference between the distances covered by columns one and two in each simulation. This is an artefact of the way that the simulation assigns exterior waypoints outside the start and destination camps. It usually results in a shorter route for column 1 but this is not always the case as the route planner only calculates the best route from waypoint 1, outside the starting camp, to waypoint 2, outside the destination camp. It ignores the camping locations of units within the camp, leaving some waypoints more convenient than others for different units. In both cases, column 3 has the longest route.

We can also easily see the difference in elevation between the area around Leukai and Dorylaion. The route into central Anatolia climbs up to the Central Anatolian Plateau and, once there, levels off somewhat. The route from Leukai starts at 91m and ends at 534m giving a difference of 443m, whereas the one out of Dorylaion starts at 855m and ends at 1,001m, a difference of 146m. We can also easily see that the route

---

[527] Devienne and Guezennec 2000, 501

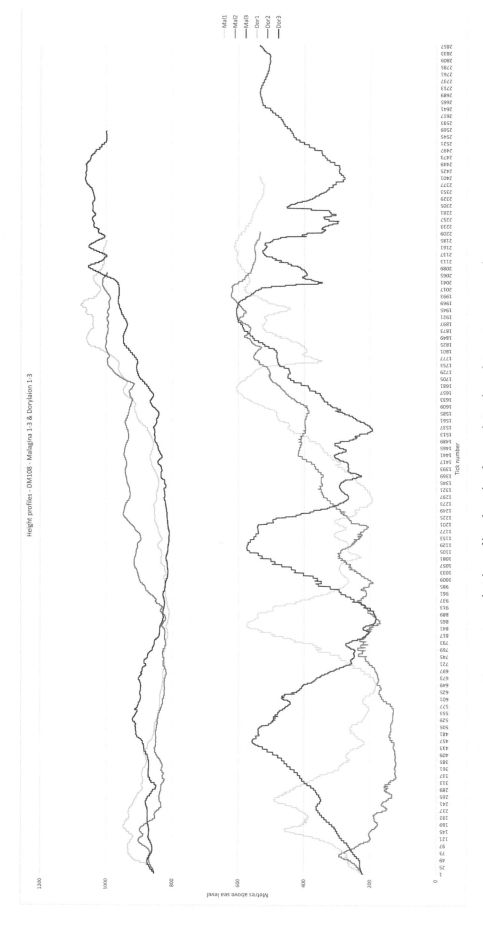

Figure 34: DM108 height profiles of marches from Leukai and Dorylaion using 1, 2 or 3 columns.

from Leukai is much hillier than that out of Dorylaion. This is reflected in the height profile but is also seen in the values for kilocalories expended (Table 25).

Although there is some concern for the accuracy of the energy expenditure calculations on flat terrain, as previously mentioned, the values broadly correspond to what we would expect. Whereas the average kilocalories expended in marching across perfectly flat terrain are around the 900 kcal mark for all three models, these rise to the 1200 mark for the march out of Dorylaion and to almost 2000 for the march from Leukai. This reflects both the longer distance travelled and the greater time spent climbing slopes.

The DM108 scenarios only model some of the factors involved in travelling over 3D terrain. They have taken into account the increased distance involved in travelling between two points that differ in their height values. If an agent travels between one 5m cell and an orthogonally adjacent cell in a 2D environment then the travel distance is 5m. The same movement in a 3D environment where the cells differ in height by 1m results in a distance travelled of around 5.1m. The DM108 scenarios also plot routes which are not straight lines as a result of their attempts to optimise the route taken. This optimisation can be achieved using various criteria, which can be explored with more simulations if required. Nevertheless, within the DM108 scenarios, the best route between two points may no longer be a straight line, as it has been in scenarios DM101-107.

The DM108 scenarios also took into account the increased calorie expenditure of travelling uphill. What they did not do is use a different speed for agents travelling either up or downhill. This would undoubtedly have an effect in real life, though the extent is hard to quantify and military sources of all ages are curiously averse to mentioning it, except with regard to carts which travel slower uphill and even slower downhill due to the problems associated with braking.

Although the DM108 scenarios only model calorie expenditure as a result of movement on the march and not the expenditure resulting from any of the other activities performed during the day, they allow us to produce comparative data which can be useful. The differences between the three routes modelled here are likely to be similar to the actual differences in calories expended, with amounts of calories expended outside the actual march likely to be similar. Thus the 500-700 kilocalorie difference between the simulated marches out of Leukai and Dorylaion is probably indicative of an actual increase in the real world. This would have consequent effects on food requirements and therefore the supply and transportation situation as a whole.

DM111 – The Mantzikert campaign

Introduction

Given the functionality within the MWGrid ABM it is possible to consider the march to Mantzikert as a whole. The model did not, as originally intended at the start of the project, simulate the whole of the march from start to finish. In addition to requiring a massive amount of computing resources, this would also quickly result in a bewilderingly complex parameter space. We instead looked at each section of the proposed route and examined the logistical context of each. We determined whether a hypothetical army would be able to reach Mantzikert within the time taken by the real army in 1071. This provides an indication as to whether an army that was considered realistic at the outset of the research was capable of making the march across Anatolia in a similar time to that recorded in historical accounts. We also started to look at what the differences were likely to be between our hypothetical army and the actual Byzantine army of the Mantzikert campaign. The uncertainties inherent in such an undertaking quickly manifest and compound themselves, but though these models are 'wrong', they are also 'useful'.

There are important limitations with constructing just one hypothetical army and selecting only one particular hypothetical route. As previously mentioned, the goal of the project is not to reconstruct what happened on the Mantzikert campaign but to use simulation to explore some of the processes and issues around the campaign specifically, and with moving large numbers of people across a pre-modern landscape more generally. Nevertheless, the DM111 scenarios provide a quick sanity check on our model as a whole and provide an opportunity to examine the local context of the march. Whether our simulated army can march across Anatolia in the same time, or less, than the actual army acts as a form of validation of the model, demonstrating that it is not obviously flawed in one of the few ways available to us.

We used individual day's marches as a way of estimating progress along the route and comparing this with what we know from the historical accounts. A comparison between the model and the historical account starts to raise interesting questions which have not previously been raised by historians using more traditional research methods. In fact, it could be said with a degree of truth that historical simulation is a much better question generating machine than it is an answer generating machine, and we hope that new questions will be raised within the mind of the reader.

The DM111 scenarios deal with a hypothetical route which has been generated with reference to pre-

Figure 35: DM108 relationship between distance covered and kilocalories expended.

Table 26: DM111 distances and army composition along the hypothetical route

Leg of route	Distance (km, approx. by road)	Cavalry	Infantry	Officials (mounted)
Constantinople – Helenopolis	boat	3,000	-	250
Helenopolis – Nikaia	36	3,000	-	250
Nikaia - Leukai	40	5,000	2,000	290
Leukai – Dorylaion	96	9,000	10,000	410
Dorylaion - Charsianon	576	9,250	10,750	420
Charsianon - Sebastea	106	9,500	11,500	430
Sebastea - Theodosiopolis	446	10,500	16,500	490
Theodosiopolis - Mantzikert	178	11,250	20,750	540

existing research. This has relied on routes plotted on a somewhat larger scale than would be considered ideal when planning an individual day's march. Fine detail regarding local topography and road conditions which may affect the army's progress is undoubtedly missing. A combination of historical research, computer simulation and fieldwork, in which simulated journeys are traced by archaeologists examining the specific areas of Anatolia over which a journey took place, has the potential to deliver new insights regarding the fine detail of movement across the Byzantine landscape. This approach has been successfully taken using GIS least cost path analysis, instead of ABM, on the area around the settlement of the northern Anatolian town of Euchaita.[528] It would be a very interesting avenue for future work to take this approach for sections of the Mantzikert campaign route, especially pinpointing areas in which terrain may constrain the free movement of the column.

Army composition

For the purposes of these scenarios we created a hypothetical army to travel across our hypothetical route. Like the route, the army composition is based on historical research, but there is even more uncertainty regarding the size of the army and at what points along the route its various elements join the main column. The parameter space here is far too large to explore extensively but there is value in creating a single hypothetical army as a starting point against which alternatives can be compared. The hypothetical army which has been produced is plausible within the parameters created by the historical accounts, consisting of different types of troops joining the campaign at different locations (Table 26). It should

always be remembered, however, that the reality was likely to have been a much more heterogeneous mixture of units. It should also be noted that a continual reduction in numbers from disease, illness and the strains of the journey is not modelled, though it would undoubtedly have occurred on the march to Mantzikert in 1071.

Within this hypothetical army, the following units join at the following locations:

Constantinople - The units from the palace leave Constantinople with the Emperor. These are the Hetaireia, Scholai, Stratelatai and the Varangians.

Nikaia - Pecheneg mercenaries and Balkan allies.

Malagina (Leukai) - Frankish mercenaries under Roussel de Bailleul, German and Oghuz mercenaries, units from Bulgaria the thematic tagmata (regional field armies) from Bithynia and the five tagmata of the west.

Dorylaion - Thematic tagmata from the Anatolikon theme.

Charsianon - Thematic tagmata from Cilicia.

Sebastea - Thematic tagmata from Cappadocia, Koloneia, Charsianon, Armeniakon along with the Armenian infantry.

Theodosiopolis - Thematic tagmata of Chaldia plus the tagmata from Syria.

In addition, the German mercenaries were sent back at Krya Pege, between Dorylaion and Charsianon, and the army was split in two between Theodosiopolis and Mantzikert with half the force being sent to Khliat (Figure 36).

Nomadic and Frankish mercenaries would have differed from Byzantine units, with the emperor's household being of a different character than the

---
[528] Haldon *et al.* 2018

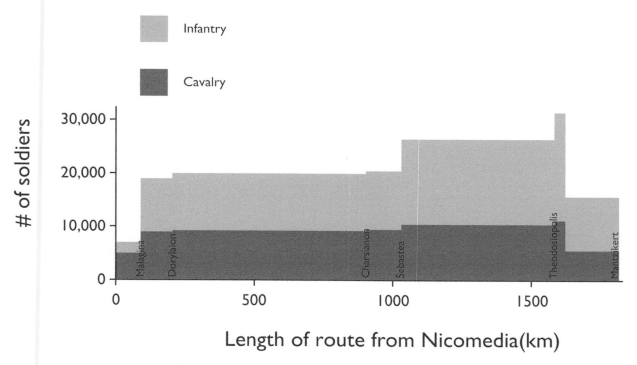

Figure 36: The size of the hypothetical army as it progresses towards Mantzikert.

thematic tagmata. Within the model we have assumed that Frankish and nomadic troops are represented solely by cavalry, along with the emperor's household. Other Byzantine troops consist of 25% cavalry and 75% infantry. Armenian and Balkan troops comprise solely of infantry. In addition to these troops there will be a number of mounted individuals travelling at the front of the column that represent the bureaucrats, functionaries, servants, officials and generals who would have found their place with the emperor, rather than with the units further back. There are 250 of these at the start and they increase by 1% of the number of troops added at each stop (Table 26).

During these scenarios we did not simulate the baggage handling capacity on either the squad, unit or army level. This gave us something close to a 'best case' scenario in which adding baggage handling capacity can only make the army slower, making it fairly straightforward to account for in our conclusions. We examine different levels and methods of supplying the army during the DM112 scenarios.

Weather and daylight

The amount of daylight within which the army had to move would have differed as it crossed Anatolia. Although the differences in latitude are fairly minor, the march took almost six months which would have

resulted in considerable variation in the number of daylight hours. The values recorded in Table 27 are based on data from the Australian Government[529] and are for dates in 2010. These obviously differ from sunrise and sunset times in 1071, but any differences are likely to have minimal impact on our interpretations and, again, precise numerical values are required within the ABM.

Timing

There are few fixed temporal points on the Mantzikert campaign. We know that the emperor left Constantinople in late February or early March, had reached Theodosiopolis by late June and fought the battle at Mantzikert on August 26th, very soon after arrival. If we set March 1st as the start date and June 30th to represent late June, we have 122 days from leaving Helenopolis to arriving at Theodosiopolis and 56 days from that point to arriving at Mantzikert on the day before the battle. It seems almost certain that the army spent some time at Theodosiopolis as Skylitzes Continuatus records a major strategic discussion at which the decision to move on to Mantzikert was made.[530] He also records that the order was given to gather 3 months' worth of supplies. Engels' work shows that this is unlikely to have included food for the whole

---

[529] Geodetic Calculators
[530] Friendly 1981, 171

Table 27: Sunrise and sunset data used in DM111

Location	Co-ordinates	Date	Sunrise (UTC +3)	Sunset (UTC +3)	Minutes of daylight	Ticks @ 3.729 secs/tick
Helenopolis (Hersek)	40° 46'N, 29° 55'E	01/03/10	07:36:00	18:53:00	677	10893
Ankyra (Ankara)	39° 52'N, 32° 52'E	15/04/10	06:11:00	19:27:00	796	12809
Sebastea (Sivas)	39° 45'N, 37° 01'E	05/05/10	05:28:00	19:29:00	841	13532
Theodosiopolis (Erzurum)	39° 54'N, 41° 16'E	01/07/10	04:51:00	19:48:00	890	14320
Theodosiopolis (Erzurum)	39° 54'N, 41° 16'E	01/08/10	05:14:00	19:29:00	855	13757
Mantzikert (Malazgirt)	39° 48'N, 42° 19'E	26/08/10	05:34:00	18:53:00	799	12856

three months,[531] but it does at least indicate that the stop at Theodosiopolis was more than just a flying visit.

Throughout the written account of the DM111 scenarios which follows we keep track of how our hypothetical army is progressing compared to the historical record. This is a valuable method of validating the models, as if the simulated army substantially underperforms the actual army it implies that the simulated army, free of unexpected delays and baggage, has some significant factor or factors causing its lack of speed. Considering we are modelling something close to a 'best case' scenario, we would expect the opposite, and our simulated army to reach Mantzikert ahead of the historical schedule.

Results

Helenopolis to Nikaia

Start – day 1.

The route from Helenopolis to Nikaia is likely to have headed due south to the northern shore of the lake now called İznik Gölü, before heading east to Nikaia (Figure 37). The distance between the two settlements was around 32km, the route being closer to 36km on the ground. Nikaia was 'one of the greatest Byzantine cities'[532] and would have been well supplied, with ample facilities. The need to transport goods such as lentils from areas around Nikaia to Constantinople via the ports at Helenopolis or Pylai implies a well-maintained road between the two places.[533] Although our hypothetical army at this point is small and entirely made up of cavalry, it is just beginning its expedition and some leeway is probably required to account for

the members of the expedition adopting the routine of life on campaign. It is therefore likely that the march would be split over two days, with the north shore of İznik Gölü being roughly halfway between Helenopolis and Nikaia.

Modelling the march of our hypothetical army from Helenopolis to the northern shore of İznik Gölü, around the location of the modern Turkish town of Boyalıca, presents this section of the campaign as a comfortable journey. At this stage the army numbers 3000 cavalry and 250 officials, therefore all simulated agents travel on horseback. The final unit arrives at its destination on the 7279th tick, around 7 hours and 32 minutes after the start of the simulated day (Figure 38). If the first unit sets off at sunrise, the last unit arrives just after 3 o'clock in the afternoon.

The second part of the journey is a shorter march along the shores of the lake and can be assumed to have been finished even earlier in the day than the first part. Our hypothetical army has marched from Helenopolis to Nikaia in a very comfortable two days and it would be plausible to add an extra day at Nikaia to cope with the organisational efforts required to accommodate the new troops and the need for the emperor to satisfy the niceties of diplomacy with local notables.

Nikaia to Leukai

Start – day 4.

Our hypothetical army picks up Pecheneg mercenaries and Balkan allies at Nikaia and moves on towards Dorylaion via the district of Malagina (Figure 39). Malagina was an important mustering point for the Byzantine army although the district itself lies a little to the north of the road that travels from Nikaia, through Leukai, to Dorylaion. Leukai itself would be a suitable

---

[531] Engels 1978, 20
[532] Kazhdan *et al.* 1991, 1463
[533] Belke 2017, 37

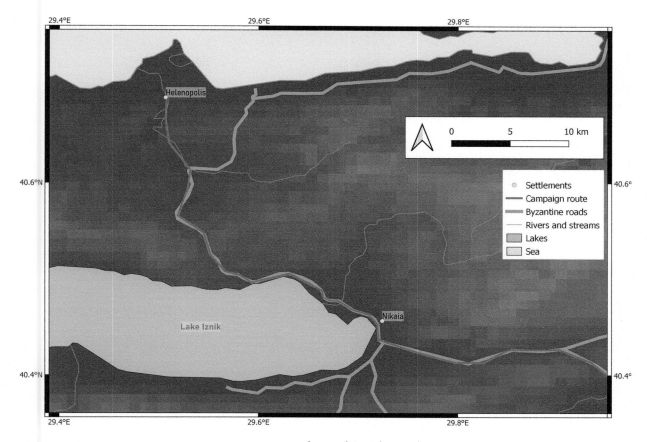

Figure 37: Route map from Helenopolis to Nikaia.

point for the troops gathered at Malagina to join the rest of the army as it marched along its route.

As the 32km between Nikaia and Leukai as the crow flies is closer to 40km along the ground, with the vast majority of the journey uphill and a bridge to be contended with, it is likely that this journey, like the one between Helenopolis and Nikaia, would be split across two days despite theoretically being possible in one. Breaking the journey at Schinae results in two fairly comfortable marches. The last members of the mounted portion of the army arrive at Schinae at around the same time as they reached camp after the first day's march from Helenopolis. The infantry arrive later, but still well within the hours of daylight (Figure 40).

The route between Nikaia and Schinae rises steadily (Figure 41) and the roads are likely to be well used and therefore in decent condition. Modern weather data for March from the town of İznik[534] gives temperatures between 5-13 degrees Celsius, along with 26mm of rain spread across 7 rainy days. A cool start for the army and maybe an increase in weight due to wet clothing and equipment. Again, arrival at Leukai after 2 days

on the march would probably require a further day of organisation and local bureaucracy as the troops which were mustered at Malagina were incorporated into the army.

Leukai to Dorylaion

Start – day 7.

The journey from Leukai to Dorylaion along our hypothetical route covers a distance of 71 miles or 114 km (Figure 39) and involves travelling from 91m above sea level up to 799m. At Leukai the hypothetical force increases from around 7000 troops to around 19,000 with the addition of the Frankish, German and Oghuz mercenaries and the five tagmata of the west, among others. There would have to have been at least a day for these forces to be introduced into the army's organisational structure. The supply situation at Malagina will almost certainly have been affected by the length of time that these troops will have been waiting in the area, although Malagina itself was a fertile plain with good transport links, presumably explaining its use as a mustering point.[535]

---

[534] Iznik Annual Weather Averages

[535] Foss 1990

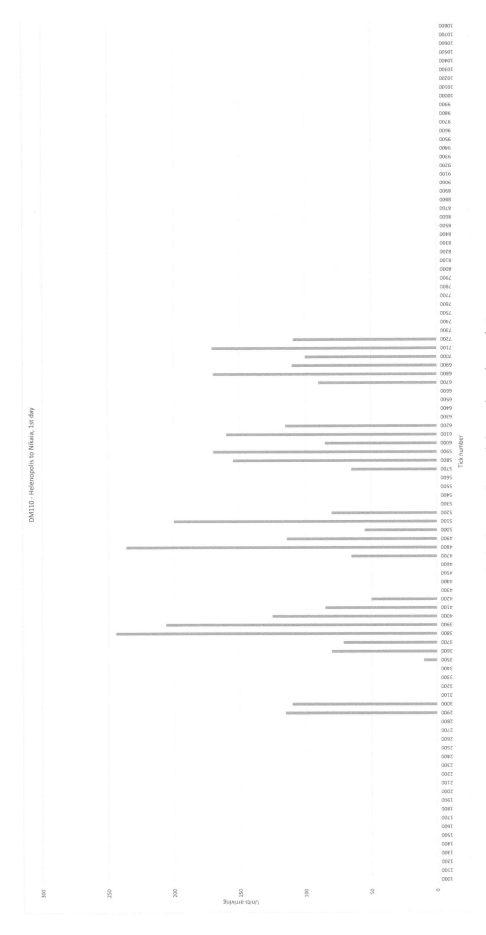

Figure 38: Arrival tick of units on the march from Helenopolis to Nikaia – Day 1.

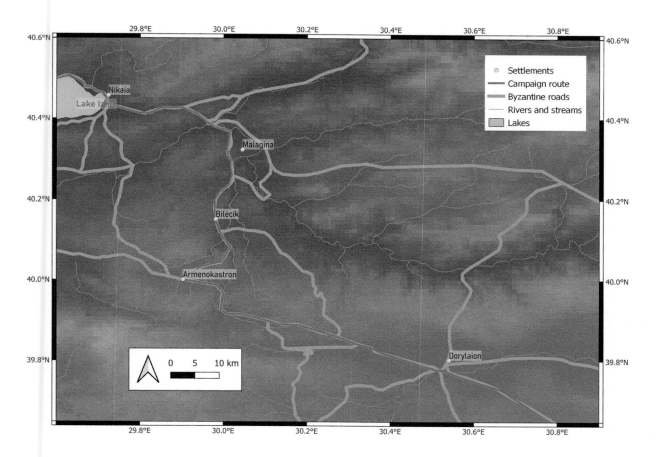

Figure 39: Route map from Nikaia to Dorylaion.

Our hypothetical Mantzikert campaign route travels south to Armenokastron, before heading east towards Dorylaion, located in the area of the modern Turkish city of Eskişehir. This mirrors the start and end points of a march undertaken by the Crusaders of the First Crusade although, as with the Mantzikert campaign, there is uncertainty regarding the actual route taken. The journey from Leukai to Armenokastron is the part of the journey in which the majority of the increase in altitude occurs, the journey eastwards from Armenokastron to Dorylaion being much flatter. The route to Armenokastron is likely to have been more constrained by the terrain, with little scope for splitting the army along parallel routes until just after the modern Turkish town of Bilecik. For this reason, we will simulate our entire hypothetical force marching in a single column to investigate the likely progress to Bilecik, before discussing the options from there.

The distance between Leukai and Bilecik is around 24km but this is likely to have been over 30km along the road. The newly expanded army would have found this a challenging march to have completed in a day, especially considering the requirement for new troops to be accommodated by the existing organisation. The

graph of unit arrival time (Figure 42) shows an army arriving throughout the day. What it does not show are the units who are spread out across the whole route by the end of the day. In fact, just over half the army (11,580 agents out of a total of 19,556) has not arrived by the end of the day and around 20% (4,190) have not even set off from Leukai.

The simulated army is unable to travel between Leukai and Bilecik in a single column in one day and the emperor would have had to make a decision as to whether the army would camp at a location before Bilecik, split itself into parallel columns or split into two groups who travel the same route on subsequent days. Due to the restricted nature of the terrain and the fact that the troops joining the column would probably already have a camp set up in the area of Leukai as a result of the mustering process then it seems reasonable to march our hypothetical army along a single route from Leukai to Bilecik along subsequent days. Absent any need to stay at either Bilecik or Armenokastron, and assuming the army can make the smaller march from Bilecik to Armenokastron in a day and the 67km between Armenokastron and Dorylaion in three days, this would result in the front portion of the army

Figure 40: Arrival time of units on the march between Nikaia and Leukai - Day 1.

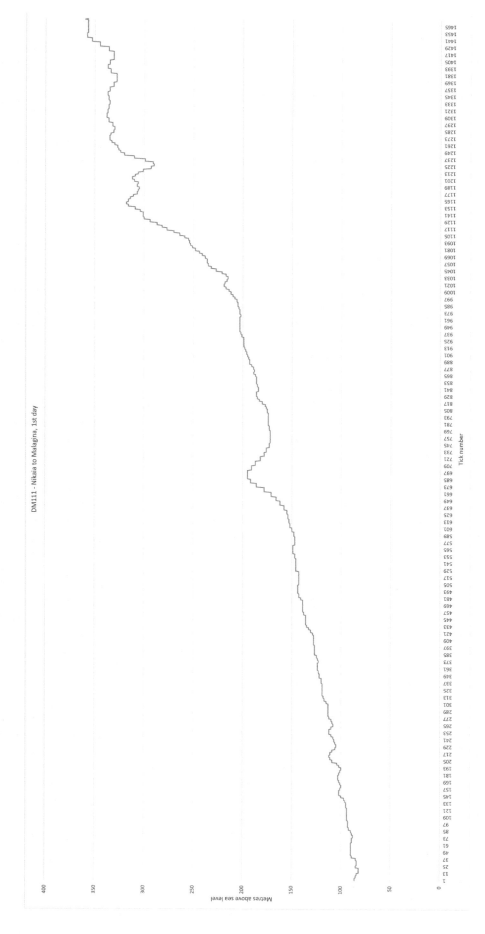

Figure 41: Cross section of the first day's march between Nikaia and Leukai.

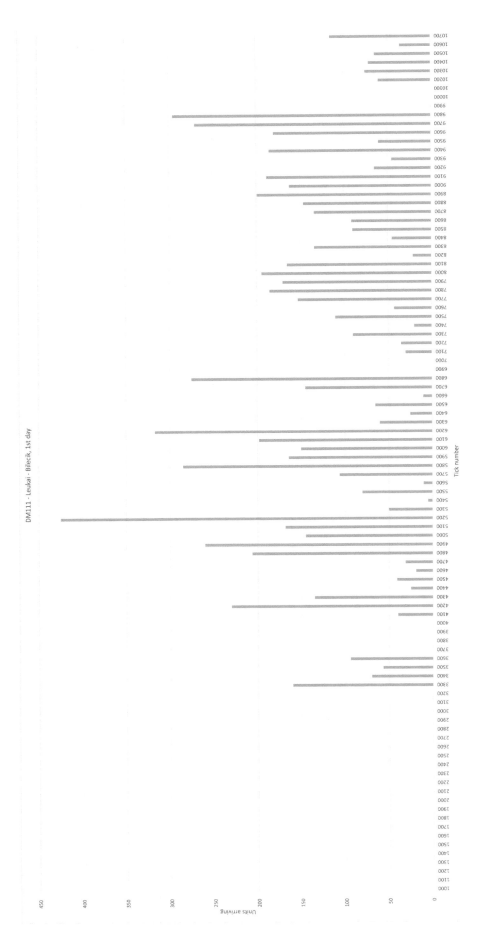

Figure 42: Unit arrival time on march between Leukai and Bilecik.

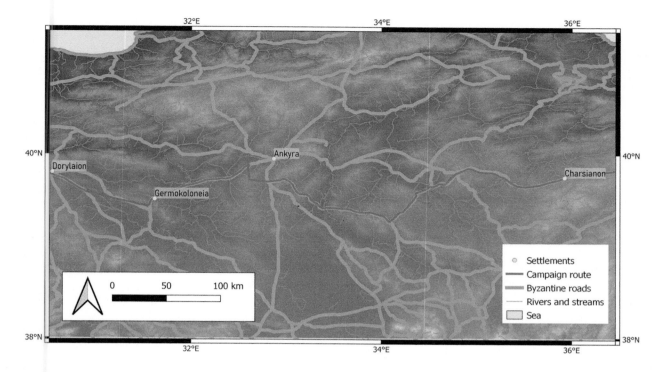

Figure 43: Route map between Dorylaion and Charsianon.

arriving in Dorylaion on day 12 and the remainder on day 13. Allowing a rest day from the arrival of the tail of the army, this would ensure the next leg of the journey commenced on day 15.

Unmodelled here, however, is the possibility that the majority of the army which left Nikaia travelled on the route directly south instead of via Malagina, joining up with the forces from Malagina at either Armenokastron or Dorylaion. This would have resulted in a smaller army travelling the rougher terrain south of Leukai towards Armenokastron but is unlikely to have saved any time overall. It is also possible that the troops mustered at Malagina could have travelled to Dorylaion either in advance of, or behind, the other parts of the army.

Dorylaion to Charsianon

Start – day 15.

The march between Dorylaion and Charsianon would have covered a distance of around 576km across the Central Anatolian Plateau (Figure 43). As the size of the simulated army is static over this leg of the journey it would be expected that our virtual soldiers would be becoming accustomed to the routine of life on the march. On the actual campaign there would likely have been a constant coming and going of stragglers dropping out of, and rejoining, the column, and merchants and

hangers on joining for a while until their curiosity or financial aims had been satisfied. Nevertheless, our simulated army picks up no troops along this stretch of the journey.

The requirements of the animals, particularly horses, would have necessitated a rest day every 6 or 7 days. This area of Anatolia would have had a certain amount of open countryside which would have been crossed by a number of roads or tracks, therefore splitting the army up into parallel columns would have been a viable tactic during parts of this leg of the journey. For this reason, we have modelled the march of our hypothetical army across a section of the route, organised into one, two and three columns.

In this section of the route the army travels almost directly east and passes just south of Ankyra. A simulated day's march of 20km was attempted, with the army split into one, two and three columns. As the march takes place later in the year than the previous marches, an increase in the number of simulation ticks was made, although, as the previous days on this leg of the journey have not been simulated, a best guess has to made regarding the length of the day. For these scenarios we chose the data from Table 27 for the modern city of Ankara in the middle of April, giving a total of 12,809 ticks.

Table 28: Simulation data from a day's march between Dorylaion and Charsianon

Columns	1	2	3
Average arrival time	9696.1404	7093.9387	6940.9947
Average distance covered	14629.13	22170.813	23221.692
Average arrival time (Officers only)	8885.0281	6577.2285	6350.3461
Last arrival tick	12809	10700	10783
Squads	3062	3062	3062
Agents	20686	20686	20686
Column Leaders	1	1	1
Cavalry Officers	1987	1987	1987
Infantry Officers	1075	1075	1075
Cavalry Soldiers	7948	7948	7948
Infantry Soldiers	9675	9675	9675
Mules	0	0	0
Donkeys	0	0	0
Horses	0	0	0
Camels	0	0	0
Carts	0	0	0
Baggage Handlers	0	0	0
Average kilocalories expended	749.09593	1128.8346	1189.4755
Average travel time	2296.244	3347.3493	3507.7486
Agents still in transit	10351	0	0
Agents not set off	399	0	0

As can be seen from Table 28, our army of 20,686 agents has comfortably completed a march of 20km when split into two or three columns. The differences between the two are minimal, with a slightly later last arrival tick (only just over five minutes later) and longer average travel distance for three columns but an earlier average arrival tick. The arrival of the last unit into camp equates to just after 17:15, over two hours before sunset, when using the sunrise and sunset time of mid-April.

As can be seen from the graph of arrival times (Figure 44), there are minimal differences between splitting the army across two (red) and three (yellow) columns. With the army marching as one column (blue), the last of the cavalry arrives at around the same point in the day as the last units of infantry from the other scenarios, but the infantry is all still yet to arrive, and 399 of them have not even set off.

The implications for our hypothetical army are not necessarily as straightforward as this model implies. It is clear our hypothetical army can comfortably march 20km per day when split into parallel columns, with the difference between two columns and three being minimal. The number of occasions for which this would have been practical remain unknown without considerably more research on the specific parts of terrain being crossed and a large dose of speculation regarding placement and condition of roads. In areas where multiple columns would have been impractical, a single column would have to be used, although this could be spread out over consecutive days as has been hypothesised for the march between Malagina and Dorylaion. If it were not spread out across consecutive days, the total distance covered per day would have to be less than 20km.

This is where we start to run up against the limits of this kind of simulation in such a large parameter space. In the DM111 scenarios we are attempting to chart the progress of a hypothetical army across the route, once only, using day's marches which we believe tell us something about the historical campaign. Yet important factors such as the road network are unknown, and the fact that we are not simulating every day's march means we have a degree of uncertainty regarding at what point the modelled day's marches occur and therefore how long the modelled day is. How much do these factors matter? It is clear from the above example that the precise length of the day does not make much difference to our conclusions in this particular instance. A slightly shorter day would still result in both the two and three column armies arriving in time and it would take an unreasonably long day for the single column army to successfully complete the march.

There are likely to be other situations along this leg of the march in which it would turn out to be more significant, though. 20km was chosen as a somewhat arbitrary length for these scenarios but in reality, the length of each day's march would have been determined by the practicality of splitting the column and the availability of good camping locations. Yet one of the benefits of the DM111 scenarios is that we have an explicit model against which people can compare their own ideas and models. Our hypothetical army travels its hypothetical route in one particular way so that there are values against which other ideas can be compared, rather than to dogmatically declare that this is exactly how the Mantzikert campaign progressed.

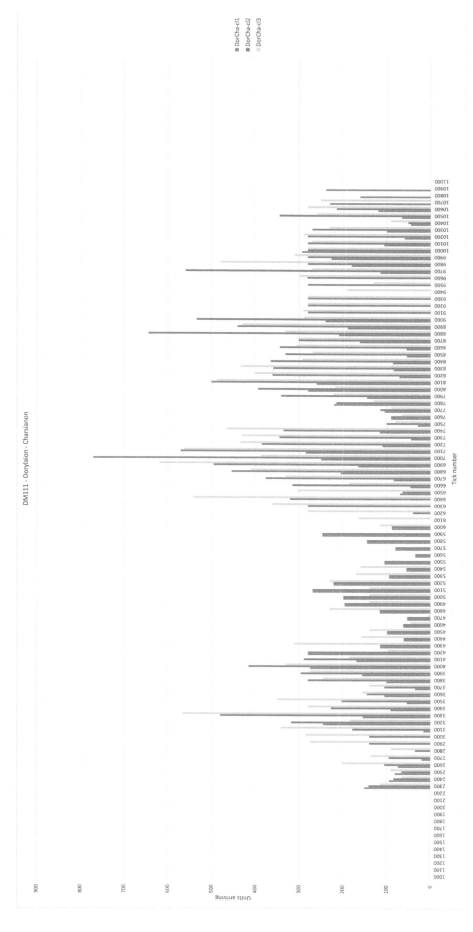

Figure 44: Unit arrival time for march between Dorylaion and Charsianon.

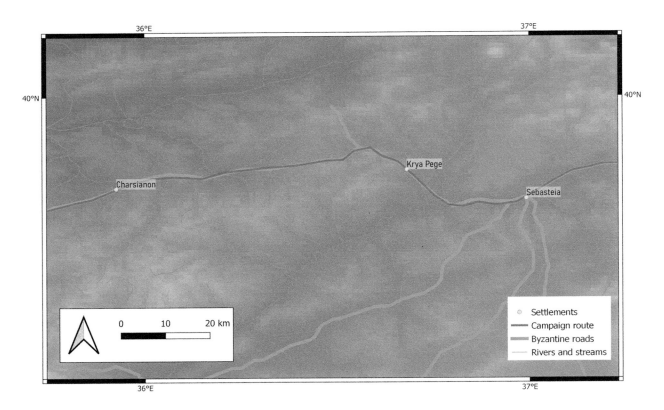

Figure 45: Route map between Charsianon and Sebastea.

Regarding the progress of our hypothetical army, our distance of 576 km between Dorylaion and Charsianon is traversed in marches of 20 km per day, with a day of rest every six days to allow animals to recover. This day of rest, taken on different days by separate halves of the army, facilitates the splitting of a single column into two parts which march the same route on consecutive days. This scheme gives a total travel time of 35 days for the march from Dorylaion to Charsianon. Allowing an extra day for the crossing of the River Halys by bridge and another day for local pleasantries, the next leg commences on day 52, around two thirds of the way through April.

Charsianon to Sebastea

Start – day 52.

By the time the army arrived at Charsianon, around halfway between Nicomedia and Mantzikert, it had climbed a total of over 1km from sea level to the Central Anatolian Plateau. The travel distance between Charsianon and Sebastea is around 106km (Figure 45) however Attaleiates records that the army spent several days at Krya Pege, around two thirds of the way between the two. This stay involved dealing with some badly behaved German mercenaries, but it is uncertain exactly why an extended stay here was required. Maybe this covered the tasks of interacting with the local

notables and introducing the local troops into the army. Our hypothetical army grows by over 5000 troops at Sebastea and it could be that some of these troops were late to arrive, leaving Romanos with the decision to either gather and wait at Sebastea, where other troops had already gathered for an unknown period of time, or wait a little further back up the road at Krya Pege. Attaleiates records that the army stayed long enough at Krya Pege to start to exhaust the resources of the area, a situation we will return to in the DM112 scenarios.

The 74km between Charsianon and Krya Pege, as with the previous leg of the journey, would have been more comfortably accomplished by either two parallel columns or by marching along the same route split over two consecutive days. This journey could have been accomplished in four days if parallel routes were used and five if consecutive days were used to march different halves of the army. If the emperor already knew he would spend some time at Krya Pege then it would not have mattered much either way. There are so many possibilities surrounding how the army marched from Charsianon, how long the army stayed at Krya Pege and how and where the troops from Sebastea were integrated into the army that a cursory treatment cannot hope to do justice to the intricacies, and any attempt to reduce the situation to a single chunk of time is a largely arbitrary exercise. At this point, allocating five days to get the whole of the army from

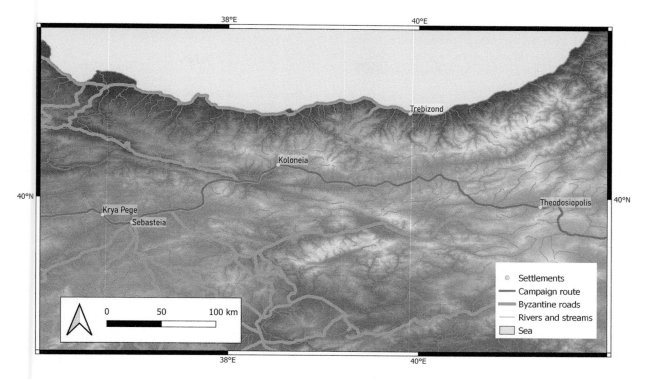

Figure 46: Route map between Sebastea and Theodosiopolis.

Charsianon to Krya Pege in two halves and marching on consecutive days with seven days for the stay at Krya Pege and three days to move the army the 32km to Sebastea and integrate the forces is a plausible decision.

Sebastea to Theodosiopolis

Start – day 66.

At this point, in early May, the simulated army has travelled around 850 km, with another 450 km to go until it reaches Theodosiopolis, yet the days are getting longer and the army has only taken 65 days out of the 122 assigned for this task. It has travelled around two thirds of the distance between Helenopolis and Theodosiopolis in only around half of the time taken by Romanos' army. On the face of it, it looks like our simulated army is comfortably outperforming its historical counterpart, however the army is now nearly 30,000 strong and movement has become more complex.

The terrain between Sebastea and Theodosiopolis rises a total of around 600m, which is not significantly problematic over a distance of around 450 km. It has areas in which the route passes through hilly terrain, and areas which are flatter, more open and more amenable to spreading the army out. Our hypothetical route heads out ENE from Sebastea towards Koloneia before heading eastwards towards Theodosiopolis, although there are other routes by which the army may have travelled between the two towns.

The road to Koloneia would be roughly 150km on the ground, with the journey between Koloneia and Theodosiopolis around twice as long. At this point, progress would have depended heavily upon the terrain and the road network, with any opportunity to split the army likely to aid progress. To what extent this could have assisted the progress of the army is the focus of the simulation of the route between Sebastea and Theodosiopolis.

The simulated army from Sebastea to Theodosiopolis numbers 10,500 cavalry, 16,500 infantry and 490 mounted officials. The difference between the distance that is able to be covered by the entire army and that able to be covered by half the army may be a significant factor in the decision-making of the emperor and his staff. This section of the march is represented by five simulated day's marches. Half the simulated army, comprising 5,250 cavalry, 8,250 infantry and 245 officials, were marched to three locations along the largely flat road out of Sebastea, eastwards and slightly north. As this road largely follows a route which travels a distance north that is 25% of the distance east, the three destination points are chosen for ease of calculation, giving march distances of 10,308m (10km east, 2.5km north), 15,462m (15km east, 3.75km north) & 20,616m (20km east, 5km north). At this point, the simulated day is 13,532 ticks long. These three marches were also attempted with the full army although the failure to complete the day's march were so pronounced in the shortest two scenarios that the longest march was not even attempted.

Table 29: Arrival data for half the army - Sebastea to Theodosiopolis

	10km east	15km east	20km east
Average arrival time (tick)	7416	8509	9643
Average distance covered (m)	11555.22	17687.12	24162.35
Average arrival time (Officers only)	6468	7454	8494
Last arrival tick	11378	12685	13532
Squads	1940	1940	1940
Agents	13826	13826	13826
Column Leaders	1	1	1
Cavalry Officers	1115	1115	1115
Infantry Officers	825	825	825
Cavalry Soldiers	4460	4460	4460
Infantry Soldiers	7425	7425	7425
Average kilocalories expended	651	973	1420
Average travel time (ticks)	1810	2797	3837
Agents still in transit	0	0	1719
Agents not set off	0	0	0

Half the simulated army performed well, with a total of 13,826 agents easily travelling the two shorter distances in the daylight allowed and the majority of them arriving before sunset in the longest march (Table 29). Noting the actual distances travelled, there is an element of inefficiency in the way the route out of and into camp is calculated which inflated the distance beyond the shortest distance between two points. In order to travel 20km east and 5km north the average agent travels almost 25km. In these conditions it is not far fetched to claim that a 20km march in an efficient and organised manner by this force would be practical.

Table 30: Arrival data for the full army - Sebastea to Theodosiopolis

	10km east	15km east
Average arrival time (tick)	7238	7662
Average distance covered (m)	7743.59	10743.35
Average arrival time (Officers only)	8303	8919
Last arrival tick	13532	13532
Squads	3872	3872
Agents	27611	27611
Column Leaders	1	1
Cavalry Officers	2222	2222
Infantry Officers	1650	1650
Cavalry Soldiers	8888	8888
Infantry Soldiers	14850	14850
Average kilocalories expended	559	758
Average travel time	1487	2104
Agents still in transit	5410	9321
Agents not set off	6480	6480

The situation is very different for an army twice the size (Table 30), with the '10km east' march resulting in 11,890 agents not having arrived in time with 6480 of those not even having set off. This could be offset by splitting the army into columns, which should be possible for a lot of the route between Sebastea and Theodosiopolis, although there are stretches in which the route travels through more mountainous areas in which multiple parallel columns may not be practical.

The simulated army needs to travel 450km in 56 days, which, if one day in seven is taken as a rest day to allow horses and other animals to recuperate, leaves 48 days for the simulated army to reach Theodosiopolis at around the same time as the real army. This is clearly achievable if the army splits into two parts, either along entirely separate routes or along the same route on subsequent days, however it is very unlikely if the army travels in a single column. Bearing in mind that these scenarios model an army without baggage requirements or unexpected delays it seems clear that the entire simulated army cannot travel over a single route in a single day and still match the historical army's performance.

The possibilities, though, are almost endless, with an enormous parameter space encompassing different routes, organisational schemes and possible events along the way. Yet at least this modelling gives a base upon which to discuss the options. If the army splits into two separate routes it would arrive at Theodosiopolis early, but one half would need to wait there for the other to catch up.

Theodosiopolis also presents us with the problematic assertion by Attaleiates that the emperor commanded the soldiers to supply themselves with 'provisions for two months'.[536] Did the area of Theodosiopolis contain this quantity of resources, considering that it was an area subject to Seljuk raids over recent years? Are we to interpret Attaleiates' words as an order for each soldier to carry two months' food for himself? The evidence from both Engels and the Victorian military literature argues against this. Attaleiates also mentions siege equipment carried on almost a thousand wagons and herds of animals, which could also double as meat on the hoof if required. Neither of these constituents of the army's marching column are mentioned before and it is tempting to think that their introduction occurred at Theodosiopolis, but is this plausible?

One explanation is that the siege machinery had travelled with the army all the way from Constantinople, possibly a number of days behind the army due to the disruptive effect that so many wagons would have on the main column. The meat on the hoof could have also been a regular component of the support train, fluctuating in size as the army progressed along the route. Another explanation is that the siege machinery came from Trebizond, with the meat on the hoof also provided at Trebizond, Theodosiopolis and places in between. Although the march from Trebizond to Theodosiopolis is 260 km, mostly uphill, siege machinery could have been transported by sea to Trebizond, leaving the wagon transportation to Theodosiopolis to take place independently of the march of the main army. The meat on the hoof could theoretically have been gathered from the Theodosiopolis region, although this will be discussed during the DM112 scenarios.

Theodosiopolis to Mantzikert

Start – day 123.

Due to the army's presence in Theodosiopolis in late June being a fixed historical point, our simulated army now knows that it needs to reach Mantzikert in 56

days, the same amount of time it had to travel around 450km from Sebastea to Theodosiopolis. On this leg of the journey, however, the route is approximately 180km (Figure 47). It is uncertain whether the time spent at Theodosiopolis should be taken from this leg of the journey or the previous one, so the 56 days could be much less if the army spent a considerable time at Theodosiopolis. Nevertheless, it is likely that the pace of the army was much slower between Theodosiopolis and Mantzikert. This should come as no surprise. From Theodosiopolis, the simulated army is at its largest with 11,250 cavalry, 20,750 infantry and 540 officials, until it splits into two at the point at which some units are sent off to Khliat. If this army was split across multiple routes or on separate days it would arrive at Mantzikert long before August 26th, especially as the army was around half the size for the latter part of the march. There are still many reasons for progress to be slower, however. The army was approaching the enemy and therefore would have moved cautiously in comparison to the more relaxed movement in friendlier territory. Romanos might not have known that Alp Arslan was in the area with a sizeable army, but he would have expected a Turkish presence in the fortress of Mantzikert. The army would have had a larger quantity of supplies and a wagon train of siege machinery to cope with, and the proximity of the enemy may have necessitated a marching column which contained these units in the protected middle rather than at the vulnerable rear. Some of the supplies gathered in Theodosiopolis would have taken the form of meat on the hoof, which would have contributed its own particular problems to movement.

Any army beyond a certain size encounters a problem which was seen in the simulated march from Sebastea. The scheme which determines how often a unit sets off has a maximum number of units which may leave camp during the daytime. If, for example, one unit sets off per 10 seconds and there are 12 hours in the simulated day then only 4320 units will ever set off in that day, regardless of how short or easy the subsequent march is.

Measures which would have mitigated this problem include splitting the army into different parallel columns, shortening the gap between units setting off, lengthening the marching day by setting off before sunrise and/or clustering smaller units into a smaller number of larger units. In this respect, the model points to a real world problem, but has limited power to explain which options may have been pursued. One solution would have been to treat the two parts of the army, the one which went on to Mantzikert and the one which veered off towards Khliat and played no part in the battle, as discrete forces, with one marching a day behind the other. That way they could both march in a

---

[536] Attaleiates 2012, 277

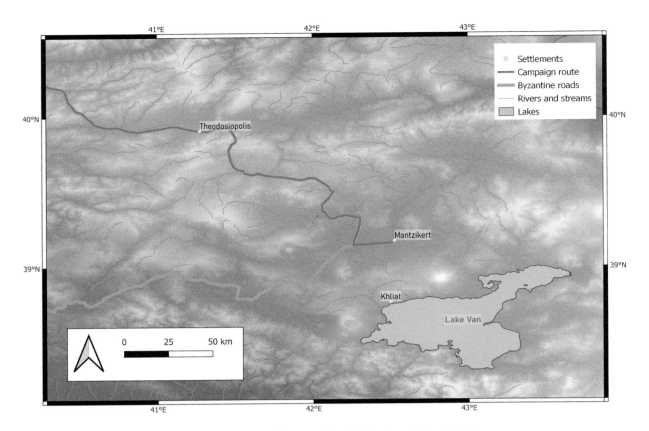

Figure 47: Route map between Theodosiopolis and Mantzikert.

manner which left them less vulnerable to attack, with their baggage within the line of march, and avoiding the problems associated with marching the whole army as a single block. It would also make splitting the forces easier on the road, as the separation of equipment and food would have been done before setting off from Theodosiopolis. This simple expedient would make the march of the armed forces from Theodosiopolis to Mantzikert in the manner which we have simulated the DM111 scenarios, easily achievable within 56 days.

Yet the addition of extra supplies and siege equipment was likely to be the biggest factor in the progress of the army on this leg of the journey. As the supply situation is likely to be a problem which cannot be simply punted to the rear of the column, it will be dealt with in the DM112 scenarios. With such a large army, relatively small changes in organisation and numbers of days for which supplies are transported can have significant effects.

Conclusions

The simulated army marched across Anatolia, albeit via a relatively small number of sample day's marches. We can draw several conclusions from simulating this best-case scenario involving an army moving without a baggage train.

The variables vary too much, and the constants are not constant enough

The possible combinations of circumstances surrounding the march of an army across Anatolia are almost infinite, and careful contextualisation is required to be able to make sense of the results. From an early point in the march, the increasing number of possible permutations renders the progress of our simulated army increasingly uncertain. Keeping track of the number of days since the start of the campaign becomes difficult as decisions made regarding the organisation of the army in the earlier stages would have had a knock-on effect on the later progress of the army. Fixed points such as Theodosiopolis help add some degree of certainty to the comparison between the simulated army and the historical campaign. Nevertheless, this exercise has emphasised the role of simulation as a sandbox of hypotheses as opposed to a recreation of a historical event. Distilling the DM111 scenarios down to a final result regarding the progress of the army is less useful, and less interesting, than reflecting on how the scenarios do and do not relate to the historical event.

Some form of method beyond just marching the whole army in a group is required if the army size and route are accurate

This is a big 'if', but if an army of the size of our hypothetical army travelled the route which we have suggested in the same time as the historical accounts record, it cannot have moved as a single mass along a single route in a single column. The progress of the army becomes too slow if that is the only method of organisation used throughout the whole route. The fact that a single column may have been required beyond Theodosiopolis is one possible explanation for the army making significantly slower progress at that point of the route. The alternatives to marching in a single column on a single day are plausible, effective and are highly likely to have been used at certain points during the Mantzikert campaign. We cannot prove that the Byzantine army did march across separate routes, or along the same route on different days, but we have demonstrated that it is such an effective aid to movement that its utility cannot have escaped the notice of an experienced campaigner like Romanos.

The notion of the army moving along a certain route or arriving at a certain time may hide a lot of detail

Byzantine historical accounts are terse when it comes to the movement of the army, in a manner common to many other pre-modern sources. In actual fact, when not clustered together for the purpose of security, the army was likely to be a sprawling beast using multiple routes, consisting of straggling columns, and resulting in disruption to the communication routes of many of the communities through which it travelled. When Attaleiates refers to the progress of the army it is likely he is referring to himself, the emperor and his household. The location of the majority of the baggage or some segments of the army are likely to be pieces of information that were not regarded as important enough to note. A bias towards the upper echelons of the army is liable to be transmitted to modern historians, making the development of a computer model through which our assumptions can be tested an important step in getting at the detail behind the written accounts. 'The Byzantine army' as a single coherent spatial entity is likely to become more relevant as it approaches Mantzikert, and possible contact with the enemy, but it is likely to represent something much more distributed and diffuse in earlier sections of the march.

Our simulated army has made it to Mantzikert

This test of both the model and our assumptions which factored into its design resulted in a simulated army which could travel across Anatolia to Mantzikert in, or under, the time taken by the historical army. This certainly does not make the model a recreation of the army that marched to Mantzikert, we know that it is not. It lacks many things, including a baggage train, the disruption caused by the digging of a camp each night, delays caused by broken equipment, sick or lame troops, illness of horses and baggage animals and any consideration of the agency of the emperor, on whose whim the army moved, or did not. Nevertheless, it demonstrates that the gaps between the performance of the simulated army and that of the real army are not catastrophic. This in itself tells us something about this best-case model. If organisational help is required to move a simulated army across Anatolia, how much more must the real army have relied upon experienced generals, quartermasters, officials and a comprehensible set of procedures that were able to be communicated to the heterogenous troops of the Byzantine army. It also draws an explicit line in the sand, framing debate about the campaign. Anyone disputing any aspect of the simulated army, and there is much to dispute, now has a solid example against which to argue. If our simulated army is deemed too large, or too small, by others then we hope we have at least given enough information to start to examine the implications of any suggested changes. Simulation has begun the process of situating the march in a world of complex interrelationships in which altering one aspect affects multiple other systems, rather than one in which statements may be made with no reference to how they would affect other parts of the Byzantine world.

DM112 – Supply systems

So, our simulated army made it to Mantzikert, but without supply requirements or baggage handling capabilities, and its progress has raised a number of questions which can be addressed by further models. One of the strongest conclusions from the DM111 scenarios is that the many possibilities surrounding the logistics of the march to Mantzikert create a parameter space that is much too large to explore thoroughly. The number of simulations required to cover all possible army sizes, travel routes, organisational schemes and supply systems would be colossal. Running them would take huge amounts of computing resources and, absent AI assistance, analysing the results would take an age. We can, however, select certain aspects of the march and produce focussed scenarios which may help provide a new perspective on specific problems.

We have split the DM112 models into three separate research questions:

- How would a three-tier system of baggage transportation (squad, unit and army level capacity) affect the progress of the army?

Table 31: Quantities and organisation of mules in the DM112 system

Days worth of food	Total mules	Mules with squads	Total mule squads with units	Mule squads per unit	Mule squads in rear baggage train
1	2540	1250	125	25	132
10	7140	1250	580	116	584
20	20590	1250	1905	381	1913

- How long would it have taken the army to deplete the resources around Krya Pege?
- How would an army with excess supplies and a siege train have moved between Theodosiopolis and Mantzikert?

Answering these questions has implications beyond the specific circumstances we are modelling. From here we can start to explore more innovative ways of supplying the army, taken from the Victorian literature, along with more flexible ways of transporting goods and we can start to look at the impact of the army as it passes through each settlement along the way.

How would a three-tier system of baggage transportation affect the progress of the army?

Splitting the baggage handling capacity of the army between the squad, unit and army level seems to make sense in that it ensures frequently accessed equipment is conveniently located yet enables the bulk of the army's needs to travel away from the main body of men. However, this comes at the cost of inserting more baggage animals within the column of march itself. As previously detailed, this approach is endorsed in the Victorian military literature. Furse draws a distinction between 'absolutely indispensable' and 'occasionally required' equipment and recommends that occasionally required items travel a 'short day's march' behind, citing the Prussian and German armies of 1866 and 1870-71 as users of this particular method.[537] He also states that 'the conclusion I have formed is that the Turkish system of attaching one pack horse for the special purpose of carrying the implements attached to each company, is that which is most likely to be useful in modern war'.[538]

In order to assess the effects of the three-tier baggage system, this section of the DM112 scenarios reruns the DM107 scenarios in which 10,001 agents travel 10km with enough mules to carry food for 1, 10 and 20 days. In these scenarios, the number of baggage animals was

split into three sections. Each squad had a single mule to carry commonly required items. The remaining mules were split into two, with 50% forming the mules travelling with the units and 50% with the baggage train at the rear of the column. For the purposes of this simulation, each section of the camp was treated as a separate unit so there were five unit baggage trains. The number of mule squads per unit was allocated equally, with any remainder placed in the baggage train. The total number of mules differed to those in scenario DM107 because a muleteer was considered not required for the mules attached to squads so the food required for that muleteer was subtracted from the total. Muleteers (referred to by the more general term 'baggage handler' in the MWGrid ABM, covering the handlers of all transport animals) were still attached to mule units within the unit and army baggage trains. We refer to the system of baggage organisation in which all goods are carried in a single train of mules behind the army as the DM107 system and the tripartite organisational scheme recommended by Furse as the DM112 system.

Enough food for 1 day

Table 32: DM112 and DM107 aggregate stats with enough food for 1 day

	DM107	DM112
Average arrival time	6536.51	5891.59
Average distance covered	10453.07	10339.56
Average arrival time (Officers only)	4809.45	4943.55
Last arrival tick	10967	10154
Squads	1250	1250
Agents	13049	12793
Column Leaders	1	1
Cavalry Officers	500	500
Infantry Officers	750	750
Cavalry Soldiers	2000	2000

---
[537] Furse 1882, 30
[538] Furse 1882, 75

	DM107	DM112
Infantry Soldiers	6750	6750
Mules	2540	2535
Donkeys	0	0
Horses	0	0
Camels	0	0
Carts	0	0
Baggage Handlers	508	257
Average calories expended	444.53	430.50
Average travel time	2103.35	1979.32
Agents still in transit	0	0
Agents not set off	0	0

As can be seen from the arrival graph and the accompanying table (Figure 48, Table 32), there was only a small difference in the number of mules between the two scenarios. Using the movement scheme of DM107, with all baggage being carried by mules in a train which travels behind the cavalry and infantry, 2540 mules were required to carry the food for the entire army's animals and men. Using a tripartite organisation of the baggage, with each squad having its own mule, without muleteer, and each army section having its own baggage train, and a further train travelling behind the whole army, 2535 mules were required. The five fewer mules is accounted for by the slight reduction in food required due to the lower number of muleteers (257, which is 251 fewer than the 508 required in the DM107 system). The average arrival tick was a little lower for all agents when using the DM112 system, though it was a little higher for officers only. This is a technical issue within the simulation software, resulting from the baggage handlers not counting as officers. Having baggage animals in the main body of the army slowed down the average arrival of the army squads a little but the smaller baggage train at the rear meant that the army as a whole arrived earlier using the DM112 system. The difference, however, was not great; only 813 ticks, which is just over 50 minutes on a march taking around 11.5 hours.

Enough food for 10 days

Table 33: DM112 and DM107 aggregate stats with enough food for 10 days

	DM107	DM112
Average arrival time	5493.93	5151.53
Average distance covered	11737.01	11486.20
Average arrival time (Officers only)	3594.97	3915.71
Last arrival tick	9531	9268
Squads	1250	1250
Agents	18569	18235
Column Leaders	1	1
Cavalry Officers	500	500
Infantry Officers	750	750
Cavalry Soldiers	2000	2000
Infantry Soldiers	6750	6750
Mules	7140	7070
Donkeys	0	0
Horses	0	0
Camels	0	0
Carts	0	0
Baggage Handlers	1428	1164
Average calories expended	506.18	489.41
Average travel time	2572.73	2515.57
Agents still in transit	0	0
Agents not set off	0	0

When the baggage handling capacity of the army was increased to carry enough food for 10 days, the effects were slightly pronounced (Table 33, Figure 49). Here the army had been split into two columns to ensure it finishes the march within a day. Again, the average arrival tick of an agent was reduced in the DM112 system, as was the arrival tick of the last agent. Here the difference was reduced due to the earlier arrival overall, caused by splitting the army into two forces. The extra mules in the DM107 system, caused by the higher number of baggage handlers, had risen to 70 but this imposed no significant extra strain on the army's movement. In these scenarios, the DM112 army arrived 263 ticks earlier, which is just over 15 minutes on a total march time of just less than 10 hours.

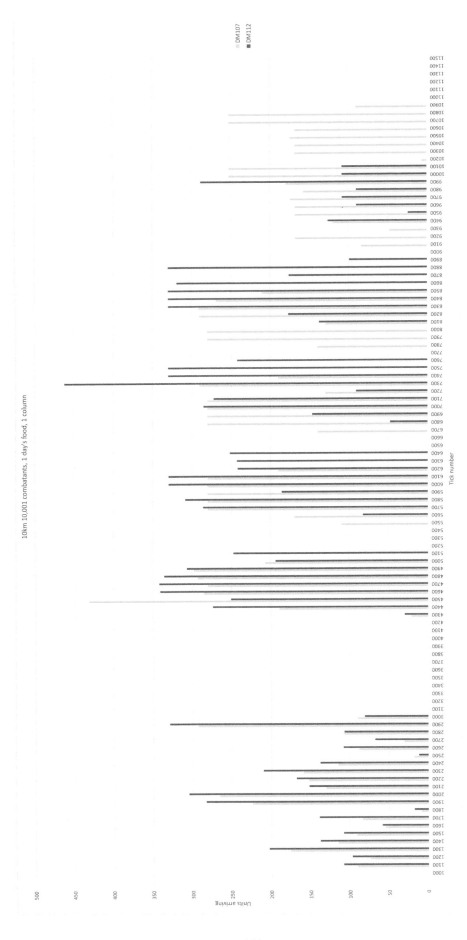

Figure 48: Comparison of arrival times between DM107 & DM112 baggage setup with food for 1 day.

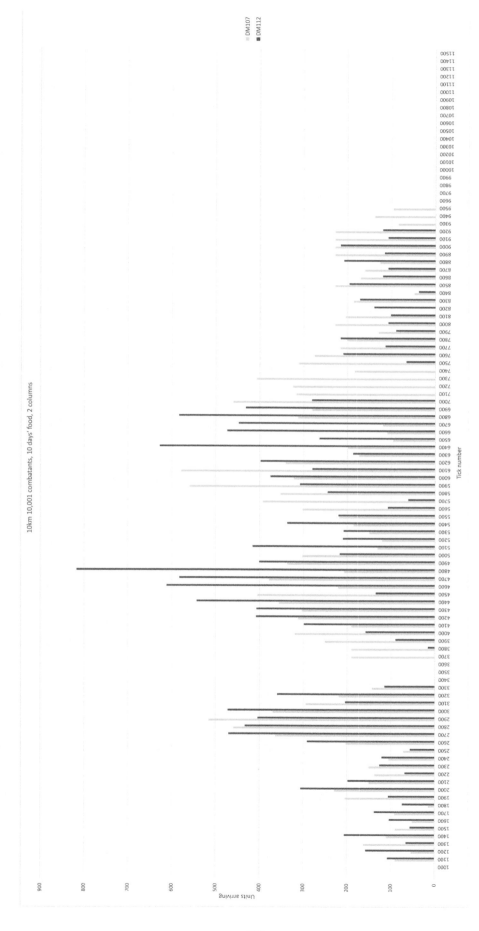

Figure 49: Comparison of arrival times between DM107 & DM112 baggage setup with food for 10 days.

Figure 50: Comparison of arrival times between DM107 & DM112 baggage setup with food for 20 days.

Enough food for 20 days

Table 34: DM112 and DM107 aggregate stats with enough food for 20 days

	DM107	DM112
Average arrival time	6322.73	5700.48
Average distance covered	11971.03	11992.15
Average arrival time (Officers only)	2978.78	3483.81
Last arrival tick	11586	9114
Squads	1250	1250
Agents	34709	32131
Column Leaders	1	1
Cavalry Officers	500	500
Infantry Officers	750	750
Cavalry Soldiers	2000	2000
Infantry Soldiers	6750	6750
Mules	20590	18650
Donkeys	0	0
Horses	0	0
Camels	0	0
Carts	0	0
Baggage Handlers	4118	3480
Average calories expended	526.17	523.08
Average travel time	2772.41	2853.99
Agents still in transit	833	0
Agents not set off	0	0

When the army was asked to carry enough food for 20 days (Figure 50, Table 34), a couple of interlinked factors caused more problems for the DM107 system. The mules carried more food for themselves and therefore had less spare capacity for the food of others. The effects of this were dealt with in the DM107 scenarios, so we will highlight the differences caused by the smaller number of baggage handlers in the DM112 system. There are 1,940 fewer mules and 638 fewer baggage handlers in the DM112 system. With the army split across three columns, there were still 833 agents in transit at the end of the day with the DM107 system, whereas the army using the DM112 system had all arrived with around

two and a half hours of the day to spare. The pattern in which the whole army arriving earlier but the actual infantry and cavalry squads arriving later in the DM112 system still held.

As we can see, a tripartite system of baggage organisation within the simulation has pros and cons which may map onto real world situations. It could lead to a slight reduction in the number of mules and baggage handlers if these roles are taken on by the squads which have a mule attached. It also ensures that frequently needed goods are more accessible than they would be if all goods are carried by a train at the rear of the army. It could also really make a difference on the army's progress if large distances were to be covered without resupply. It is likely to lead to the combat portions of the army having, on average, a later arrival in camp, however. This was the case in a model which does not account for delays caused by either baggage animals or their handlers, loads or equipment. If so, the real world effect is likely to have been even greater.

Of course, the emperor would have had his own requirements for baggage handling and these would have been distinct from those of the rest of the army. The more important members of the army's hierarchy would also have travelled with more significant amounts of equipment, albeit much less than the emperor. How the emperor's baggage was ordered is a matter for speculation, although Constantine VII Porphyrogenitus provides a data point with his record of the Imperial household requirements, these totalling 1086 mules and 30 saddled horses.[539] If we take this at face value, the requirements for muleteers alone would have added another 220 or so non-combatants to the army, beyond the emperor's possibly extensive requirements for servants. It would not be unrealistic to add the equivalent of 225 mule squads and 10 cavalry squads to the army list to cope with the emperor's need for a lavish lifestyle on the march.

When adding this to the requirements for the DM107 scenario of an army of 10,001 agents marching 10km in 1 column, we see that the increase in mules and baggage handlers caused a single column to finish the day with some units yet to arrive (Table 35, Figure 51). The main difference within the simulation lies in the fact that the emperor's baggage train, positioned between the central section of cavalry and the following units of infantry, travels slowly enough to end up at the head of the main body of the army rather than the tail of the vanguard. How this would have worked in practice is uncertain. Did the leading units travel no faster than the emperor's baggage to ensure that the emperor had access to his equipment at all times? Was the emperor's baggage spread across enough animals to ensure that

---

[539] Constantine Porphyrogenitus 1990, 101–121

in travelled faster than the usual baggage units? The questions are many, and it would take many more scenarios to properly explore the parameter space. One thing that is demonstrated is that whilst the emperor's baggage train served the needs of the emperor, it generated potential problems to the units held up behind it, and also to the baggage units at the very rear of the column who may not reach camp before sunset. The extent to which these problems would have influenced the emperor's decision making is left to the reader.

Table 35: Aggregate data from two scenarios: 'NoEmp' without the emperor's baggage train and 'Emp' with.

	NoEmp	Emp
Average arrival time	6530.91	7002.35
Average distance covered	10436.69	10568.18
Average arrival time (Officers only)	4804.47	5316.20
Last arrival tick	10991	11586
Squads	1250	1260
Agents	13049	14449
Column Leaders	1	1
Cavalry Officers	500	510
Infantry Officers	750	750
Cavalry Soldiers	2000	2040
Infantry Soldiers	6750	6750
Mules	2540	3665
Donkeys	0	0
Horses	0	0
Camels	0	0
Carts	0	0
Baggage Handlers	508	733
Average kilocalories expended	443.68	452.25
Average travel time	2095.87	2239.06
Agents still in transit	0	510
Agents not set off	0	0

How long would it have taken the army to deplete the resources around Krya Pege?

Attaleiates records that the army on the Mantzikert campaign stayed at Krya Pege long enough to start to exhaust the resources available in the area. Although vague, this piece of historical information provides us with a fixed point against which we can design models. The variables in this case include the size and composition of the army, the size of the local population, the agricultural productivity of the landscape and the amount of surplus food which was available to be stored. The amount of surplus food itself would be dependent on a number of variables including storage infrastructure, recent weather and the demands placed on the area by previous military campaigns. Therefore, the variables are too numerous and too variable to permit a firm statement approaching 'the army on the Mantzikert campaign stayed at Krya Pege for X days', whichever value we could assign to X. Nevertheless, we have no reason to doubt the one piece of information we do have, that the army stayed until it exhausted the local resources.

It is unclear which resources are being referred to. These could have been clean water, animal fodder, human food, firewood, some other unknown essential or any combination of the above. It is also unclear how the resource situation was affected by the proximity of Krya Pege to Sebastea, which was only 32km away by road. As our hypothetical army gained troops at Sebastea, the total number of troops requiring supplies in the Sebastea/Krya Pege area in our simulation is 9,500 cavalry, 11,500 infantry and 430 mounted officials. Without baggage handling capacity, this gives a total of 20,430 humans and 9,930 horses, which at 1.3kg for humans and 2.5kg for horses gives a daily requirement for 26,559kg of human food and 24,825kg of animal fodder. Of course, this picture would be complicated by the potential availability of grazing land for the horses. If horses are not being worked and have good grazing, they need far less supplementary food, and in some cases none at all. Other sources of uncertainty include the populations ordinarily supported by both Sebastea and Krya Pege, the amount of grazing land and firewood available in the area and the ability of the inhabitants of the area to accumulate food surplus during the previous years. Food availability would also have been affected by the types of food grown in the area and the time of year, with availability fluctuating with harvest times and the performance of the storage techniques used to preserve food.

The fact that Sebastea and Krya Pege are relatively close, and that the army was apparently static for some period of time results in this being a situation which may benefit from a supply arrangement most closely

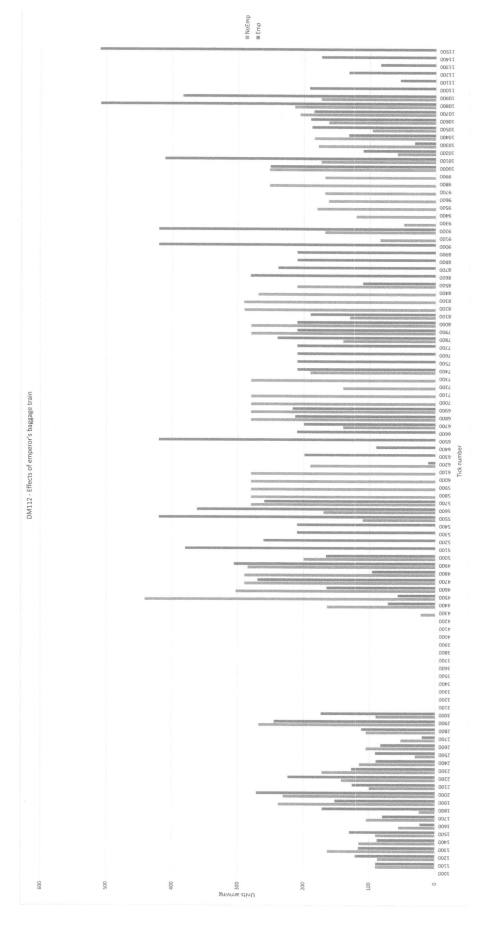

Figure 51: Arrival times of units with (blue) and without (orange) the emperor's baggage train.

resembling the staging system of transport between depots described by Furse and Sharpe.[540] Furse describes a staging system in which a string of depots is set up and pack animals or wagons shuttle supplies between the depots as 'a system which will always be found to be the most expeditious and economical'.[541] The use of depots can be omitted from this system, or at least be replaced in function by the settlements of Charsianon and Sebastea, with baggage trains which cover different sections of the route meeting up and transferring goods between them.[542] The staging system is claimed to have multiple benefits over a single baggage train that followed an army all the way through from the start of the march to the finish. The animals and handlers work the same sections of the route each day and therefore would be familiar with the conditions. They could have been based at home providing the route was nearby, and therefore be able to supply their own food and shelter. The animals would spend half their time unladen as they return to the start of their route to pick up goods and therefore would be more rested compared to animals following the army, which may be laden on all or most days. This system would also remove some of the need for repair workers to travel with the army as they could remain in place and have broken wagons, harnesses and equipment brought to them.[543]

The 32km between Krya Pege and Sebastea could be a day's march for a small, well organised transport unit. The 74km between Charsianon and Krya Pege could be done in two days by a similar group. Split into two by a staging system, the army could be supplied at Krya Pege by three groups of transport units: one travelling between Krya Pege and Sebastea every day, one covering half the journey from Krya Pege back to Charsianon and the other working out from Charsianon and meeting the other unit halfway. This would allow the whole stretch between Charsianon and Krya Pege to be supplied from local transportation, removing the need for the army to provide these animals and their handlers themselves. With this setup, each journey would have to carry two day's worth of supplies, as resupply would be every other day. The requirements can be further reduced by splitting the transportation requirements into six, with each unit travelling out half a day, picking up some goods, and returning in the second half of the day.

Using the values from the DM107 scenarios, each mule in the staging system would be able to carry its full capacity (91.kg, minus 19.5kg for a pack saddle) each day, rather than a reduced amount which takes into account the food requirements of itself and its muleteer.

The benefits of the staging system also include the fact that the route between Charsianon and Sebastea was a 7-8 day journey as part of our hypothetical Mantzikert army yet would involve only three days of travel for the smaller mule trains used in a staging system, meaning that each mule could use the roughly 16kg-18kg of capacity that it would need for carrying its own food to carry food for the army. An army of 9500 cavalry, 11,500 infantry and 430 mounted officials would need 6460 mules to carry seven days of food from Charsianon to Sebastea in one trip, yet the same food requirements could be serviced by 5031 mules in six teams, working from Charsianon, Krya Pege, Sebastea and a point roughly halfway between Charsianon and Krya Pege. This is a saving of 1429 mules, which rises to 1946 if eight days of food would have been required from Charsianon to Sebastea.

The availability of food and other resources would have, as previously mentioned, depended on other factors, the investigation of which may lead to interesting areas of further study. Our simulated army arrives in the area in late April/early May. If this was the case on the Mantzikert campaign, what implications would this have for resource availability? If not, what real life factors caused the difference in the arrival date? Could the real-world army have significantly outperformed the simulated army? If not, and the army arrived at Krya Pege later, what implications would this have for the later sections of the march?

A 1920 British Foreign Office publication on Armenia and Kurdistan, which covers the area around Sebastea, lists the Sivas *vilayet* (an Ottoman province, Sivas being the Turkish name for Sebastea) as possessing 18,000 square miles of arable land and 11,000 square miles of 'mountains, barren lands, forest and pasture'. The same publication lists the area around the town of Sivas as being the source of a particularly valuable variety of wheat, and speculates that the agricultural potential of the arable land in Eastern Anatolia was constricted more by its transport links than the ability to grow cereals.[544] It also lists wine as a local product, along with fruit and Lucerne, a plant used for livestock fodder. Other areas, including Erzurum (the Turkish name for Theodosiopolis) to the east, were more prominent in livestock raising, implying that cereals were the staple food product around Sebastea, although sheep tax receipts were high for the province.[545] If we take these conditions to be indicative of the area in 1071, we might surmise that there was plenty of wheat and fodder to be had around Sebastea. If this was the case, the most significant factors would then become the local demography, the climate and the time of year.

[540] Sharpe 1905, 59
[541] Furse 1882, 22
[542] Furse 1882, 32
[543] Furse 1882, 33

[544] Prothero 1920, 47
[545] Prothero 1920, 82

Demography – In examining the amount and nature of resources likely to have been available in the area around Krya Pege, it would be useful if we could make some assessment of how many people the area supported under normal circumstances. Population estimates of ancient lands, settlements and empires are problematic, however, and come with large error bars. Angeliki Laiou gives a thorough summary of past work in her chapter on the human resources available to the Byzantine economy.[546] While we might expect estimates of the number of inhabitants of the empire as a whole to be based on a large element of conjecture, even smaller areas such as the population of a town or city also involve large amounts of uncertainty. In the area around Krya Pege there were three main settlements, Charsianon, Sebastea and Krya Pege itself. Compounding the uncertainty is the unknown ratio of the rural population to that living in towns, which is likely to be comparably large, compared to modern, urban, settlement patterns. Estimates for small urban settlements tend towards the very low tens of thousands, which would mean that the total population of these towns would be broadly similar to the size of our hypothetical army.

Climate – The year 1071 is within a period known as the Medieval Climate Anomaly, a period from 900 – 1250 in which temperatures were generally as warm as those in the mid-20th century.[547] Its effect during this period was not uniform across all regions though, and the effects on Central and Eastern Anatolia are poorly understood, suffering from a comparative lack of data. Without further research, the unfortunately imprecise 'similar to the mid 20th century' may be the most accurate statement we can make.

Time of year – The British Foreign Office report lists some of the wheat of the area as being sown in September, being protected by the winter snow and making early growth in spring.[548] If this was the case in the time of the Mantzikert campaign then it would present an interesting factor in the provisioning of the army. If grain was available in early May, along with animal fodder in the form of the stalks of the wheat, with another harvest of Spring-sown wheat to come later in the year, then Sebastea may be a hospitable area for the army to stay. Otherwise, a more traditional wheat-growing regime would see the army having to rely on the previous year's stores, as the conventional model of Byzantine cereal production places the wheat harvest in June and July.[549] This would obviously reward the forward planning of military campaigns, as any reliance on the previous year's harvest would be made

more secure if the population knew in advance whether it would need to supply a travelling army.

From the above data we can propose a model of resource availability and consumption for the Byzantine army at Krya Pege. Fresh water is unlikely to be a problem due to the proximity of the cool springs that gave Krya Pege its name. Firewood is more likely to be a concern, with potentially few forests in the area. Yet firewood is a resource which can be stored more easily and with less wastage than most foodstuffs, so considerable stores may have been held in reserve.

If we produce a simple mathematical model we can start to examine some assumptions regarding the stay at Krya Pege. Our DM111 hypothetical army contained over 27,000 people and over 10,000 horses at Sebastea. This sounds like a not unreasonable estimate for the population of Charsianon, Sebastea, their environs and the land in between. This being the case, the food requirements for the area would effectively double while the army is in the area. On the one hand, the area will have been tasked with providing food for the army and would therefore have stores built up specifically for this purpose. On the other hand, these stores may have been partly composed of available surplus, leaving fewer supplies to be drawn upon if the army stays longer than expected. This presents a complex situation in which assumptions regarding one aspect of the puzzle affect our view of the other aspects. On the face of it, an area with a population of around 27,000 should be able to accommodate an extra 27,000 from surplus for a short period without too much problem. One would hope that the area had more than a week's surplus food, so if the army stayed a week then it should have resulted in no critical shortages. If shortages occurred, they can be explained by some plausible hypotheses:

- The army was much larger than supposed.
- The population of the area was smaller than supposed.
- The length of time that the army stayed in Krya Pege was longer than the seven days accounted for in the DM111 scenarios.
- The food gathered for the army was drawn from the pre-existing surplus, giving little margin for an extended stay.

Added to this is the fact that, of the many resources required, only one resource needed to run low to constitute a problem. Maybe food was still abundant but firewood was almost exhausted.

The effects of the army on the economy of the areas through which it passed are likely to have been complex, but one significant change would be an enhanced ability for the inhabitants of an area to turn surplus into cash.

---

[546] Laiou and Morrisson 2007, 46–55
[547] Xoplaki *et al.* 2016
[548] Prothero 1920, 51
[549] Xoplaki *et al.* 2016, 5

This may factor into the conversation regarding the source of the area's provisions for the army. Maybe the plan was always to convert existing surplus into cash, which could be used to procure supplies from areas away from the route of march. The extent of the monetisation of the Byzantine economy is debated, but the passage of the army is likely to have enabled a rural population whose focus was mainly on subsistence to more easily convert excess into money.[550] This then may have inflated regional prices, especially in a situation in which local stocks of food were depleted but local stocks of money were increased. Such a situation would have knock on effects in neighbouring areas upon which the burden of feeding the army fell more lightly and who therefore had a larger surplus of food to sell on.

An explicit, computerised, model regarding this situation is complicated by the sheer number of variables and the large areas of uncertainty. Nevertheless, without a digital simulation this still serves as an example of what Innis termed 'conceptual utility'.[551] By working through the steps required to begin designing a model we have raised many pertinent questions regarding the supply situation around Krya Pege and identified many areas about which we need more data. We do have enough data to state that a staging system of supply, with food ferried between smaller mule teams would have resulted in fewer mules required for the journey between Charsianon and Sebastea, but this has to be fitted into the context of the campaign as a whole. If the army requires enough pack animals to cover other, more problematic areas of travel, then little may be gained by implementing a staging system on this leg of the journey. As is often the case, we cannot use either our agent-based models or the simpler mathematical models to state what did happen as the variables are too numerous and too variable. We can, however, raise interesting new questions.

How would an army with excess supplies and a siege train have moved between Theodosiopolis and Mantzikert?

Everything about siege machines is difficult and hard to understand[552]

The requirements of our hypothetical army changed over the course of the campaign that was modelled in the DM111 scenarios, but the organisational requirements of the army must have been at their highest in the first part of the journey from Theodosiopolis to Mantzikert. The area would have been very sparsely inhabited and have had few resources to collect. Siege machinery would have been required in advance of the anticipated attempt to take the fortress at Mantzikert. The army would have been at its most numerous, at least until the force was despatched to take Khliat. The DM111 scenarios speculated that the splitting of the army may well have occurred at Theodosiopolis for practical purposes, albeit with both forces travelling the same route at different times up to the point that their routes diverged. Attaleiates states that the force sent to Khliat went ahead of that travelling to Mantzikert, and with an army this size it must have travelled on a preceding day.[553] This made the travel of the 180km between Theodosiopolis and Mantzikert within the 56 days time limit in the DM111 scenarios a relatively trivial matter. Yet this did not take account of the full baggage requirements of an army on its way to a potential siege.

The presence of siege machinery implies carts, and it is likely that some carts would have been used before this point anyway, whether as permanent fixtures within the column or as hired local transport along the more amenable stretches of roads. The 10th-century manual on siegecraft, commonly attributed to Heron of Byzantium but actually of unknown authorship, specifies a series of siege machines which may be representative of those taken to Mantzikert. As the majority of the siege machines described by Heron are made predominantly or entirely of wood and are reasonably quick to build, it seems highly likely that any machinery was transported in component form and intended to be assembled on site. The siege machinery described by Heron consist mainly of tortoises, a term which covered a variety of portable shelters designed to protect teams of sappers and engineers whose task is to fill in defensive ditches and undermine the walls using tunneling, fire or both. Towers and ladders are also mentioned to aid in any assault on the walls.

Of the components specified in Heron's manual, the most interesting are the largest timbers, some reaching around 24 *podes* in length (roughly 7.5m)[554] and fresh cattle skins to serve as anti-incendiary protective coverings.[555] Timbers of around 7.5m would be too large to be transported by pack animal and would have either required carts or to be sourced in the area around Mantzikert. The fresh cattle skins required to protect the siege machines from burning substances could be easily obtained if some of the supplies collected in Theodosiopolis consisted of meat on the hoof.

This leaves us with two important variables when constructing a model of the march from Theodosiopolis: the amount of siege machinery and the amount of meat on the hoof to be transported. Attaleiates provides us with some details regarding each in the following section:

---

[550] Harvey 2003, 80
[551] Innis 1972
[552] Sullivan 2000, 27
[553] Attaleiates 2012, 271
[554] Sullivan 2000, 59
[555] Sullivan 2000, 53

As the emperor approached Mantzikert, he ordered a fortified camp and palisade set up in the usual manner with all their equipment someplace nearby. With a select contingent of his army he rode around the city to look for the best place to launch an assault on the walls and move up his siege towers. These had been carefully prepared of huge logs of various kinds of wood and transported on a thousand wagons. Innumerable flocks and herds of animals were also driven along for the use of the army.[556]

Attaleiates does not provide any quantification of the animals but provides a number for the wagons. This number is suspiciously rounded, and may be used to mean 'a large number' rather than a literal thousand wagons, though what the actual number of wagons would be if it was not literally a thousand is uncertain.

By now, of course, we should be familiar with this kind of situation, in which the complex relationships between the variables preclude a simple resolution. The size of the army and the amount of other supplies available affects the amount of meat on the hoof required. The amount of siege machinery is dependent on the nature of Mantzikert's defences and the amount of timber likely to be available in the area surrounding the fortress. It is also dependent on whether the emperor considered an assault on the walls to be likely or not. In the end, no such assault was required as the Seljuk garrison vacated the fortress without a struggle. Whether the Byzantine preparedness for a siege was a factor in their decision is unknown. Therefore, the amount of siege equipment transported in component form from Theodosiopolis is likely to be highly speculative, if we avoid taking Attaleiates' one thousand wagons at face value. The amount of meat on the hoof is also unknown, but can at least be plausibly modelled.

The historical record gives a roughly 56-day period between the army's presence in Theodosiopolis and the Battle of Mantzikert. The work of Engels, our own modelling and the historical accounts from various places give around 20 days as a practical maximum for the amount of food able to be transported by an army, not including meat on the hoof which transports itself. Given that our 56-day period does not necessarily start at the point at which the army set off from Theodosiopolis, we at least have to transport enough food to sustain the half of the army for the length of time it would take to travel the 180km from Mantzikert to Theodosiopolis. We cannot reach a definitive conclusion on the duration of travel and the amount of food required but we can examine some of the possibilities. We modelled the supplies required for the maximum travel time (56 days), a minimal travel time (10km per day plus a rest day every week for the pack and draft animals, which gives a total of 21 days) and

an intermediate duration (38 days). Likewise, there can be no certainty regarding the amount and nature of the siege machinery so. In the absence of a plausible method to create an alternative, we modelled the army with the thousand carts specified in Attaleiates.

In order to create a plausible model of how many animals on the hoof the army would have required, we must find plausible values for how much food can be gained from the types of animals that may have been available to them. This is another area in which the variables are many, including species of animal, condition, nutrition, butchery methods and the amount of time available to make the most of each carcass. Meat such as beef and mutton were attested as being eaten during campaigns of the Roman army in antiquity[557] and these, along with goats, would have been the easiest to transport on the hoof. Pack animals such as horses, mules and donkeys could also be eaten, but these are unlikely to have been high on the list of food preferences for an army that would have assumed a triumphal return from the campaign. The Food and Agriculture Organization of the United Nations has published 'Technical Conversion Factors For Agricultural Commodities', a document detailing, among other things, average weights of animals and yields of meat, offal and fat from them.[558] Taking modern data from Turkey, with the usual caveats regarding how modern data relates to that from the time of Mantzikert, we can compile the following data (Table 36).

Table 36: Average weights of animal products from cattle and sheep

	Average weight of animal (kg)	Average weight of meat (kg)	Average weight of offals (kg)	Average weight of fat (kg)
Cattle	302	151	13	2.5
Sheep	34	15	2	1

In order to generate a simple mathematical model of how many animals could sustain the army then we have used the simple method of counting calories. This requires a calorie requirement (dependant on exercise as shown in the DM108 scenarios) and a calorie per kg amount for each type of edible animal product. The Turkish Food Composition Database gives us average values for the meat of beef and sheep at around 134 kcal/100g. This gives totals for the meat of 202,340 kcal and 20,100 kcal for individual cattle and sheep respectively. The fat and offal can be crudely approximated by using the same value of kcal/100g for the offal and trebling that value for the fat. This gives us

[556] Attaleiates 2012, 275–277

[557] Roth 1999, 28
[558] Sukhatme 1960

Table 37: Meat on the hoof requirements for our simulated army.

Journey time	Officials	Cavalry (squads of 5)	Infantry (squads of 10)	Pack mules (squads of 5)	Siege engine carts	Mule squads for 15 days food	Sheep on the hoof required	or	Cows on the hoof required
21 days	300	1210	1100	225	1000	4855	15,071		1,757
38 days	300	1210	1100	225	1000	4855	57,771		6,735
56 days	300	1210	1100	225	1000	4855	102,983		12,006

final totals of 229,810 kcal and 26,800 kcal for individual cattle and sheep respectively. It should be stressed that these values are crude approximations and entirely fail to capture the complexity of the situation, as the animals themselves will fluctuate in calorie provision as they both travel (burning calories) and eat (taking calories on board) on the march. If we assume a kcal/day requirement of 3000 per person, then each simulated sheep will feed 8.93 people per day and each simulated cattle will feed 76.6 people per day.

For our hypothetical army on the journey from Theodosiopolis to Mantzikert, the troop totals at Theodosiopolis were 540 officials, 11,250 cavalry and 20,750 infantry. Dividing the force into two parts and rounding the officials up a lot (with more wanting to stay with the emperor) and the others up a little, we can assess the supply requirements of a new hypothetical force of 300 officials, 6000 cavalry and 11,000 infantry. To this we added the 225 mule squads and 10 cavalry squads that we used to represent the emperor's train as described by Constantine VII Porphyrogenitus. We also require enough pack animals to carry the army's equipment and other foodstuffs. We assumed there were enough mules to carry the food and fodder for the whole army for 15 days, with any extra being covered by meat on the hoof. This meat on the hoof is fed solely by grazing so has no requirements of its own. We also assume that any food requirements of the draft animals and drivers of the carts would be carried on the carts, along with the siege engine parts. Each official was treated as a squad for equipment purposes to cover their likely higher requirements for personal effects. From this, we produced a series of possible scenarios (Table 37).

As we can see, the fact that cattle take up more space in the column of march is compensated by the fact that fewer animals are required to feed the army in comparison to sheep, and they must have been the preferred choice when available. Hannibal is reputed to have had over 2000 cattle travelling along with a force of 30,000 men in 214 BC,[559] which lines up quite well with the lowest level calculated here, which is designed to

feed a force consisting of 22,430 people. For this reason we only model the army travelling with live cattle, not live sheep. It is clear that if the simulated army makes poor progress with cattle, then switching to sheep will not assist movement. In reality, however, the choice of animal would have been affected by availability in the areas travelled through.

The relationship between individuals and units becomes significant when we count the number of individuals who arrive at the following day's camp by the end of the day. The size of an individual agent and the number of individuals within each unit can affect how we see the progress of the simulated army depending on whether we count individuals or units within our statistics. The individuals of our hypothetical army break down into categories in Table 38.

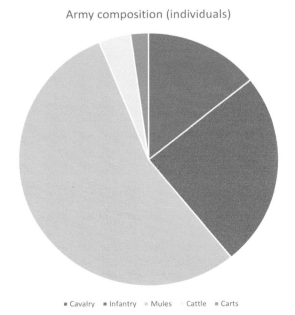

Army composition (individuals)

■ Cavalry ■ Infantry ■ Mules Cattle ■ Carts

Figure 52: Pie chart showing army composition in individuals, with matching colours to Figure 53

---

[559] Roth 1999, 214

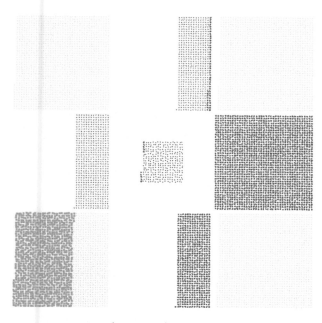

Figure 53: Visualisation of camp layout, with agent types coloured as in Figure 52

Table 38: Number of individuals in DM112 hypothetical army

Type of agent	Number of individuals
Cavalry	6,351
Infantry	11,000
Mules	24,275
Cattle	1,758
Carts	1,000

Comparing the pie chart (Figure 52) with the visualisation of the army (Figure 53) highlights the fact that certain types of agent take up greater space in camp and in the column of march than others.

The difference is particularly noticeable in the comparison between the cavalry and the infantry. There are nearly twice as many infantry as cavalry, yet the cavalry occupy a much greater area. As can be seen from the camp visualisation, the cattle on the hoof occupy a negligible amount of space in the simulation, especially compared to the pack mules. This affects our interpretation of the statistical output of the model. If X agents fail to make it into camp, our interpretation of how successful a particular day's march may have been is affected not only by which value replaces X, but by who X are. In this scenario, the agents largely go in speed order, with the fastest agent types at the front. In this scenario, this means that the order is Cavalry – Infantry – Mules – Cattle – Carts.

But how fast can our hypothetical force move from Theodosiopolis? If it can travel 10km per day then it should be possible to travel between the two settlements in the 21 days. If not, we need to reassess our army, supply regime, route or timings. One obvious tradeoff in the movement of the army between Theodosiopolis and Mantzikert lies in the number of live food animals that are transported. The faster the march, the fewer animals required, but the longer each day's march must be. Marching between the two locations in 21 days requires a rate of around 10km per day, assuming that one day per week is needed to rest animals. Marching in 38 days requires a rate of around 6km on the same basis. Which is most likely?

Within the simulation, the main problem with our hypothetical army at this stage lies in the number of squads. Our smallest army, one with enough supplies for 21 days, contains a total of 8690 squads, plus cattle. To ensure a squad of cattle can fit within a cell, they are split into squads of five, which adds another 362 squads. If each squad set off from camp on the tick after the proceeding squad and was perfectly organised with optimal, robot precision, it would be nine hours after the first squad moves that the last squad will start moving. Then would come the cattle, whose organisation is highly speculative and whose movement may be problematic, but in our five cattle per squad organisation would add another 23 minutes.

Table 39: DM112 squads marching from Theodosiopolis with siege machinery and cattle

	Total squads	Squads in following day's camp at end of day	Squads in transit	Squads not yet set off
21 days' food (10km)	9052	3855	2577	2620
38 days' food (6km)	10711	4513	1865	4333
21 days' food (10km, only carts)	6461	3957	2421	83
38 days' food (6km, only carts)	8120	4585	1761	1774

Given these parameters, our simulated army made the progress highlighted in Table 39.

The cavalry and infantry all make it into camp within the simulated day, with some of the mules and none of the cattle or carts. Splitting the column across two consecutive days would easily solve this problem, though this would require some organisation to ensure that the day's beef supply was within reach. If we switch the mule transport to carts using Xenophon's 646.5kg-load ox carts, we can substitute 2264 carts for our 4855 squads of mules. With simulated armies of this size, it is clear that the biggest barrier to successful marching is ensuring everyone can set off within a day. Although the setup for our ABM has started to map poorly onto the likely organisation of the heterogenous mix of people and animals which make up the army at this point, ensuring all units could leave camp in time to manage a day's march would have been a problem for the real army too. Earlier in the march such situations were solved by marching along parallel routes or on the same route on subsequent days. How confident were the Mantzikert campaign's leaders that the enemy were not a threat at this point? If they were confident that they would not encounter the enemy, it seems likely that the army was split over a couple of days, giving it enough space to march at 10km per day with 21 days' supplies or 6km per day with 38 days' supplies.

If not, we have to look outside our ABM for answers. Does the 3.7285 second tick resolution of the ABM constrain the army and render the setoff timings unrealistic? Could squads have been expected to set off quicker than one tick behind the previous squad? Sometimes this may have happened, but it would take an incredibly well-drilled force to do so with regularity until the camp was emptied. We also have to reiterate that our simulated army is a group in which no carts break down, no pack saddles fail or have to be readjusted, no road blockages are encountered. A less perfect, real-world, army in which these events happened would have had to be of smaller size, be split across two routes or be split across two days. The value of simulation in this case is in providing a documented comparator against which our expectations and hypotheses can be tested. The end result, as here, is usually a different, and hopefully more interesting, set of questions rather than a set of answers.

Chapter 8 – Conclusions

Synthesis of results

At the end of this particular piece of research we have provided a different view of the march towards Mantzikert, based on the contemporary accounts, enhanced by the new data that computer simulation can provide but also incorporating information from 19th-century military writing. The simulations have suggested conclusions of their own, but they have also prompted us to reassess existing data from a fresh perspective. We have some new answers to old questions but we also have a new and interesting set of questions. What, then, does our updated view of the Mantzikert campaign look like?

The Emperor Romanos IV Diogenes will have departed from Constantinople with a force consisting of units stationed in and around the great city. The route will have been planned and officials would have prepared the way well in advance, informing the authorities along the intended route of march of their responsibilities regarding military units, equipment, foodstuffs and transportation. Certain categories of equipment may well have also been transported along with the baggage. The emperor's personal baggage train would have been with the army from the start, although parts of it may well have left the column whenever he did, on the occasions when Attaleiates mentions that he went to inspect his estates.[560] Siege engines, or at least certain critical parts of siege engines, may well also have been brought from Constantinople although there remains a possibility that such heavy items with no practical function on the march could have been taken by ship to Trebizond and transported overland to Theodosiopolis. That the siege equipment travelled separately to the main body of the army on a day-to-day basis seems certain, even if it travelled the same route on succeeding days and caught up with the army at Theodosiopolis. The majority of baggage may also have travelled a day or more behind the army as the movement of the army was problematic enough, without the transport infrastructure adding to congestion. Foodstuffs would probably have been tailored to fill gaps expected further along the route. Commodities such as olive oil and wine would have been cheaper and more plentiful in Constantinople while meat would have been easy to procure throughout the Anatolian plateau. Meat on the hoof was transported from Theodosiopolis but there

are no circumstances before this in which the army could not be fed by more conventional means.

Until the incorporation of the forces gathered at Malagina, the column would largely have consisted of cavalry and baggage, with few enough of each to march in a single column and still cover a reasonable amount of distance each day. From Leukai to Sebastea, a distance of around 950km, the army would probably have been large enough to necessitate splitting the column across different routes. This would definitely have been the case after Sebastea, with no realistic prospect of moving the entire army across a single route on the same day while keeping to the generally accepted timescale of the march. Given that the army is recorded to have taken on a large amount of supplies at Theodosiopolis, an area likely to have been ravaged by Seljuk raids, it is possible that some of the supplies picked up at Theodosiopolis had come from Trebizond and had either made their way there by boat or were intended to be replaced via Black Sea trade.

From Theodosiopolis, and until the army splits to take both Khliat and Mantzikert, the army would have been at its largest, though the split is likely to have happened very early in that journey and maybe even at the start. The baggage train would also have been large considering the supplies picked up at Theodosiopolis. At this point the full army, siege equipment, baggage train and meat on the hoof would have been well beyond what could be moved on a single route in a day, and the army may have passed from relatively safe land to those where the threat of enemy action was possible. Even with half our total hypothetical force, this final leg of the march may have necessitated that the army was split over two subsequent days. It is probably worth returning to one of the original questions raised when formulating the Medieval Warfare on the Grid project in 2006. How large was the Byzantine army at the Battle of Mantzikert? The army simulated in the DM111 scenarios is able to make it to Mantzikert in the time taken by the historical army. The results of our simulation do not render a Byzantine force equal to our simulated army of 17,351 impossible. The mechanisms suggested by the simulations would allow a greater number, whether this is facilitated by moving the army on parallel routes, on subsequent days or with higher levels of discipline and organisation. However, some of these methods are likely to have been practiced for reasons other than that they were essential to enable a sensible end to each day's march. The extent to which

---

[560] Attaleiates 2012, 267

they were used and how they were combined are critical factors in deriving a figure for the size of the Byzantine army that faced the Seljuks.

What the simulations do show is that all the factors governing the movement of a force interact in complex ways. Factors unmodelled, such as the increasing familiarity with marching in column and the daily routine of setting up and breaking camp, would have improved efficiency as the march went on. Disease would have reduced the army size by an unknown amount and equipment failure, such as deteriorating footwear and broken pack saddles, would have created delay. The space, or lack thereof, between the individuals and units in the column would have affected both the number of individuals able to reach the following day's camp and also the column's robustness to delay and blockage. A system in which baggage animals travelled within the column would have slightly reduced the size of the army but added even more potential for delay.

What has been presented during the DM111 scenarios is a narrative version of a possible course of events, however there is something fundamentally disingenuous about presenting the data in this manner. Modelling, and the relationship it has with the events of the past, is uncertain and conditional. We cannot definitively say that the Byzantine army on the march to Mantzikert numbered 10,000, 40,000 or 100,000. We can, however, start to assess probabilities and assign boundaries. We can incorporate quantitative data into our hypotheses, but we can also discuss the implications of competing hypotheses. The utility of modelling has hopefully been demonstrated in this book, but its true potential will only be realised when critics can suggest corrections, refinements and brand-new scenarios that can feed into a second wave of modelling. We have only just started to explore our parameter space, productive areas of which will be much more apparent to others with viewpoints and specialisms different from our own. Hopefully the inherent uncertainty involved with modelling (by now it should be obvious that no single model presented in this work is the 'correct' model) will emphasise the role of modelling as a sandbox for testing ideas as opposed to a magic answer-generating machine.

Advantages over previous work

The quantitative work on pre-modern military logistics which started with Engels provided a valuable, new perspective on how armies moved and were fed. *Alexander the Great and the Logistics of the Macedonian Army* remains a remarkable contribution to the subject and its methods are still useful, as evidenced by their reuse for other campaigns. The ability to calculate the transport requirements of an army with nothing more

technologically advanced than a pencil and paper will ensure that Engels' methods continue to be used, as indeed they are within this work. Nevertheless, they lack the ability to examine the dynamic aspects of an army's march that involve complex behaviours. The models presented in this work have demonstrated the ability to not only calculate how much food an army needs and consequently how many pack animals and wagons are required but also to examine the implications of any changes. They can compare different methods of marching and start to set boundaries on what is possible when moving an army.

The main advantage of using ABM is the ability to generate 'what if?' scenarios that allow the comparison of two different sets of circumstances. Neither may correspond to historical reality but in examining what would happen if changes were made, we can begin to understand the processes involved and identify markers for these processes rather than simply quantify totals of pack animals or lengths of columns. Indeed, one of the significant conclusions of this research is that concepts such as army size, size of baggage train and length and speed of the marching army are crude abstractions of dynamic processes, and that these abstractions can be misleading or unhelpful. It should come as no surprise that a more dynamic model produces more dynamic conclusions but the extent to which the somewhat simplistic details given in historical accounts are liable to be reassessed is an unintended result of this project. When al-Turtushi gives a total for the Byzantine armies of 600,000 warriors,[561] what does he mean? At what point is this figure intended to be accurate, given that the army's size will have fluctuated constantly on the march to Mantzikert? Maybe Matthew of Edessa's 'more numerous than the sands of the sea' is not simply poetic but more accurately reflects the shifting nature of the subject. Maybe the Byzantine historians' reluctance to provide a total size of their army stems from an acknowledgement of the arbitrary nature of such a total? Maybe not, but we can now add appropriate uncertainty regarding army sizes, as modern historians have been doing for some time, and also start to examine the circumstances under which an army's size might fluctuate, and by how much. Travel times too can also be treated more sceptically, with an appreciation that a description of an army moving between two points in a certain amount of time may be a drastic, but convenient, oversimplification of a very complex reality.

An expedition of Basil II from Constantinople to Aleppo in 995 was recorded as taking 15 days instead of the usual 60, albeit with the original 40,000 troops reduced to 17,000 by the time they arrived.[562] The distance

---

[561] Hillenbrand 2007, 27
[562] Haldon 2005, 144

between these two cities is 891km as the crow flies. On the ground this was likely to be more like 1200km, giving a marching rate of 80km per day. What are we to make of this given the information contained in this book? Treating the army as a monolithic entity we can express scepticism of this seemingly impressive feat. 80km per day for 15 days without a rest day would be punishing for both humans and animals. Previously we may have expressed scepticism regarding the total number of troops, the number that reached their destination or the timescale, or maybe all three. Hopefully we now have a framework within which we can examine such accounts in more detail. Were there really 40,000 troops starting from Constantinople or were some collected on the way? If so, how many and where? How many of the 40,000 were cavalry, and what proportion did they make of the troops who actually arrived? Was the march made under threat of enemy action? 40,000 troops would almost certainly have to be split across separate routes or along the same route on subsequent days. Accomplishing the task in 15 days rather than 60 may have simplified the food supply arrangements as fewer days on the road would have meant less food required and therefore fewer pack animals. And so, without even modelling the march we can start to gain a different perspective on the historical account.

Simulating Furse

The work of George Armand Furse, and a number of contemporary authors, was clearly significant to this study. Consequently, it is worth considering how this work reflect those factors that Furze considered significant. In the Art of Marching, Furze lists the conditions that influence marching. These are:

a. The general nature of the country – its roads, defiles, desert tracts, etc.
b. The season of the year and the atmospheric influences.
c. The physical and moral state of the troops, and the discipline maintained on the line of march.
d. Defects in the equipment – bad boots, badly balanced valises, overloading, etc.
e. The insufficiency of provisions, forage, fuel, or water.
f. The size of the trains which follow the combatants.'[563]

Of these, we have been able to directly model *b*, *f*, some elements of *a* and part of *c*, while considering *e* in a less direct manner. That still leaves plenty of work to do to cover all of the conditions which Furse lists as influences on marching.

Reassessing Engels

It seems clear that a reassessment of Alexander the Great's campaigns is overdue in the wake of the information contained within the 19th-century military literature and the new technology pioneered within this research. Donald Engels' book stands as a significant milestone in pre-modern military logistics research and the model he used was as complex as could be achieved given the tools available at the time. It will likely remain a useful model for easily calculated accessible sanity checks on transport arrangements for campaigns in many different situations. Nevertheless, now that the data and tools available to researchers have advanced, other approaches are now feasible, that allow novel questions to be asked of the data we have. With this in mind, reassessing Alexander's transport needs and remodelling the logistics of his campaign using the opportunities provided by new technology and a variety of different organisational schemes would be of considerable interest.

Individual variation

The models presented here use identical characteristics for each agent of a particular type. Each soldier, officer and animal is identical to all others of the same type. This is in stark contrast to life, and variation between individuals no doubt played an important role in how the army moved and fed itself. The extent to which the pace of the army was moderated to accommodate slow moving individuals, and what happened to them if they dropped out of the column, is something that is not modelled here but would have been an ever-present factor in the march of a real army. The extent to which this is unappreciated by researchers but important for people involved in moving an army in real life can be seen in the difference between the US Special Forces training documents for the use of pack animals and the work of Engels, Haldon, France etc. People who need to work with pack animals are told that each animal is an individual and should be treated and fed as such.[564] In contrast, pack animals are treated as identical examples of their species in previous work centred on logistics, although this approach is acknowledged and justified by Engels.[565] ABM has the capacity to explore the differences created by individual variation but this would require further models designed specifically for this purpose. This would be another interesting topic for further research.

Biographies of simulated people

Contemporary military history, particularly Byzantine military history, is written by a very select group of

[563] Furse 1901, 159

[564] U.S. Army 2004, 2–17
[565] Engels 1978, 128

individuals. The presence of the emperor and other high-ranking officials looms large in accounts of Byzantine military campaigns. Military treatises give us a subtly different perspective as, although they are written by and for the people at the top, their advice is tailored to the wellbeing of the troops as a whole and therefore they are often concerned with the health and comfort of the lesser members of the army. They still, however, give us more of an insight into what daily life is like for a general than what it is like for a common infantryman.

ABM can help give us a glimpse of what life is like behind these biases. By tracking the differences between individual agents within a simulation we can start to examine how these may have related to the diverse experiences of the members of the army in the real world. The fact that the cavalry lead the column is a method of organisation which has solid practical reasons behind it, but the cavalry are generally higher status individuals, able to equip themselves with more expensive equipment than the infantry. This situation has implications for their lifestyle on the march. Rising early, travelling fairly quickly on roads that have not already had the majority of the army marching over them, setting up camp around midday, getting to the fresh water first and having the rest of the day to themselves may have seemed a relatively privileged schedule in comparison to the infantry or those in other parts of the column. Practically speaking it would make sense for the cavalry to be the ones to dig the ditch around the camp, but this is overwhelmingly likely to have been the job of the early infantry arrivals. One can imagine the feeling of marching into camp in one of the first infantry units and arriving to find the cavalry relaxing by their tents after a good lunch, the area around the local source of fresh water trampled by horses and the prospect of setting up the defences still to come.

ABM is in some ways inherently egalitarian in that it is as easy to track the agents at the head of the column as it is to track those at the tail, and comparisons can easily be made. Obviously, the track of an agent through the simulation does not give us their whole life on the march, as it also does not definitively give us an actual day on the march of any actual individual. It does, however, give pointers towards typical daily experiences, often of people whose lives are otherwise absent from history.

Technical achievements

Technically, the models contained within this project break little new ground. With the exception of the modified version of A* route planning that is the backbone of the means for getting agents from A to B,

there is nothing innovative about the software used. It is the use to which this software is put, and the results obtained that are novel. The combination of Java ABM, OpenOffice spreadsheets for data analysis and Python scripts in Blender for visualisation is relatively unusual within archaeology, though each element is individually conventional. Within archaeological ABMs, where Netlogo[566] is the most common choice of platform, the construction of a completely bespoke environment is still relatively rare. The demands of route planning and the number of agents render Netlogo inappropriate for models of this scale, but Netlogo is by far the most commonly used ABM software in archaeology for a reason. Its simplicity and gentle learning curve make it the best introduction for users with no detailed programming knowledge. If this book has stimulated any desire to learn about ABM, Netlogo is a common and obvious place to start.

Although much is made of ABM's modular nature and the possibility of reusing individual elements for future work, this rarely happens in practice. Indeed, the even easier step of rerunning other models in order to check their conclusions and further explore their parameter space is not often done, or at least not often published, Marco Janssen's *Understanding Artificial Anasazi* being a very rare example.[567] All the software used to run and analyse the models contained in this book has been uploaded to Philip Murgatroyd's Github repository where it can be freely downloaded and is also intended be archived in the CoMSES network's computational library. Unfortunately, there is a large difference in effort between making the models functional and documenting the models on the one hand and providing a user interface to make them easy to use on the other. Consequently, some patience and technical ability will be required to rerun these models with bespoke parameters. Making simulation software truly accessible, that is releasing it in a state in which it can easily be found, downloaded, run, understood and modified, is something which we have gained an increasing appreciation for as this project has progressed. We hope that any future work will focus significant effort in this direction.

Advanced technological considerations

The models, as originally envisaged, involved the entire army and context and the whole of the march being modelled from beginning to end and at a high levels of granularity. Typically, the computational requirements for models of such scale and granularity, far exceed the performance and storage capabilities of a single computer. In such cases, Distributed Simulation techniques, whereby the simulation model

---

[566] Tisue and Wilensky 2004
[567] Janssen 2009

is partitioned in multiple computing nodes, provide a viable solution. Such approaches however come with their own challenges. Firstly, the simulation infrastructure has to provide solutions to fundamental problems which increase the complexity and overhead, such as partitioning and distributing the model and synchronisation; these problems are particularly challenging for ABMs which are data-centric and not easily parallelisable.[568] Secondly, the specification and programming of the models requires substantial knowledge of the underlying infrastructure on behalf of the modeller. In the course of this project we did utilise and evaluated Distributed Simulation approaches,[569] particularly the PDES-MAS system,[570] a pioneering ABM distributed simulation engine developed under the leadership of Professor Theodoropoulos at the University of Birmingham.

However we quickly concluded that this additional complexity and overhead introduced by Distributed Simulation was not really necessary in our case. The march to Mantzikert took almost six months but this was split into discrete atomic units of a single day's march. Simulating an individual day's march allowed a lot of issues surrounding the march to be adequately investigated on a single sequential computer, thus removing the need for distributed simulation. Longer periods could be simulated by daisy-chaining individual day's marches together, but there are few benefits and many drawbacks to simulating the whole march in a single model.

Future work

The easiest way to expand on the models used within this project are to either continue modelling the march to Mantzikert or to examine other campaigns which took place across the same landscape. Significant historical questions also remain about several military campaign with logistics-critical components in Anatolia. The Crusades in particular have numerous situations in which armies moved in circumstances that were inadequately described in primary accounts. But there is also still much surrounding the Mantzikert campaign left to model, including areas of the landscape not virtually traversed and combinations of types of organisation and supply that were not simulated. Due to the nature of complex systems, one can never be sure that potentially significant non-linear relationships are being missed due to the selective nature of the simulations being run.

Due to the sporadic nature of the evidence for the Byzantine road system, the ability to determine optimal routes across the landscape, where 'optimal' can be relative to a variety of characteristics, may form a useful tool. This ability is already provided by GIS software[571] but being able to model different types of traffic and the effect of different types of road upon their progress may prove significant in reconstructing a route system that could have been designed to accommodate anything from small merchant caravans to whole armies.

The only modifications needed to simulate movement in other parts of the world would be a new set of terrain data, which would be relatively easy to incorporate. With this, armies of similar technological complexity, from Alexander onwards, could be simulated with the same software. Historically significant army movements such as Hannibal's march across the Alps or Marlborough's campaigns in Europe could quite easily be examined in the same way as the Mantzikert campaign. With enough computing power and some development time, this software could be made available to all via a web-based interface or a truly accessible download, allowing anyone to test their own hypotheses of any campaign, anywhere in the world.

Concluding remarks

The *Medieval Warfare on the Grid* project started in 2007 with the intention to take a bold new perspective on pre-modern military logistics by using distributed computer simulation to run large-scale models of the Byzantine army on the march across Anatolia to the Battle of Mantzikert. The project, as envisaged in the successful application for AHRC-EPSRC-Jisc e-Science funding, was in some ways very different from the results contained within this book. Some of the original goals have been met in the manner, or at least to the degree of success, that was hoped for at the start of the project. The project has indeed used computer simulation to generate new perspectives on an old problem. Those simulations have provided a valuable additional tool to existing historical research on military logistics in general and the Mantzikert campaign in particular. The end result is a combination of traditional humanities research and cutting-edge technology of precisely the kind that the e-Science grant was set up to enable, and we reiterate our gratitude to the institutions which funded this project.

What was entirely unanticipated at the beginning of the project was just how useful the 19th-century military writing would prove to be, not only for a traditional historian's analysis of pre-modern logistics but also as a base for computer simulation. The quantitative data, historical synthesis and analysis based on real world experience that is provided by writers such as

---

[568] Suryanarayanan and Theodoropoulos 2013
[569] Murgatroyd *et al.* 2012
[570] PDES-MAS

[571] e.g. McMahon 2022

George Armand Furse is of tremendous help to both conventional historians and agent-based modellers alike. The vastly increased availability of this large body of work, thanks to 21st-century document scanning programmes by the likes of Google and Microsoft, changed the content, direction and, ultimately, timescale, of the project. It is to George Armand Furse along with his predecessors and contemporaries that this project owes a great deal of thanks. What George Armand Furse would have thought of being the godfather of a new sub-discipline, computer simulation of pre-modern military logistics, is open to speculation. We think he'd be surprised but we hope he'd be pleased.

Bibliography

Aldenderfer, M.S. 1981. Computer simulation for archaeology: an introductory essay. Pages 11–49 in *Simulations in archaeology*. Edited by Jeremy A. Sabloff. Albuquerque: Albuquerque.

Andrews, Tara L. 2016. *Mattʿēos Uṙhayecʿi and His Chronicle: History as Apocalypse in a Crossroads of Cultures*. Leiden: Leiden.

Angold, Michael. 2004. The Byzantine Empire, 1025–1118. Pages 217–253 in *The New Cambridge Medieval History: Volume 4: c.1024–c.1198*. Edited by David Luscombe and Jonathan Riley-Smith. The New Cambridge Medieval History. Cambridge: Cambridge.

Angold, Michael. 2007. The Venetian Chronicles and Archives as Sources for the History of Byzantium and the Crusades (992-1204). Pages 59–85 in *Byzantines and Crusaders in Non-Greek Sources, 1025-1204*. Edited by Mary Whitby. Oxford: Oxford.

Anon. 1855. *A Remedy for the Evils That Have Caused the Destruction of a Large Portion of the British Army before Sevastopol*. London: London.

Attaleiates, Michael. 2012. *The History*. Translated by Anthony Kaldellis and Dimitris Krallis. Cambridge, Massachusetts: Cambridge, Massachusetts.

Aubry, Thierry, Bradley, Bruce, Almeida, Miguel, Walter, Bertrand, Neves, Maria Joao, Pelegrin, Jacques, Lenoir, Michel, and Tiffagom, Marc. 2008. "Solutrean laurel leaf production at Maîtreaux: an experimental approach guided by techno-economic analysis." *World Archaeology* 40:48–66.

Bachrach, B. S. 2006. Crusader logistics: from victory at Nicaea to resupply at Dorylaion. Pages 43–62 in *Logistics of warfare in the Age of the Crusades*. Edited by John H. Pryor. Aldershot: Aldershot.

Balado, Donna. 1995. *ACSM's Guidelines for Exercise Testing and Prescription*. 5th Revised edition. Baltimore: Baltimore.

Beihammer, Alexander Daniel. 2017. *Byzantium and the Emergence of Muslim-Turkish Anatolia, Ca. 1040-1130*. London: London.

Belke, Klaus. 2008. Communications, Roads and Bridges. Pages 295–308 in *The Oxford Handbook of Byzantine Studies*. Edited by Robin Cormack, John F. Haldon, and Elizabeth Jeffreys. Oxford: Oxford.

Belke, Klaus. 2017. Transport and Communication. Pages 28–38 in *The Archaeology of Byzantine Anatolia: From the End of Late Antiquity Until the Coming of the Turks*. Edited by Philipp Niewohner. Oxford: Oxford.

Billings, John D. 1887. *Hardtack and Coffee*. Boston: Boston.

Bowley, Arthur Lyon. 1900. *Wages in the United Kingdom in the Nineteenth Century*. Cambridge: Cambridge.

Box, G.E.P. 1979. "Robustness in the strategy of scientific model building." *Robustness in Statistics. Academic Press, New York*.

Bryennios, N. and Gautier, Paul. 1975. *Histoire, Ed. and Trans*. Bruxelles: Bruxelles.

Carpenter, Thorne Martin. 1921. *Tables, Factors, and Formulas for Computing Respiratory Exchange and Biological Transformations of Energy*. Washington: Washington.

Chatzelis, Georgios and Harris, Jonathan. 2017. *A Tenth-Century Byzantine Military Manual: The Sylloge Tacticorum*. London: London.

Cheynet, Jean-Claude. 1980. "Mantzikert: un desastre militaire?'." *Byzantion* 50:410–438.

Cheynet, Jean-Claude. 1990. *Pouvoir et Contestations à Byzance (963-1210)*.

Cioffi-Revilla, Claudio, Luke, Sean, Parker, Dawn C., Rogers, J. Daniel, Fitzhugh, William W., Honeychurch, William, Fröhlich, Bruno, De Priest, Paula, and Amartuvshin, Chunag. 2007. Agent-Based Modeling Simulation of Social Adaptation and Long-Term Change in Inner Asia. Pages 189–200 in *Advancing Social Simulation: The First World Congress*. Edited by Shingo Takahashi, David Sallach, and Juliette Rouchier. Tokyo: Tokyo.

Connolly, Peter. 1986. "A Reconstruction of a Roman Saddle." *Britannia* 17:353–355.

Connolly, Peter and Van Driel-Murray, Carol. 1991. "The Roman cavalry saddle." *Britannia* 22:33–50.

Constantine Porphyrogenitus. 1990. *Three Treatises on Imperial Military Expeditions*. Translated by John F. Haldon.

Contreras, Daniel A., Bondeau, Alberte, Guiot, Joel, Kirman, Alan, Hiriart, Eneko, Bernard, Loup, Suarez, Romain, and Fader, Marianela. 2019. "From paleoclimate variables to prehistoric agriculture: Using a process-based agro-ecosystem model to simulate the impacts of Holocene climate change on potential agricultural productivity in Provence, France." *Quaternary international* 501:303–316.

Conway, Richard Walter. 1964. *An Experimental Investigation of Priority Assignment in a Job Shop*. Santa Monica: Santa Monica.

Copeland, B. Jack. 2004. "Colossus: its origins and originators." *IEEE Annals of the History of Computing* 26:38–45.

Crowley, Patrick and Sheffield, Gary. 2009. *Kut 1916: Courage and Failure in Iraq: The Forgotten British Disaster in Iraq*. Cheltenham: Cheltenham.

Dalkey, Norman. 1967. *Simulation of Military Conflict*. Santa Monica: Santa Monica.

Davis, Reed Ellsworth. 1967. *A Dynamo Simulation of an Assault River Crossing*.

Dawson, Timothy. 2007. "Fit for the task': equipment sizes and the transmission of military lore, sixth to tenth centuries." *Byzantine and Modern Greek Studies* 31:1–12.

Dennis, George T. 2001. *Maurice's Strategikon: Handbook of Byzantine Military Strategy*. Philadelphia: Philadelphia.

Dennis, George T. 2010. *The Taktika of Leo VI*. Washington: Washington.

Dennis, George T. 1985. *Three Byzantine Military Treatises*. Washington: Washington.

Devienne, M.F. and Guezennec, C.Y. 2000. "Energy expenditure of horse riding." *European journal of applied physiology* 82:499–503.

Doran, James. 2005. Iruba: An agent-based model of the guerrilla war process. Pages 198–205 in *Representing social reality, pre-proceedings of the third conference of the European social simulation association (ESSA)*.

Doran, James. 1970. "Systems theory, computer simulations and archaeology." *World Archaeology* 1:289–298.

Dostourian, A.E. 1972. *The Chronicle of Matthew of Edessa: Translated from the Original Armenian, with a Commentary and Introduction*.

Dungworth, David and Wilkes, Roger. 2007. "An investigation of hammerscale." *Research Department Report* 26.

Engels, D.W. 1978. *Alexander the Great and the Logistics of the Macedonian Army*. Berkeley: Berkeley.

Epstein, J.M. and Axtell, R. 1996. *Growing Artificial Societies: Social Science from the Bottom Up*. Cambridge, Massachusetts: Cambridge, Massachusetts.

Feather, John. 2005. *A History of British Publishing*. London: London.

Foss, Clive. 1990. "Byzantine Malagina and the Lower Sangarius." *Anatolian Studies* 40:161–183.

France, John. 2006. Logistics and the Second Crusade. Page in *Logistics of Warfare in the Age of the Crusades*. Edited by John H. Pryor. London: London.

French, DH. 1981. *Roman Roads and Milestones of Asia Minor*. Oxford: Oxford.

Friendly, A. 1981. *The Dreadful Day: The Battle of Manzikert, 1071*.

Furse, George Armand. 1882. *Military Transport*.

Furse, George Armand. 1901. *The Art of Marching*. London: London.

Gabrovsek, Stanislas, Colwill, Ian, and Stipidis, Elias. 2016. "Agent-based simulation of improvised explosive device fragment damage on individual components." *The Journal of Defense Modeling and Simulation: Applications, Methodology, Technology* 13:399–413.

Gardner, Martin. 1970. "Mathematical games." *Scientific american* 223:120–123.

Geodetic Calculators. https://geodesyapps.ga.gov.au/sunrise Accessed 10/2/2020

Geyer, Bernard. 2002. Physical factors in the evolution of the landscape and land use. Pages 31–45 in *The Economic History of Byzantium, from the 7 th through the 15 th centuries*. Edited by Angeliki E. Laiou.

Gilbert, G.N. and Troitzsch, K.G. 2005. *Simulation for the Social Scientist*. Maidenhead: Maidenhead.

Gotts, Nicholas M. 2017. Agent-Based Modelling of Military Communications on the Roman Frontier. Pages 143–148 in *Advances in Social Simulation 2015*. Edited by Wander Jager, Rineke Verbrugge, Andreas Flache, Gert de Roo, Lex Hoogduin, and Charlotte Hemelrijk. Advances in Intelligent Systems and Computing. Cham: Cham.

Graham, S. 2009. "Behaviour Space: Simulating Roman Social Life and Civil Violence." *Digital Studies/Le champ numérique* 1.

Grose, Francis. 1786. *Military Antiquities Respecting a History of the English Army: From the Conquest to the Present Time*.

Grose, Francis, Williamson, John, and Townshend, George Townshend Marquis. 1867. *Advice to the Officers of the British Army*.

Haldon, John. 2014. *A Critical Commentary on the Taktika of Leo VI*. Washington: Washington.

Haldon, John. 2003. Approaches to an alternative military history of the period ca. 1025–1071. Pages 1025–1081 in *The Empire in Crisis (?): Byzantium in the 11th Century (1025-1081)*. Athens: Athens.

Haldon, John. 2005. Feeding the Army: Food and transport in Byzantium, ca 600-1100. Pages 85–100 in *Feast, Fast or Famine: Food and Drink in Byzantium*. Edited by Wendy Mayer and Silke Trzcionka. Byzantina Australiensia.

Haldon, John, ed. 2006a. *General Issues in the Study of Medieval Logistics: Sources, Problems and Methodologies*. Leiden: Leiden.

Haldon, John. 2006b. Introduction: Why model logistical systems? Pages 1–36 in *General issues in the study of medieval logistics: Sources, problems and methodologies*. Edited by John Haldon. Leiden: Leiden.

Haldon, John. 2015. Late Rome, Byzantium, and early medieval western Europe. Pages 345–89 in *Fiscal Regimes and the Political Economy of Premodern States*. Edited by Andrew Monson and Walter Scheidel. Cambridge: Cambridge.

Haldon, John. 2006c. Roads and communications in the Byzantine Empire: wagons, horses, and supplies. Pages 131–58 in *Logistics of Warfare in the Age of the Crusades*. Edited by John H. Pryor. London: London.

Haldon, John. 2008. *The Byzantine Wars*. Cheltenham: Cheltenham.

Haldon, John. 1999. *Warfare, State and Society in the Byzantine World, 565-1204*. London: London.

Haldon, John, Elton, Hugh, and Newhard, James. 2018. *Archaeology and Urban Settlement in Late Roman and*

Byzantine Anatolia: Euchaïa-Avkat-Beyözü and Its Environment. Cambridge: Cambridge.

Haldon, John, Gaffney, Vince, Theodoropoulos, Georgios, and Murgatroyd, Phil. 2011. "Marching across Anatolia: Medieval Logistics and Modeling the Mantzikert Campaign." *Dumbarton Oaks Papers* 65:209–235.

Haldon, John, Roberts, Neil, Izdebski, Adam, Fleitmann, Dominik, McCormick, Michael, Cassis, Marica, Doonan, Owen, Eastwood, Warren, Elton, Hugh, and Ladstätter, Sabine. 2014. "The climate and environment of Byzantine Anatolia: integrating science, history, and archaeology." *Journal of Interdisciplinary History* 45:113–161.

Harari, Yuval Noah. 2007. "Military Memoirs: A Historical Overview of the Genre from the Middle Ages to the Late Modern Era." *War in History* 14:289–309.

Harari, Yuval Noah. 2000. "Strategy and supply in fourteenth-century western European invasion campaigns." *The Journal of Military History* 64:297–333.

Harvey, Alan. 2003. *Economic Expansion in the Byzantine Empire, 900-1200*. Cambridge: Cambridge.

Haynes, I. P. 2015. Marking Time: Temporality, routine and cohesion in Rome's armies. Pages 113–120 in *Understanding Roman Frontiers: a celebration for Professor Bill Hanson*. Edited by David Breeze, Rebecca Jones, and Ioana Oltean.

Head, George. 1837. *A Home Tour through Various Parts of the United Kingdom, a Continuation of the "Home Tour through the Manufacturing Districts". Also, Memoirs of an Assistant Commissary-General*.

Hendy, Michael F. 2008. *Studies in the Byzantine Monetary Economy c. 300-1450*. Cambridge: Cambridge.

Hill, Raymond R., Champagne, Lance E., and Price, Joseph C. 2004. "Using agent-based simulation and game theory to examine the WWII Bay of Biscay U-boat campaign." *The Journal of Defense Modeling and Simulation: Applications, Methodology, Technology* 1:99–109.

Hillenbrand, Carole. 2007. *Turkish Myth and Muslim Symbol: The Battle of Manzikert*. Edinburgh: Edinburgh.

Holliday, L. P. and Gurfield, R. M. 1968. Viet Cong Logistics.

Holmes, Catherine. 2008. Political-Historical Survey, 800–1204. Pages 264–279 in *The Oxford Handbook of Byzantine Studies*. Edited by Robin Cormack, John F. Haldon, and Elizabeth Jeffreys.

Home, Robert. 1882. *A Précis of Modern Tactics*.

Horne, Gary E. and Leonardi, Mary L. 2001. *Maneuver Warfare Science 2001*. Quantico: Quantico.

Huston, James A. 1966. *The Sinews of War: Army Logistics; 1775-1953*.

Hutton, E.T.H. 1893. "The Art of Marching." *Royal United Services Institution. Journal* 37:621–654.

Ilachinski, Andy. 2000. "Irreducible semi-autonomous adaptive combat (ISAAC): An artificial-life approach to land combat." *Military Operations Research* 29–46.

Innis, George. 1972. "Simulation of ill-defined systems: some problems and progress." *Simulation* 19:33–36.

Iznik Annual Weather Averages. *WorldWeatherOnline. com*.

Jacoby, David. 2010. *Mediterranean Food and Wine for Constantinople: The Long-Distance Trade, Eleventh to Mid-Fifteenth Century*.

Janssen, Marco A. 2009. "Understanding Artificial Anasazi." *Jasss-the Journal of Artificial Societies and Social Simulation* 12:A244–A260.

Kazhdan, A.P., Talbot, A.M., Cutler, A., Gregory, T.E., and Sevcenko, N.P. 1991. *The Oxford Dictionary of Byzantium*. Oxford: Oxford.

Kirby, Major Troy T. 2014. *The Duke Of Wellington And The Supply System During The Peninsular War*.

Kohler, T.A. 2010. A New Paleoproductivity Reconstruction for Southwestern Colorado, and Its Implications for Understanding Thirteenth-Century Depopulation. Pages 102–127 in *Leaving Mesa Verde: peril and change in the thirteenth-century Southwest*. Edited by T.A. Kohler, Mark D. Varien, and Aaron Wright.

Kohler, T.A. and van der Leeuw, S.E. 2007. *The Model-Based Archaeology of Socionatural Systems*. Santa Fe: Santa Fe.

Kohler, Timothy A., Bocinsky, R. Kyle, Cockburn, Denton, Crabtree, Stefani A., Varien, Mark D., Kolm, Kenneth E., Smith, Schaun, Ortman, Scott G., and Kobti, Ziad. 2012. "Modelling prehispanic Pueblo societies in their ecosystems." *Ecological Modelling* 241:30–41.

Kohler, Timothy A. and Varien, Mark D. 2012. *Emergence and Collapse of Early Villages: Models of Central Mesa Verde Archaeology*.

Kroll, Henriette. 2012. "Animals in the Byzantine empire: an overview of the archaeozoological evidence." *Archeologia Medievale* 39:93–121.

Laiou, Angeliki E., ed. 2002. *The Economic History of Byzantium: From the Seventh through the Fifteenth Century*. Washington: Washington.

Laiou, Angeliki E. and Morrisson, Cécile. 2007. *The Byzantine Economy*.

Land Warfare Development Centre. 2017. *Land Operations. Army Doctrine Publication AC 71940*.

Lauxtermann, Marc D. and Whittow, Mark. 2017. *Byzantium in the Eleventh Century: Being in Between*.

Lazenby, J. F. 1994. "Logistics in classical Greek warfare." *War in History* 1:3–18.

Lefort, Jacques. 2002. The rural economy, seventh-twelfth centuries. Pages 231–310 in *The Economic History of Byzantium: From the Seventh Through the Fifteenth Century*. Edited by Angeliki E. Laiou. Washington: Washington.

Leighton, Richard M. and Coakley, Robert W. 1955. *Global Logistics and Strategy, 1940-1943*.

Lessing, Gotthold Ephraim. 1889. *Selected Prose Works*. London: London.

Lippitt, Francis James. 1869. *Field Service in War: Comprising Marches, Camps and Cantonments, Outposts,*

Convoys, Reconnaissances, Foraging, and Notes on Logistics. New York: New York.

Lippitt, Francis James. 1902. *Reminiscences of Francis J. Lippitt: Written for His Family, His Near Relatives and Intimate Friends*. Providence: Providence.

Luttwak, E.N. 1993. Logistics and the aristocratic idea of war. Pages 3–9 in *Feeding Mars: logistics in western warfare from the Middle Ages to the present*. Edited by John A. Lynn. New York: New York.

McGeer, E. 1995. *Sowing the Dragon's Teeth: Byzantine Warfare in the Tenth Century*. Washington: Washington.

McGeer, Eric and Nesbitt, John. 2020. *Byzantium in the Time of Troubles: The Continuation of the Chronicle of John Skylitzes (1057–1079)*. Boston: Boston.

McMahon, Lucas. 2022. "Digital Perspectives on Overland Travel and Communications in the Exarchate of Ravenna (Sixth through Eighth Centuries)." *Studies in Late Antiquity* 6:284–334.

US Army Quartermaster Foundation, 'Major General Henry G. Sharpe - Quartermaster General 1916-1918' http://www.qmfound.com/MG_Henry_Sharpe.htm Accessed 11/1/13

Miller, Dean A. 1966. "The logothete of the Drome in the Middle Byzantine period." *Byzantion* 36:438–470.

Miller, Walter. 1914. *Xenophon: Cyropaedia*.

Muhammad, Tarek M. 2009. Had the Arabs Military Skills or Tactics during their Early Conquests of Bilād al-Shām? Pages 83–96 in *East and West: Essays on Byzantine and Arab Worlds in the Middle Ages*. Edited by Juan Pedro Monferrer-Sala, Vassilios Christides, and Theodoros Papadopoullos.

Murgatroyd, Philip, Craenen, Bart, Theodoropoulos, Georgios, Gaffney, Vincent, and Haldon, John. 2012. "Modelling medieval military logistics: an agent-based simulation of a Byzantine army on the march." *Computational and Mathematical Organization Theory* 18:488–506.

Murgatroyd, Philip Scott. 2012. *Medieval Warfare on the Grid*.

O'Connor, Stephen. 2013. "The Daily Grain Consumption of Classical Greek Sailors and Soldiers." *Chiron* 327–356.

O'Connor, Stephen. 2015. The Problem of the 400 Wagons: The Provisioning of the Ten Thousand on the March to Cunaxa. Pages 124–146 in *Ancient Warfare: Introducing Current Research*. Edited by Geoff Lee, Helene Whittaker, and Graham Wrightson.

Orr, Robert. 2010. "The history of the soldier's load." *Australian Army Journal* 7:67.

PDES-MAS. *PDES-MAS*. https://pdes-mas.github.io/ Accessed 16/1/2024

Perjés, Geza. 1970. "Army provisioning, logistics and strategy in the second half of the 17th century." *Acta Historica Academiae Scientiarum Hungaricae* 16:1–52.

Premo, L.S. 2010. Equifinality and Explanation: Thoughts on the Role of Agent-Based Modeling in Postpositivist Archaeology. Pages 28–37 in *Simulating Change: Archaeology into the Twenty-First Century*. Edited by Andre Costopoulos and Mark Lake. Salt Lake City: Salt Lake City.

Prinzing, Friedrich. 1916. *Epidemics Resulting from Wars*. Oxford: Oxford.

Prothero, G.W. 1920. *Armenia and Kurdistan*. London: London.

Pryor, John H. 2006. *Logistics of Warfare in the Age of the Crusades: Proceedings of a Workshop Held at the Centre for Medieval Studies, University of Sydney, 30 September to 4 October 2002*. London: London.

Psellus, M. 1966. *Fourteen Byzantine Rulers: The Chronographia*. London: London.

Reynolds, Craig W. 1987. Flocks, herds and schools: A distributed behavioral model. Pages 25–34 in *Proceedings of the 14th annual conference on Computer graphics and interactive techniques*.

Rogers, Clifford J. 2007. *Soldiers' Lives through History - The Middle Ages*. Westport: Westport.

Roth, J.P. 1999. *The Logistics of the Roman Army at War (264 BC-AD 235)*. Leiden: Leiden.

Rubio-Campillo, X., Cela, J. M., and Cardona, F. X. H. 2013. "The development of new infantry tactics during the early eighteenth century: a computer simulation approach to modern military history." *Journal of Simulation* 7:170–182.

Rubio-Campillo, Xavier, Matías, Pau Valdés, and Ble, Eduard. 2015. "Centurions in the Roman legion: computer simulation and complex systems." *Journal of Interdisciplinary History* 46:245–263.

Runciman, S. 1951. *History of the Crusades, Volume 1: The First Crusade*.

Sharpe, Henry Granville. 1896. "The Art of Supplying Armies in the Field as Exemplified During the Civil War." *Journal of the Military Service Institution* 18:45–214.

Sharpe, Henry Granville. 1905. *The Provisioning of the Modern Army in the Field*. Kansas City: Kansas City.

Sharpe, William F. 1965. The Army Deployment Simulator.

Skylitzes, John and Wortley, John. 2010. *John Skylitzes: A Synopsis of Byzantine History, 811-1057: Translation and Notes*.

Smith, E.A. and Choi, J.K. 2007. The emergence of inequality in small-scale societies: Simple scenarios and agent-based simulations. Pages 105–20 in *The model-based archaeology of socionatural systems*. Edited by Timothy A. Kohler and Sander E. van der Leeuw.

Spiers, Edward M. 2004. *The Victorian Soldier in Africa*. Manchester: Manchester.

Sukhatme, P. V. 1960. *Technical Conversion Factors for Agricultural Commodities*. Rome: Rome.

Sullivan, Denis F. 2000. *Siegecraft*. Cambridge, Massachusetts: Cambridge, Massachusetts.

Suryanarayanan, Vinoth and Theodoropoulos, Georgios. 2013. "Synchronised range queries in distributed simulations of multiagent systems." *ACM Transactions on Modeling and Computer Simulation* 23:25:1–25:25.

Talbot, A.M. and Sullivan, D.F. 2005. *The History of Leo the Deacon: Byzantine Military Expansion in the Tenth Century*. Washington D.C.: Washington D.C.

Thompson, P.A. and Marchant, E.W. 1995. "A computer model for the evacuation of large building populations." *Fire Safety Journal* 24:131–148.

Tiede, Roland V. and Leake, Lewis A. 1971. "A Method for Evaluating the Combat Effectiveness of a Tactical Information System in a Field Army." *Operations Research* 19:587–604.

Tisue, Seth and Wilensky, Uri. 2004. Netlogo: A simple environment for modeling complexity. Pages 16–21 in *International conference on complex systems*.

U.S. Army. 2004. *FM 3-05.213 (FM 31-27) Special Forces Use of Pack Animals*. Washington D.C.: Washington D.C.

Van Tilburg, J. A. and Ralston, T. 2005. Megaliths and Mariners: Experimental Archaeology on Easter Island. Pages 279–303 in *Onward and Upward: Essays in Honor of Clement W. Meighan*. Edited by Keith L. Johnson. Baltimore: Baltimore.

Van West, Carla R. 1994. *Modeling Prehistoric Agricultural Productivity in Southwestern Colorado: A GIS Approach*. Tucson: Tucson.

Vegetius. 2011. *Epitome of Military Science*. Second Revised Edition. Translated by N.P. Milner. Liverpool: Liverpool.

Von Neumann, J. 1951. The general and logical theory of automata. Pages 1–41 in *Cerebral mechanisms in behavior; the Hixon Symposium*. Edited by L.A. Jeffress. New York: New York.

Vratimos, Antonios. 2018. Greek Secondary Sources on Romanos IV Diogenes (1068-1071 a.d.).

Vratimos-Chatzopoulos, A. 2005. *The Two Expeditions of the Byzantine Emperor Romanos IV Diogenes in 1068 and 1069*.

Watson, Moira M. 2022. "Stability and Utility of a First Century AD Roman Cavalry Saddle and the Influence on an Alternative Design for the Saddle." *Cheiron: The International Journal of Equine and Equestrian History* 1:31–45.

Wellington, Arthur Wellesley. 1838. *Vol. 8: The Dispatches of Field Marshal the Duke of Wellington: During His Various Campaigns in India, Denmark, Portugal, Spain, the Low Countries, and France, from 1799 to 1818*. London: London.

Wilkinson, TJ, Christiansen, JH, Ur, J., Widell, M., and Altaweel, M. 2007. "Urbanization within a dynamic environment: modeling Bronze Age communities in Upper Mesopotamia." *American Anthropologist* 109:52–68.

Wintjes, Jorit. 2015. "Europe's Earliest Kriegsspiel? Book Seven of Reinhard Graf zu Solms' Kriegsregierung and the 'Prehistory' of Professional War Gaming." *British Journal for Military History* 2:15–33.

Wittek, Peter and Rubio-Campillo, Xavier. 2012. Military reconstructive simulation in the cloud to aid battlefield excavations. Pages 869–874 in *Cloud Computing Technology and Science (CloudCom), 2012 IEEE 4th International Conference on*.

Xenophon. *Hellenica*.

Xoplaki, Elena, Fleitmann, Dominik, Luterbacher, Juerg, Wagner, Sebastian, Haldon, John F., Zorita, Eduardo, Telelis, Ioannis, Toreti, Andrea, and Izdebski, Adam. 2016. "The Medieval Climate Anomaly and Byzantium: A review of the evidence on climatic fluctuations, economic performance and societal change." *Quaternary Science Reviews* 136:229–252.

Zamoyski, Adam. 2004. *1812: Napoleon's Fatal March on Moscow*. London: London.

Zhuge Liang and Liu Ji. 2005. *Mastering the Art of War: Zhuge Liang's and Liu Ji's Commentaries on the Classic by Sun Tzu*. Translated by Thomas Cleary. Boston: Boston.